Hippies of the Religious Right

HIPPIES
OF THE
RELIGIOUS RIGHT

Preston Shires

BAYLOR UNIVERSITY PRESS

Book Design by Diane Smith
Cover Design by Pamela Poll
Cover Image: "Hippies In Park" is from the Hulton Archive. Photograph by John Minihan. Used by permission of Getty Images.

Library of Congress Cataloging-in-Publication Data

Shires, Preston, 1956-
Hippies of the religious right / Preston Shires.
p. cm.
Includes bibliographical references and index.
ISBN 978-1-932792-57-7 (pbk. : alk. paper)
1. Christians--United States--Political activity. 2. United States--Church history--20th century. 3. Religious right--United States. 4. Christian conservatism--United States. 5. Hippies--United States. 6. Counterculture--United States. I. Title.

BR517.S39 2007
305.6'7730825--dc22

2007001124

Printed in the United States of America on acid-free paper with a minimum of 30% pcw recycled content.

To Orlin and Louise Shires,

parents who kept the faith
with the younger generation

Table of Contents

Preface

This book is an investigation of the countercultural youth who ended up in the Religious Right movement of the late 1970s, 1980s, and 1990s. It seeks to explain how and why such youth were attracted to evangelicalism and what countercultural values they took with them into what most historians have described as a purely reactionary movement. In analyzing this phenomenon, I have examined the Christian message of fundamentalists, Pentecostals, new evangelicals, and charismatics prior to the rise of the counterculture in order to find connections between their biblically grounded worldview and the perspectives of sixties youth. After establishing that both the biblically grounded Christians and the countercultural youth shared certain profound beliefs, I next analyzed how the two subcultures blended together, especially in the Jesus movement, and how this mixing not only changed the nature of evangelicalism but also affected biblically grounded politics.

In conducting this investigation, I have taken the participants' perspectives on religion, the world, and politics at face value. I have not sought ulterior motives or reinterpreted their explanations for their teachings and behavior. Neither have I based this study upon the judgments of people who were once a part of the Religious Right and then later rejected and condemned it. This is a history of the Religious Right movement and not of opposing movements except inasmuch as the latter incited a response from the former. I have attempted to understand the Religious Right as it was and is, not how others would like it to have been or to be. Therefore, I have elected not to enclose in quotation marks such characteristic Religious Right concerns as "family values" (except here), because such a practice tends to convey the message that advocates of the Religious Right were somehow insincere or hypocritical. In sum, it is best simply to allow the facts to speak for themselves.

This is not to say this history lacks critical judgment. Indeed, its very thesis disputes the way members of the Religious Right have perceived themselves as well as the way their political opponents have perceived them. It is my hope that readers of both parties will come to a shared recognition that the Religious Right owed no small debt for its political success in the late seventies to the hippie movement of the sixties.

As for myself, I owe a debt as well to several people who helped me along with this work. In the first place, I am indebted to several friends in the early seventies who had entered the counterculture in their youth and then came to accept Jesus as their Savior. It was in pondering their experience that I suddenly realized that there was something more to the Religious Right than reactionary fundamentalism. I owe as great a debt to Ben Rader of the University of Nebraska, Lincoln. As a student at UNL, I noted that while some professors could see through a student's good ideas to all their flaws, there were a few professors who could clear away the flaws and expose the ideas. Ben is of the latter sort, and his insights guided my pursuit of this topic. Of course there may be errors yet within this work, and I alone bear full responsibility for them.

Appreciation is also extended to Larry Eskridge, Associate Director of Wheaton's Institute for the Study of American Evangelicals, who graciously sent me his dissertation entitled "God's Forever Family," hopefully to be soon published, which greatly enhanced my knowledge of the Jesus movement. Of course, I would also like to thank Carey C. Newman of Baylor University Press, whose exuberance and prodding filled me with both new ideas and the sense of urgency necessary to bring a book to fruition. Finally, I must thank Sylvie, my wife of twenty-seven years, who has been proofreader, taskmaster, and above all, my inspiration.

Introduction

In the mid-1970s, America's raucous counterculture, which had raged since the mid-1960s, faded away. Ignited by racism, poverty, war, and government oppression, the fires of the counterculture subsided as the effects of the Civil Rights Act of 1964 and of President Johnson's Great Society took hold, and then were effectively snuffed out with the 1973 withdrawal of U.S. combat troops from Vietnam and the capitulation of the establishment's Silent Majority leader Richard Nixon in 1974. True, the Great Society had not eliminated poverty, but an experiment in that direction had been attempted; and although minorities still suffered discrimination, progress in achieving equality had been made. More definitive were the end of the Vietnam War and the demise of Richard Nixon's presidency.

The year 1974 may be considered a turning point, putting an end to what had been called the "sixties"—a decade stretching from the assassination of John F. Kennedy to the resignation of his old rival Nixon—and opening up a new era charged with religio-political zeal. This pivotal year's spiritual significance may be instanced in a conversation between evangelist Billy Graham and a young hipster man of twenty-two who had been living a desultory life. Graham told him that no matter "what he did, where he went, or how he ended up," he would always be loved.[1] The young man was rebellious, fast with cars and girls, easy with drugs and drinking, and he was also Billy Graham's son. William Franklin Graham III, called Franklin, had plunged into the sixties counterculture as a teenager, but in July of 1974, the same month in which Richard Nixon faced impeachment, young Franklin converted to his father's faith. The counterculture had lost its antiwar and antigovernment impetus, but its activist soul would live on in another avatar.[2]

Billy Graham's son was one of millions of youth who to some degree succumbed to the sixties' counterculture. Many, including those who had not been born into a religiously conservative household like Franklin, would surprisingly end up in the robust evangelical movement of the late 1970s and early 1980s. These new conservative religionists brought with them the radical activism of the counterculture and gave American institutions—whether religious, economic, social, or political—a vigorous rank and file filled with a new dynamism. This activism was not simply a vibrant and politically motivated imitation of the New Left by young conservative religionists, although political reporter Nina Easton makes just such an argument in her analysis of baby-boomer rightist Ralph Reed. Conservative activism was actually a faithful expression of a commitment to radical engagement that had been engendered and nurtured by sixties' youth during the counterculture and then authentically and persistently lived out by them, albeit for different causes, after they converted to a biblically grounded Christianity.[3]

The beliefs and behavior which coalesced into the Religious Right in the 1970s may have been fed by many different streams of thought and style—and certainly everyone recognizes the influence of fundamentalism—but one of those streams had its source in the counterculture.[4]

1

Modern Culture—Mainstream and Mainline

Some of the more salient characteristics of the counterculture that grab our attention today are exactly those things that seemed so rebellious and antimainstream during the sixties: experimentation with new ways of thinking, believing, behaving, and relating to one another. A confidence in and desire for novelty was pushed to unprecedented heights during the sixties. So important was this phenomenon that historians such as Roland Stromberg who analyzed the intellectual drift of civilizations lamented that a culture of *neophilia*, or love of things new simply because they were new, tainted the minds and fired the passions of too many Americans.[1]

There were reasons for this obsession for newness. By the fifties, the conventions and constraints of American mainstream society had become onerous and stultifying for many, especially for young Americans. These conventions and constraints had served a purpose immediately before and after World War II and gave many middle-class Americans a sense of place and stability.[2] The way people dressed, addressed one another, spent their weekdays (and weekends), and established their homes were all, for the most part, carefully defined. It was proper to wear a suit and tie to work, to call someone *Mr.* Smith or *Mrs.* Jones; it was proper for Mr. Smith to be home for the evening meal and to read the paper after supper; it was proper for the farm family to go to town on Saturday, for city folk to move to the suburbs and live in a house with a front lawn. And it was proper for all to go to church on Sunday.

Most middle-class people aspired to live in this way, and their sense of freedom resided in their opportunity to do so. But with the more affluent postwar era, young people especially realized they had both the means and the leisure to move beyond these conventions. What was freedom for the parents became shackles to the young.[3] Postwar youth, then, if they wanted to experience freedom in the new economic context, needed to go beyond the fetters forged by convention. That they did so is evident in the ways youth developed their own culture during the fifties and sixties. By the end of the sixties, they dressed in jeans and muscle shirts, called professors by their first names, stayed out late at night and soaked up the vibes of the latest rebellious music; Saturdays and Sundays blended into the nightlife of those weekdays, and the home they envisioned was, in some cases, no more than a pad in a commune.

The countercultural youth who practiced the new freedom were not, for the most part, simply practicing it for the sake of being different. They practiced freedom as a protest against what they understood to have been irrational conventionality. Many of these defiant youth were searching to ground their new practices in something concrete; they wanted something to justify their freedom. Neophilia, as Stromberg presented it, was actually a caricature, or at best an exaggeration, of the countercultural spirit. This is not to say novelty for its own sake did not become a habit among many, especially in academia, but it was not what generated the counterculture. Sixties' youth were after something deeper, something psychologically reliable, even if that something proved elusive. And this is why the sixties were about more than rebellion: they represented a quest for a new reality.

The Younger Generation and Modernism

In spite of the adversarial relationship that existed between the younger and older generations during the fifties and sixties over their contrasting views of reality, and their equally contrasting practices of freedom, the sixties' rebellion actually had its origins in mainstream culture. This should come as no surprise: the term most often used to describe the spirit of mainstream culture during the first half of the twentieth century is *modernism*, and modernists were very concerned about keeping up with the latest knowledge, trends, and ideas. It is not a difficult step, then, to forge a link between the "updating" theme of modernism and the "freedom" theme of the counterculture, or, ultimately, the "anarchist" theme of Stromberg's neophilia.

However, if one considers the genesis and evolution of modernism, one can detect and identify not only modernism's positive contribution to the counterculture but also the characteristics that irritated and finally infuriated sixties youth. One is tempted to consider in this regard a number of antecedents to modernism—in religion, science, and other aspects of culture—but the discussion needs to begin with economic trends, because one of the most spectacular changes in America during the second half of the nineteenth century, out of which modernism emerged, was the nation's industrialization and incorporation.[4] The expansion of industry not only created more jobs for more Americans, it also provided more goods for consumption, and this new affluence took its toll on conservative Victorian values. Because of periodic fluctuations in prosperity, people shared a certain persistent anxiety about their economic welfare, but they also shared an unprecedented capacity to purchase and consume.[5]

Some latter-day "Victorians," born around the turn of the century, who had experienced or even grown up in periodic prosperity, and later lived in the urban affluence of the twenties, participated to some degree in a counterculture of their own when they rebelled against the Victorian mantra of propriety and self-control that had been chanted into their childhood ears by teachers and parents born before the apex of industrialization. The opportunity to buy new things, which induced one to behave in new ways, tempted these middle-class Americans to challenge convention long before the sixties.[6]

The dialectical synthesis of American audacity in challenging convention in the 1920s and simultaneous quiescence to certain parts of the Victorian tradition resulted in what the cultural observers dubbed modernism. And though modernism's hunger for newness, its embryonic practice of neophilia, would be tamed by the Great Depression of the thirties and the wartime rationing of the forties—to say nothing for the moment of the lingering but increasingly disparaged creeds of a sober Protestant past—such deep deprivation would also build an intense but suppressed appetite for consumption, which, when once unleashed after the Second World War, stimulated the desire and capacity to create new forms of thought and behavior.[7]

Because radically reduced economic circumstances prevented modernist audacity from flourishing just prior to the Second World War, the mainstream culture of the World War II generation differed in some respects from that of the World War I generation. Nonetheless, there were commonalities. Like the older Victorians, who had faced economic downturns, global war, and the chimerical prosperity of the twenties, the younger World War II generation was caught up in a concern for self-preservation. This was not, however, a concern for individual self-preservation so much as for the collective preservation of the nation's hard-won prosperity. It was a preservation of the community premised upon conventions and constraints that enhanced social stability. Given the Great Depression and the Nazi threat and then the looming Soviets and their bombs, this concern with self-preservation seemed validated by past and present events for both the aging Victorians and the younger World War II generation.

To ensure continued prosperity, without returning to the excesses of the twenties that arguably provoked the Depression, America's mainstream highlighted those aspects of its heritage that seemed to have brought about dependable good times and that did not appear to threaten economic growth.[8] But what beliefs supported this preoccupation with economic self-preservation? After all, the sixties' generation would rebel not only against the behavior the older generation daily engaged in to "make a buck," but especially against the older generation's rationalizations for its daily behavior.

Drawing upon residual Victorian beliefs and practices and their own experience, members of the World War II generation by and large assumed that there existed one good and perfect system for economic progress. There may have been disagreement about the details of that one system, but it was often summed up as the "American way"; and most agreed as to what that system entailed—private property, capitalistic and consumer opportunity for all, the right to adhere to a religion that respected a Judeo-Christian ethos, and the right to vote in a democracy that supported the former criteria.[9]

Devoted to the American way, the mothers and fathers (and grandparents) of the Boomer Generation constructed a rather monolithic education system, media-information system, and, as best they could, propagandistic entertainment industry to nurture their American way.[10] There was still room for individualism, but the modern individual expected not only to achieve personal goals, but to participate in and support the American way of life. These precepts created and sustained the host of mainstream conventions, which resulted in, among other things, the suit-and-tie man and the suburban housewife. And it would seem to sixties' youth that there emerged a whole army of suit-and-tie men, seconded by subservient stay-at-home moms, that constituted an establishment, the Establishment, that was bent on compelling all Americans to abide by its rules and regulations to ensure economic stability and progress.

Modernism as Technocracy

The formula for economic success in the postwar era was based upon the efficient and productive use of technologies. There was nothing really new about this formula, except that the degree of attention lent to efficiency and productivity surpassed in breadth and depth whatever consideration had been given these elements prior to the industrial revolution. The commitment to technology was so profound and pervasive that cultural critics of the era referred disparagingly to their society as a *technocracy,* a society ruled by technocrats.

In its laconic style, *Webster's New International Dictionary* defined technocracy in 1934 as "Government or management of the whole of society by technical experts, or in accordance with principles established by technicians." That definition merits elaboration if we are to see how technocracy was viewed by radicals in the sixties. In order to achieve this, it is worth revisiting the arguments of postwar social critics.[11]

Although the concept of technocracy had been introduced by the end of World War I, French scholar Jacques Ellul fleshed out its meaning for modern society in his postwar work *La Technique* (1954), introduced to the English-speaking world in 1964 as *The Technological Society*.[12] In the sixties, professors Herbert Marcuse and Theodore Roszak, among others, borrowed the term to describe American society. As they used the term, it was not limited to technological development per se, but rather centered on the pragmatic but often haphazard construction of a society around the goal of continuous economic growth and prosperity, without regard for human aspirations unrelated to such a goal.[13]

Although most cultural critics believed men and women constructed the technocracy without any master plan and worked toward a common goal only because they agreed to common presuppositions about what constituted success, there were those who imagined the technocracy to be an imposed societal system, on a par with the one described in Aldous Huxley's *Brave New World* (1932). Such views may, in retrospect, seem paranoid, but one has to recall that this was an era marked by the totalitarian shadows of Italian fascism, Nazism, and Stalinism.

Although the technocracy was perhaps not as pervasive as Ellul, Marcuse, and Roszak claimed, one can easily argue that some measure of technocratic behavior and thinking did exist.[14] More importantly, however, many young people in the sixties ardently believed it existed, and saw it as conspiratorial; to describe it, they used suggestive epithets like "the System" or "the Establishment" or simply, and just as condescendingly, "Capitalism."[15] Whatever they termed it, sixties' rebels saw technocracy as an unfortunate consensus of thought among middle-class Americans (usually starting with their parents) that held forth that the pursuit of economic prosperity within the form of a technocratic ideal was the legitimate purpose and objective of the individual and of American society in general. Many young people rejected this subservience to the technocratic ideal because they perceived it as a mechanism for dehumanization.[16]

The Cold Scientific Heart of Modernism

Since efficient production, of the type Frank Bunker Gilbreth of *Cheaper by the Dozen* fame would have been proud, was the engine of the prosperity that the postwar establishment hoped to preserve, one is obliged to consider the presuppositions that fueled it in order to get at what prompted such deep opposition in the sixties.[17] First, it is evident that the technocracy was, by its very nature, materialistic. The knowledge or science that drove technocratic production did not dabble in the supernatural or pause over spiritual and moral questions but kept focused on measurable sensorial phenomena. In identifying this secularly based science that not only explained natural phenomena but also, in its most aggressive form, felt compelled to reduce all phenomena, including the religious, to natural explanations, one is tempted to label it as "naturalistic" or "materialistic" or perhaps as "scientism." This materialistic and antispiritual bias of technocracy helps to explain the spiritual dimension of the countercultural rebellion of the sixties.[18]

"Scientism" has a distant pedigree, and the secular worldview from which it derives is perhaps something inherent in the human mind. As the tools of empirical observation have increased and been perfected over time, and as the religious grounding of society has given way to a more secular footing, scientism has become, for us, much more refined and sophisticated. We can easily identify it in its modern garb by the end of the Victorian era.[19]

This is not to say that scientism can only operate in a mind or world devoid of religious thought. In fact, scientism owes something of its development in the seventeenth and eighteenth centuries to scholars, such as René Descartes, who were profoundly religious. Scientism even owes something to the zealous Protestants of that era, who so vehemently despised what they termed Catholic superstitions that they came to emphasize a general and rather nonintrusive providence of God over against precise and miraculous interventions, which they regarded as too closely associated with saints' lives and rosaries. Satan was still assumed to possess supernatural powers at the end of the seventeenth century, but by the end of the eighteenth-century Enlightenment, even Satan had lost his immediate hold on the world.[20]

According to atheists, agnostics, deists, and many intellectual Christians from the Enlightenment forward, the natural world with its laws was (and is) sufficient to explain sensory reality. But in order to explain the sensory world, the observer needed to be rationalized or calibrated to it; in other words, the observer needed to divest him or herself of all superstitions, which included hitherto "divinely inspired" emotions. After purging oneself of such otherworldliness, one could proceed to correctly interpret reality.[21] It was this approach that formed the worldview of scientism and, in turn, the intellectual justification for technocracy. The technocracy, then, had very secular and materialistic elements at its foundations.

Modernism's Truncated Spirituality

The foundational secular materialism in the technocracy, with its hostility to the supernatural, brings us to consider mainstream American religion during the twentieth century, because we know that along with the technocratic values that took hold during the postwar era, mainline Christianity thrived as well. The technocracy and modern Christianity apparently coexisted in a peaceable manner. This complicity actually repulsed many of the sixties' generation and inspired the spiritual dimension of their rebellion.

There is no mystery in the fact that mainstream Christianity and the technocracy were compatible in some respects. Early nineteenth-century Christianity as a whole had few qualms with the conclusions of science, though after the publication of Charles Darwin's *Origin of Species* in 1859 many Victorian churchgoers began to have second thoughts.[22] By the modern era, however, most mainstream clergymen had come round and were grateful for the new revelations of Darwin, Pasteur, Einstein, Curie, and the like, albeit some disputed how scientific discoveries were to be put to proper ethical use. The modern religious consensus was that because God had made nature and nature's laws, natural science was but an unbiased exposition of how God's creation was put together, what it was made of, and how it functioned.[23]

However, already during the latter half of the nineteenth century, as science explained more and more phenomena, including the alleged miracles of the Bible, exclusively in natural terms, mainstream religion, in perfect Victorian style, was obliged to divide the world in two in order to save a place for human interaction with the divine.[24] In the progressive Victorian and modern world, religious knowledge and scientific knowledge were both seen as valid, but religious knowledge confined itself to the nature of God—as reinterpreted according to the parameters of modern science—and to God's expectations of human conduct (ethics). Thus redefined, mainstream religion no longer attempted to explain physical phenomena as subject to radical or miraculous supernatural alteration. At best, Providence guided world events through the medium of natural law.[25]

The compartmentalization of knowledge into secular and religious categories had tremendous impact on mainstream Christianity and hence mainstream culture. It allowed modernists to be both Christians and scientists, or even Christians and technocrats. It meant that parishioners could publicly practice spirituality on Sunday, particularly from eleven a.m. to noon, and then, during the rest of the week, shift into a secular mode. This does not mean religion was wholly divorced from the workweek: certainly Christian ethics persisted, but overt spirituality would most assuredly have appeared awkward in the day-to-day world. The heartfelt relationship between the modern Christian and his or her God became internalized and subjective, a very personal and private matter that was not discussed at the office or on the assembly line.

Religion was not abandoned as the technocratic ideal matured. In some ways the role of religion became more important as religious leaders believed it increasingly necessary to humanize an otherwise increasingly dehumanized world.[26] Without the presence of religion, the technocratic ideal would solidify into a very cold, mechanized, and heartless society.[27] But mainstream Christianity became so convinced of the compartmentalized worldview that in the early twentieth century it began to condemn any spirituality that threatened its technocratic/religious association. Personal piety was fine as long as it did not question the findings of science.[28] In this way, mainstream Christianity abetted scientism and thereby appeared to encourage certain technocratic tendencies.

By the 1920s, mainstream Christianity, because it exercised a free interpretation of both doctrine and the Bible—free, that is, in the minds of its protagonists, from obscurantist traditions—had become known as liberalism.[29] Its assumption of a physical world/supernatural world dichotomy permeated Sunday school lessons and sermons, and eventually became normative in public institutions, including America's school system, which in the 1950s included the future radicals of the sixties.[30]

What was, in practice, this message that allowed for both modern science and spirituality? According to liberal doctrine, an individual could believe in and engage a God who touched the soul, but he or she could not easily believe in and engage a God who miraculously parted the Red Sea or multiplied bread and fishes. In liberalism, these biblical stories had to be reinterpreted according to the tenets of scientism.[31] The Red Sea parting was at best the result of an earthquake. As for the bread and fish, as many vividly recall from fourth-grade Sunday school lessons in a theologically liberal church, Jesus had simply given an example of sharing when he told his disciples to distribute their bread and fish, an example which then prompted the multitude to bring forth enough bread and fish for everyone. It was still a multiplication, but one rationalized with scientism, and it kept spirituality from indulging in premodern, and scientifically nonsensical, religious beliefs.[32]

Modern "Love"

For liberals, then, the focus of Christianity was limited, but it was limited to the highest moral principle, that of infinite love. As one liberal writer put it in the sixties, "The worship of God is a cultus of love."[33] Or as it had been expressed in 1950 by the Methodist bishop Herbert Welch, who was nearly ninety-years-old at the time, "Christianity is the Gospel of Love;" indeed, "the highest quality in man is that which is most like God—namely, love."[34] The neo-orthodox theologian Reinhold Niebuhr, who followed liberal thinking regarding science and the Bible, wrote in 1951 that "The Christian faith is the apprehension of the divine love and power which bears the whole human pilgrimage, shines through its enigmas and antinomies and is finally and definitively revealed in a drama in which suffering love gains triumph over sin and death."[35] Harry Fosdick, the most renowned liberal spokesman of the first half of the twentieth century, insisted in 1956 that love overruled all else, and cited his own famous polemical sermon of 1922 entitled "Shall the Fundamentalists Win?" when he stated, "Opinions may be mistaken, love never is."[36]

For liberals, love was more than just a definition for God, it was the guiding light for ethics. Reinhold Niebuhr emphatically pointed out that love was to be at the heart of the individual demanding action; even if love became lost in the collective and impersonal behavior of a social group or nation, the individual was still responsible for expressing love and acting in love.[37] And the love Niebuhr advocated was a selfless love, a love that did not expect a return in kind; it was to be the goal of the individual because it had been the defining act of God as symbolized by the cross.[38]

As one can see, the liberal call to love—as opposed to that of conservative Victorians (especially Victorian evangelicals) and their fundamentalist and Pentecostal offspring—aimed more narrowly at supporting "this worldly" aspirations and focused less on converting others to a biblically defined faith.[39] The fundamental importance of love was so crucial to mainstream society that the well-respected historian Arnold Toynbee used this theme in an attempt to unite the whole of history, when he wrote in 1956, "The meaning of Life, Existence, and Reality is Love."[40]

Using love as a centerpiece for civilization and individual behavior came easily to liberal Christianity.[41] Jesus Christ, liberals pointed out, came into the world as a testimony of love, and even if he did not do all the things the Bible claimed he did, he was still, at the very least, a symbol of perfect love. In the Christian tradition, God the all powerful, without being bound to do so, gave himself up in Christ in order to save people who despised him. The unity of the New Testament, wrote Reginald Fuller of Seabury-Western Theological Seminary in 1957, "lies in its testimony to Jesus Christ, in whom God wrought the decisive act of redemption which the Church now enjoys, and to whose completion it looks forward in the final consummation."[42] Love was true religion; and selfless love, as exemplified in the archetypal Christ on the Cross, embodied both the goal and fulfillment of the human soul.

Modern "Freedom"

Christians have traditionally defined love by referring to the following commandment that Jesus gave his followers: "Whatever you wish that men would do to you, do so to them; for this is the law and the prophets" (Matt 7:12). This principle is summarized as the golden rule. The influential liberal theologian Paul Tillich, in his book *The New Being* (1955), explained that the golden rule is not to be interpreted by Christians as a tit-for-tat repayment for kindnesses received. With Niebuhr, Tillich argued that the authentic Christian loves others by practicing the golden rule without selfish motives.[43]

The preeminence of the golden rule in liberalism belied a liberal premise about the nature of humankind that differed radically from traditional Reformation and Catholic interpretations. According to the historic biblical tradition which had informed American religious understanding since the days of its first Puritan settlers and through much of the Victorian age, humans were indelibly tainted with original sin and in dire need of regeneration.[44] Liberals, on the other hand, drawing from a combination of post-Reformation religious and philosophical interpretations of the nature of man, saw the human being as a free moral agent, and believed that all individuals innately possessed the capacity to carry out the golden rule.[45] There was no real necessity, therefore, to alter one's natural state, just one's attitude, if it were not in line with what one naturally knew to be right and ethical. For the liberal, the traditional Calvinistic concept of "the elect," as opposed to "the damned," and the evangelical concept of "conversion" became all irrelevant.[46] No longer was there a requirement for a defining, regenerative spiritual experience in the life of the believer. So the evangelical phrase "born again" (drawn from John 3:3-8) was dropped from the liberal vocabulary.

Because liberals were convinced that people were not inherently evil and could grow into godliness, they believed that individuals ought, in accordance with the dictates of love, to be allowed to think and act as they wished. This concept contributed to the idea of individual freedom in America, what cultural historians call expressive individualism.[47] Liberalism's confidence in a person's godly potential and in that person's right to act freely, combined with the centrality of the golden rule, allowed liberalism to refine and refocus Christianity. Particular religious beliefs extraneous to the golden rule, although perhaps of interest to one's personal devotion, became of secondary importance. Liberalism was thus in one sense quite focused in its definition of belief and conduct, in that these had to coincide with the premise of God as love, but it was quite hazy in its definition of the godhead, except that God had to be true to his loving nature.

The liberality or tolerance that became popular and primary in liberalism allowed for doctrinal pluralism within the fold of mainstream Christianity, although not for the "abrasive" and "judgmental" doctrines it had inherited from Victorian evangelicalism.[48] Certainly the traditional belief in a literal hell, or any form of divine punishment, dissipated as the belief in an all-loving God took shape. No longer was a person deemed sinful because he did not believe in the virgin birth or because he doubted the doctrine of the Trinity; rather, sinfulness was thought to reside, if anywhere, in the doctrinal intransigence of certain religionists. Indeed, a dogmatic Christian who held that belief in the bodily resurrection of Christ was necessary for salvation could be condemned inasmuch as he practiced intellectual intolerance. As Harry Fosdick preached, "As one watches [fundamentalists] and listens to them, one remembers the remark of General Armstrong of Hampton Institute: 'Cantankerousness is worse than heterodoxy.'"[49]

Unfortunately for the future membership of liberal denominations in the 1960s, confining God to matters of the heart would disenchant America's youth who were on a quest for a more pervasive spirituality.[50] The liberal respect for love they understood and accepted, but the theological restrictions some could not abide.[51] The rejection did not come about because sixties' youth did not understand liberalism. On the contrary, liberalism had carried on a very vigorous effort to enlighten America as to the true value of modern religion. Liberals were not embarrassed by their theology nor shy about sharing it.

Proselytizing America's Youth

In spite of the dearth of theological absolutes, other than those immediately connected to love, liberal Christians believed their form of Christianity to be ideal, as if it were the latest link, if not the final link, in the chain of religious evolution. Indeed, they held that other more traditional forms of Christianity, such as fundamentalism, were clearly anachronistic and doomed to extinction.[52] Since liberals assumed it would be ultimately self-evident to the good and rational nature within all people that their form of Christianity was correct, and that progressive society would endorse it, one might suppose that liberals did not indulge in proselytism. This was not the case, however, for even though liberals did not initiate evangelistic crusades *a la* Billy Graham, they were nonetheless committed to bringing everyone into the fold of liberalism. What differed was their attitude and approach, not their commitment to changing the world.

Liberals, certain that the tide was with them, confidently broadcast their worldview with little regard for the religious sensitivities of dissenters.[53] They were correct about the tide; with only a few notable exceptions, such as the establishment of Fuller Theological Seminary and the journal *Christianity Today,* dissenters did very little in the forties and fifties to directly challenge the liberal worldview being propagated through the nation's most prestigious institutions. The means the liberals had at their disposal certainly outclassed anything, other than purely ecclesiastical structures, that fundamentalists or Pentecostals could tap into.

That the liberal worldview played an influential role in the mainstream culture can be substantiated by the message showcased by the entertainment industry in the thirties, forties, and fifties. Films of this period are especially noteworthy, because in the age before television's preponderance the silver screen was the most powerful trendsetting tool in the country. Liberals found that they had ready allies in Hollywood. Powerful elites from the new immigrant community—Jewish and Catholic—were very influential in the movie industry because modern entertainment had its immediate origins in the great cities populated by newly arrived Italians, Poles, and other non-evangelicals. These immigrants, some of whom were intellectuals in their own right, were desirous of cultural freedoms and made common cause with liberal intellectuals who increasingly detested residual Victorian evangelical moral and social legalisms.

Hollywood produced a number of films that put the accent on golden rule living and on the liberal understanding of modern science and modern religion. One of the more carefully crafted films that underscored the golden rule ideal was *Mr. Deeds Goes to Town,* produced and directed by Frank Capra and brought into the movie houses during the Depression year of 1936. In this film, the likeable and humble Longfellow Deeds, played by Gary Cooper, unexpectedly inherits a fortune and is obliged to move from his sleepy small town to aggressive New York City, where he tends to his new estate. Because he is a generous soul, in keeping with the spirit of the golden rule, he is taken advantage of by unethical businessmen and lawyers. Even the attractive Babe Bennett (Jean Arthur), whom he falls for, is but a calculating and conniving reporter out for a headline story, a story that will ridicule and stigmatize him as the "Cinderella Man." Disgusted with the ways of the world, he plans to divide up his wealth and share it with the down-and-out. In order to prevent this, his business associates have him presented to a lunacy commission and analyzed by experts with the intention of getting him committed to a mental institution and relieved of his possessions. As the film concludes, however, the ultimately sincere love of the female reporter for him is revealed during the inquiry; and he then fights back and proves himself sane, while his accusers appear to be less competent, and certainly less moral, than he.[54]

In the film, the golden rule ethic is easily recognized in Longfellow Deeds' persistent generosity, and especially magnified by his offer to share his fortune with the indigent. But other tenets of liberalism are also highlighted. Longfellow Deeds represents man in his natural state, untainted by fast-paced city life; and he is good. Indeed, his exemplary goodness can bring out the inherent goodness in others, even in the initially cynical Babe Bennett. Underlying this goodness is love. It is ultimately the reciprocated love of Babe Bennett that restores him to fullness.

Perhaps the most intriguing part of the film, however, is the way it portrays the relationship between the technocracy and the golden rule ethic. Lacking the spirit of selfless love and the practice of the golden rule—which translates, in this case, to empowering the poor to make it on their own—the technocracy becomes an evil system. Even the experts are ridiculed when they attempt to explain Longfellow Deeds' goodness in scientific terms alone. In the final analysis, science and the inner goodness of man, which is known by intuition or faith, cannot be separated without serious social consequences. The goodness of man is a divine given, not something to be challenged by science.

Another movie that discoursed on the dialectic between the claims of scientism and the intuition of innate human goodness was *Spellbound*, directed by Alfred Hitchcock, and shown in theaters in 1945. In this film, the protagonist J. B., played by Gregory Peck, is basically a good man, and the psychoanalyst Dr. Peterson (Ingrid Bergman) intuitively knows this, as does the viewer; but it is hard to prove since it appears he has committed a murder. Through the use of the latest science, psychoanalysis, the truth of his goodness is ultimately revealed. But without the intuitive presupposition of goodness, the technocratic expert would not have pursued her inquiry. The upshot of this is that the intuition instilled in humankind, a faith of sorts, works in conjunction with modern science.[55] Science without faith is inhuman, while faith without science is folly. Or as the world's most renowned scientist, Albert Einstein, put it in 1941, "science without religion is lame, religion without science is blind."[56]

In spite of the harmonious relationship between modern religion and modern science, science nonetheless seemed to have the upper hand, as it alone had the capacity to expand its own frontier of expertise and diminish the jurisdiction of its religious competitor for knowledge, reliability, and prestige. As if kicking an already beaten and prostrate man, Hollywood's Stanley Kramer produced and directed a film that showcased the reason and common sense of modern science and mercilessly battered the superstition and obscurantism of faith without science. His *Inherit the Wind* is a romanticized reenactment of the John T. Scopes trial, in which the fundamentalist-inspired high school curriculum was challenged by the science of evolutionary theory. *The New York Times* reviewer applauded Fredric March's carefully executed portrayal of William Jennings Bryan, the silver tongued orator who, at the historic trial in Tennessee, defended the cause of fundamentalism against the withering onslaught of scientific logic. "The artistic virtue of [March's performance]," wrote reviewer Bosley Crowther in 1960, "is that it gives a stunning comprehension of a proud, pompous, demagogic man, full of dogmatic assertion and theatrical flourishes who stands serenely encircled by ignorance until the locks of his own mind are forced."[57]

Conclusion

Liberalism did not limit itself to the entertainment industry. As already mentioned, educational institutions and the news media also provided a forum for the liberal message. And the force of the liberal propagandistic pressure upon American society only accented for youth the real limits of their own freedom.

It is true that for most of the rebellious youth of the sixties, liberalism's gospel of tolerance and pluralism would be used to defy the politically conservative establishment; but sixties' youth would also conduct a spiritual rebellion that turned the tables on liberalism.[58] The more spiritually inclined youth would defy the accommodation liberalism had made with scientism, and they would demand the right to tap into the supernatural and to allow the supernatural to tap into the world.[59] The very creativity that modernism had bequeathed to the postwar generation would be used to experiment with new forms of thought and behavior that would deny essential conventions of modernism. To be sure, the affluent middle-class youth who attended college in increasing numbers during the 1960s would retain a respect for intellectual endeavor and continue to disdain obscurantism, but of these six characteristics of the mainstream culture—liberal theology, scientism, golden rule ideal, intellectualism, affluence, and freedom—liberal theology and scientism would be radically rejected. In their stead would come a spiritual quest and ultimately a new religious identity.

2

The Counterculture

Although the youth of the sixties rebelled against many of the strictures of their parents' generation, they did retain at least two important older-generation principles. They never abandoned, in the main, a commitment to the golden rule ideal, and they never relented in their pursuit of freedom or expressive individualism.[1] What they did reject was the conformism that forbade them the right to do new things and think new ideas.

The tool they used to break the shackles of conformism was logic, and this tool could be used in two ways. In the first place, it could be used to show that if a particular thought or practice did not violate the golden rule, then that thought or practice ought not be denied. If it were denied, the overbearing moralist prohibiting it would be guilty of the true sin of intolerance. Intolerance could not be abided because the virtue of tolerance, or pluralism, was thought to be sacredly embodied in the golden rule and highlighted in certain gospel verses, such as, "Love your enemies," or "Judge not, that you be not judged."[2] Secondly, the tool of logic could be used to expose inconsistencies that existed between parental traditions and the ideals of love and freedom. Using logic in this fashion, the younger generation could accuse their parents of being obscurantists or hypocrites.[3] And whenever these accusations were compelling, they easily won over the vast majority of America's youth, which constituted the fastest growing, most activist and energetic, and soon-to-be most highly educated segment of the population.[4]

Charges of intolerance and hypocrisy became the weapons of choice for America's youth because they were so effective against a worldview that accepted tradition for tradition's sake and that compartmentalized knowledge and behavior.[5] If wearing long hair hurt no one, then why deny America's young men the freedom to do so? If rocking and rolling harmed none, if smoking or drinking damaged none but oneself, then why forbid? The rule to live by became, "If it doesn't hurt anyone else, you can do it." And this rule itself pointed toward a logical conclusion that was often reiterated and followed during the sixties, "If it feels good, do it."[6] And what was the parental rebuttal to, say, long hair to be? "Only girls wear long hair." To which the youthful rebel sniped, "And so what?" or, more biting yet, "And so Jesus and George Washington were wrong? Besides, I thought you liked Custer." These were the quibbles that went on in American homes throughout the sixties, and though they may seem trifles now, they were the stuff the counterculture was made of.[7]

The youthful challenges that seem less trifling to us today are the accusations of bald hypocrisy. Beyond the petty quibbles over mere habits of style, many young people objected to societal double standards, pointing out the actual harm perpetrated upon others by elders, in clear contravention of the golden rule ideal. To affirm, for example, during Sunday's worship hour that there was "neither Jew nor Greek" (Gal 3:28), and then to recount "nigger" jokes during the ensuing "fellowship" hour reeked of malicious hypocrisy.[8] Or to celebrate the *Declaration of Independence*, with its proclamation that all men are created equal, as the foundational statement for the American way, and then to permit segregation, was adding injury upon insult.[9] And then again, when parishioners nodded in agreement on Sunday that "the love of money is the root of all evils" (1 Tim 6:10) but then went off to work on Monday to bilk the innocent or vulnerable, they again betrayed their moral duplicity. And most disconcerting for many young males were the Sunday school teachers who recited "Blessed are the peacemakers" but then condoned the politicians who herded them off to war.[10]

The accusation of hypocrisy and the accusation of intolerance, if successfully argued, put youth on the high moral ground, at least from their perspective, and gave them a crusading confidence in whatever argument or cause they championed.[11] This often cocky and sometimes exhilarating confidence was the emotional verification that they were indeed free individuals standing firm against "the system." And the taste of freedom they experienced through argument and activism gave them greater appetite for more argument and activism, and for more freedoms.

A New Freedom

The drive for more freedoms became apparent in many areas of life by the 1960s. In art, Jackson Pollock and others had already violated American aesthetic and cultural restrictions in the 1940s. In the sixties, Andy Warhol had added again more freedom to American artwork by featuring pop culture in his works.[12] The early yearnings for expressive freedom in literature are recognizable in the fifties; at the beginning of the decade, J. D. Salinger's *Catcher in the Rye* featured the nonconformist youth Holden Caulfield. The Beats, especially Jack Kerouac and Allen Ginsberg, offered convention-breaking ideas and vocabulary to America's readership.[13] The demand for freedom hit America's campuses in a big way in the early 1960s, beginning, perhaps, with Tom Hayden's *Port Huron Statement*.[14]

During the pivotal first years of the sixties, the cause of freedom became bigger than the inspirational Civil Rights movement. In 1964 the desire to be free became vocalized with Berkeley's "Free Speech Movement."[15] Soon, freedom reached out into lifestyles, as middle-class youth dispensed with suit and tie, donned jeans and sandals, and took to living in communes. In music, rock 'n' roll, the lingua franca of youth ever since Bill Haley's 1955 "Rock Around the Clock," gave lyrics and a beat to the expressive individualism that played through the counterculture.[16] And Hollywood was no latecomer. In the fifties, in spite of Joe McCarthy's long shadow, films like *Auntie Mame* (1958) told people to get the braces off their brains and to "Live! Live! Live!"[17] In sum, the mantra of freedom echoed through art, literature, politics, lifestyle, song, and film. Its actualization seemed to be its own catalyst, as the breaking of one hypocritical convention or the challenging of one intolerance led to the breaking and challenging of others.

Amongst the various freedoms sixties' youth sought was spiritual freedom. Given the deep individualism that underwrote the American desire for freedom, the meaning of spiritual freedom spread out into numerous paths of understanding. But no matter what direction this spiritual desire took, whether toward Eastern mysticism or toward Western philosophy and religion or a mixture of these, it had one purpose: to escape the scientism that imprisoned the modern temper.[18] This was one of the most radical rejections of the establishment, even more so in some respects than the rejection of capitalism by the New Left. Here again, youth employed their well-sharpened wit and shattered the compartmentalized worldview of their elders. To affirm God's omnipresence on Sunday morning and then to find him absent on the morrow made no sense. To likewise affirm God's omnipotence and then to subsequently find him powerless to perform miracles made no more sense than his "omnipresent absence." Spiritually frustrated sixties' youth wanted a way out of the modernist prison; their countercultural adventure was nothing less than a spiritual quest.[19]

The spiritual quandary that plagued sixties' youth is illustrated in the comments made by a graduating senior in a 1963 issue of the *Princeton Weekly*: "The trouble with me is that I can't believe in anything. On Sundays, I can, but most of the time I am smarter than that. I have been taught to question, not to believe, so I never know where to stop. . . . What I want is a cause; what I cannot have is a cause, because I know that causes are the opiate of the masses. . . . I am therefore unable to define myself."[20]

This quotation was included in an article contributed to *The Christian Century* by an author who believed he had an answer for the distraught student. But when one reads Herbert Stroup's article, and when one reflects upon the decline in youth membership in the liberal church during the sixties, and the rise of youth membership in biblically grounded churches, one realizes how inadequate the liberal solution was for many young people.[21] Stroup concluded that a person would only find fulfillment in being responsible to others and in finding others who would be responsible to him. "The fulfillment of the self," he stated, "must be sought in social contexts in which self-elected purposes are achieved through responsible action."[22]

Stroup's article was another solid exposition of the golden rule ideal, but it fell short of providing spiritually disgruntled youth with a connection to the godhead. According to Stroup, fulfillment was found primarily horizontally, among one's fellow human beings; the vertical relationship with a God who acted like the God of the Bible readings on Sundays was virtually absent. Spiritually sensitive youth of the sixties, however, wanted a worldview as seamless as Christ's garment, one that had no demarcation between life and belief. In this quest, some set out in one direction, toward a secular god, like the one proclaimed in the sixties' Death of God theology, and others set out in another direction, toward a world alive with the supernatural.

The Spiritual Quest

It is hard to overestimate the spiritual element in America's counterculture, but it is nonetheless often neglected in favor of studies that emphasize the drugs, sex, rock 'n' roll, political protests, and sensational but sporadic Mansonite mayhem of the era. In reality, the quest for spiritual freedom was quite pervasive, and it stands to reason. America's middle-class youth, the rank and file of the counterculture, had been nurtured during the forties and fifties in religion's greenhouse, the Sunday school. Of those baby boomers born between 1944 and 1960, 86 percent had formal religious training.[23] The nurturing Sunday school environment, because of its alleged subservience to the technocratic establishment, seemed stifling to many youth, but at the same time, it introduced them to symbols that if viewed in a fresh way could be used as weapons with which to resist, assail, and overturn the status quo.

Contemporary cultural critics frequently noted the spiritual dimension of the conflict between mainstream culture and sixties agitation.[24] In early 1964, Jacques Ellul argued in his foreword to the American edition of his work, *The Technological Society*, that people needed to become aware of the threat that scientism (my term) posed to spirituality. The technocracy, he warned, was establishing a grip over culture, and individuals needed to "assert their freedom by upsetting the course of this evolution."[25] Even Herbert Marcuse, a neo-leftist, recognized that man was losing his humanity and was becoming one dimensional in modernistic society.[26] One of the most celebrated critics of the technocratic ideal in America during the sixties, Theodore Roszak, specifically pointed to the spiritual challenge of the counterculture.

In 1969, Roszak asserted in his highly successful book, *The Making of a Counter Culture*, "The truth of the matter is no society, not even our severely secularized technocracy, can ever dispense with mystery and magical ritual." For Roszak, and for those youth who either previously viewed society according to his interpretation or who now adopted that interpretation, scientism had become an invasive and malicious ideology shoring up a heartless mainstream culture. "Ideology is not absent in the technocracy," observed Roszak with dismay (and this, in an era when many intellectuals had proclaimed an end to ideology), "it is simply invisible, having blended into the supposedly indisputable truth of the scientific world view." Furthermore, he concluded disparagingly, "The most effective ideologies are always those that are congruent with the limits of consciousness, for then they work subliminally."[27]

According to Roszak, too many Americans thought and behaved in concert with the technocratic ideal. But America's youth, heirs to the modernistic attributes of creativity, individualism, and freedom, used their inheritance to challenge modernism itself by breaking the technocratic mold. Roszak admired this audacity in the younger generation.

In his enthusiasm, Roszak lauded the mystics who dispensed with the compartmentalized worldview of the establishment and, in his mind at least, reunified knowledge in a truly scientific way, in a way that made man whole and eliminated hypocrisy. "The mystics," he wrote, "in accepting the fullness of human experience, have been more truly scientific than the conventional scientist, who insists that only what makes itself apparent to an arbitrarily limited range of consciousness deserves attention."[28] If the closed worldview system of scientism would not open itself to the worldview of the rising generation that allowed for the spiritual, all humanity would be trapped in bondage to a machine. "An integral part of the counter culture," Roszak insisted, was the "unprecedented penchant for the occult, for magic, and for exotic ritual."[29] And he added, "The dissenting young have indeed got religion." But he concluded that it was "Not the brand of religion Billy Graham or William Buckley would like to see the young crusading for—but religion nonetheless."[30] Little did he know, in spite of his denunciation of rock 'n' roll and his itching desire to cut the hippies' hair, Billy Graham was warmer to the new spirituality than Roszak supposed.[31]

To foreign observers, the spirituality of America's countercultural youth was probably more evident than it was to most homegrown critics who, accustomed to America's religious rhetoric, did not always find youthful references to religious symbols particularly noteworthy. Michel Lancelot, a French journalist with an educational background in psychology, is a case in point. He began in earnest to investigate the American countercultural movement in 1967 and made some incisive observations. For Lancelot, coming from a country nearly devoid of evangelical traditions, the culture shock, triggered by the religious themes he felt emanating from America's youth, was so powerful that references to spirituality rippled throughout his book-length report.

In sum, Lancelot observed that the vaunted generation gap itself could be explained in terms of a spiritually motivated quest, on the part of youth, for a new worldview not beholden to scientism.[32] "As their elders journey across space or violate the ocean depths," he wrote, "these young embark on an inner exploration of their soul, and give themselves brainwashings in order to find anew a purity of thought and perception."[33] In this exploration, youth rejected the old religion that had quarantined spirituality in time and place, that is, to say, from eleven a. m. to noon on Sunday and under a church steeple. They searched for something overarching.[34] And in this search, they became eclectic and intrigued by all things religious, hoping to find a religion that quickened all aspects of life, encompassing all thought and behavior.[35] In a visit to San Francisco, Lancelot noted this avid thirst for a new spirituality when he witnessed hippies enthusiastically drinking up the words and wisdom of Jesus Christ and simultaneously reading the *Bhagavad-Gita*. But the eclecticism was not random and reckless, it had purpose; even drug use, Lancelot soon discovered, was only a means to an end for many hippies, who were really practicing a freedom to access a spiritual world founded upon the golden rule, upon love.

The first objective, wrote Lancelot of the hippies, was "to preach and to practice Love under all its forms, both individual and universal."[36] And here Lancelot was very perceptive. This was not Stromberg's neophilia in its purest definition. It was not newness for the sake of newness; it was rather experimentation with new ideas in a spiritual quest to validate a deep conviction that real achievement could only be attained through authentic fulfillment of the golden rule.

As a necessary corollary to this spiritual quest for fulfillment was the intellectual quest to rationalize the golden rule with expressive individualism; the two cherished themes that survived from modernism had to accommodate each other in the emerging countercultural consciousness. For if the golden rule were validated by divine approbation, then individualistic freedom could not be allowed to swallow up charity, lest God be seen as condoning intolerance and hatred and every other vice that might spring up out of the human heart. For many countercultural radicals, such as a John Lennon, the counterculture had limits, but for others, like Charles Manson, it did not. Our concern, in this volume, is with the former.

Spiritual Options in the Sixties

The sixties are peppered with explorations into religious thought that confirm Lancelot's observations. Some of the radical liberal theologians would even break the mold of liberalism and authenticate God by identifying spirituality with the secular. John A. T. Robinson's rather notorious *Honest to God* appeared in 1963, and by 1966 the Death of God theologians had generated a media storm.[37] Chaim Potok's *The Chosen* (1967) described the spiritual struggle young Jewish men had with the secular world and with the older generation. The narrator, young Reuven Malter ultimately decides to pursue a spiritual vocation, and he does so probably because his father left him the option not to do so. His alter ego, Danny Saunders, decides to abandon tradition and become a psychologist. The effort to validate spirituality by translating it into modern scientific concepts was a logical pursuit for liberal intellectuals.

Often the line blurred between spirituality, with its connection to the divine, and purely human psychic activity. As early as the fifties, Aldous Huxley was pointing toward new realms of consciousness; and writings such as Timothy Leary's *High Priest* (1968) and Tom Wolfe's *Electric Kool-Aid Acid Test* (1968) demonstrated that countercultural youth wanted that line to be blurred so that they might go beyond scientism.[38]

Some of the explorations sought answers in an Eastern mysticism that would eventually direct many Americans toward the New Age movement of the late seventies and eighties.[39] Allen Ginsberg's 1955 "Footnote to Howl" began by chanting fifteen times the word "Holy!" and then proceeded to claim everything holy. "Holy the supernatural extra brilliant intelligent kindness of the soul!" but holy also the sea, the desert; the very world itself.[40] Jack Kerouac, who authored *The Dharma*

Bums (1958), elicited a mystical connection with nature and called for a rejection of the technocratic mantra to "consume, work, produce, consume." His influence was still profound more than a decade later: nature-minded youth faithfully carried *The Dharma Bums* to Earth Day 1970.[41]

Robert Pirsig's popular *Zen and the Art of Motorcycle Maintenance* (1974) likewise used Eastern thought to address the spiritual interests of America's young and their desire to fulfill a spiritual quest. According to Pirsig, the end of the quest could only come when one accepted the reality at hand and ceased to pursue solutions to the problems that dualistic-minded Westerners got stuck on; otherwise, one was "endlessly pursuing questions, never seeing, never understanding that the questions will never end." For Pirsig, "Quality" could only be reached when a person dissolved the subject/object relationship, which was at the source of spiritual dissatisfaction. In other words, let the world be what it is and move with it. "An egoless acceptance of stuckness is a key to an understanding of all Quality, in mechanical work as in other endeavors." The answer would come in a feeling, and a feeling that is "not just on the surface of things, but penetrates all the way through."[42]

There was a desire in the counterculture to resolve the malaise born of the technocratic ideal and to resolve it in an emotional or spiritual way that was in harmony with love, just as Pirsig's Chris, at the close of the quest, finally gave up on hatred and found everything henceforth so different. Most youth, however, would find Pirsig's grail half full; they wanted something more than what seemed to them a mere indifference to the strictures and conventions of nature and society. Some among these dissatisfied wanted to change the world, to disrupt nature and societal conventions; in short, they wanted a connection to the supernatural that would empower them to defy and destroy the technocracy. Pirsig, the Death of God theologians, and the other sixties' guides who pointed in directions that did not really offer that connection, would simply not do.

The Spirit of Love

The countercultural youth who set out on the spiritual quest that shaped sixties' culture usually exhibited certain shared characteristics. They were spiritual, of course, and retained the golden rule ideal of their parents, but they were also affluent, for they had come out of the middle class, and being affluent, they could bask in expressive individualism. Also due to their middle-class origins, they were educated and therefore respected logical argumentation and intellectual sophistication. All these factors—their intellectual sophistication, their expressive individualism, their affluence, and their commitment to the golden rule ideal—shaped their spiritual quest.

In the songs and films of the sixties, one finds these themes cropping up again and again, which makes it possible for us to get a feel for their sixties' resonance. Perhaps the easiest theme to identify is the commitment the younger generation had to love and tolerance. For many youth, racism and war were obvious violations of the golden rule ideal and needed to be exorcised from American culture. In their public protests against these violations, youth sharpened their definition of countercultural tolerance and love.

In 1963, before Vietnam had become regular fare on the nightly news, Bob Dylan's antiwar ballad "Blowin' in the Wind" had already been rendered famous by the sweet harmony of Peter, Paul, and Mary. "How many times must the cannonballs fly, before they are forever banned?"[43] The answer would be blowing in the wind of the antiwar demonstrations. Bearing their golden rule Sunday school lessons in their grown up hearts, America's youth frowned upon war even before the Gulf of Tonkin. The direct intervention into Vietnam and the subsequent military draft, especially the coerced participation that the draft entailed, prompted youth to extend their concept of the golden rule beyond America's impoverished, beyond her racial minorities; it inspired them to extend it to the whole world. By the end of the decade, some of America's youth enthusiastically looked forward to the dawning of a better world graced with love and global harmony. The Fifth Dimension's song "Aquarius/Let the Sun Shine In" celebrated that hope, and hit the top of the charts in the spring of 1969.[44]

In practical terms, the love extolled by youth was to be manifested most nobly in the practice of tolerance and acceptance; the only people to be shunned, of course, were the intolerant ones. This aspect of the golden rule punctuated the music of the sixties. The most popular group of the decade, The Beatles, echoed the theme in their 1966 hit, "We Can Work It Out." "Life is very short," admonished the Beatles, "and there's no time for fussing and fighting, my friend. I have always thought that it's a crime, so I will ask you once again. Try to see it my way, only time will tell if I am right or I am wrong."[45] By the end of the decade Ray Stevens sang out that "Everything Is Beautiful."[46] In this hit, he told his listeners what they already knew; "[W]e shouldn't care about the length of his hair or the color of his skin. Don't worry about what shows from without but the love that lives within." If there were to be a countercultural love, it would have to accept everyone; if there were to be a countercultural spirituality, it would have to be tolerant and broad-minded.

Hollywood showed equal enthusiasm for promoting the golden rule ideal and the tolerance it entailed. It was a theme that could speak to both generations, but the films that spoke most clearly and specifically to youth were those films that turned the golden rule into a judgment against the status quo. One movie that comes to mind is *To Kill A Mockingbird* (1962), wherein lawyer Atticus Finch (Gregory Peck) proved to be not only the kindest man in a small southern town, but also the only person courageous enough to risk himself and his reputation in defending a Negro maliciously accused of rape.[47] This film faithfully echoed the civil rights cause that many youth endorsed as a spiritually meaningful expression of the golden rule ideal.[48]

Some of the movies that championed the golden rule were not overtly countercultural, but others certainly were. One does not think of *Mary Poppins* (1964), for example, as countercultural, but in a sense it was, even though its magical storyline successfully charmed both generations.[49] What one sees in *Mary Poppins* from the perspective of the young viewer is not only an endorsement of nonstop fun and games and an emphasis on the miraculous dimension to life, which in itself is a judgment against the technocratic ideal, but also an appreciation for human relationship or love rather than moneymaking. The father in the story must be convinced that excessive devotion to his job is wrong and that devotion to human beings, his family, and leisure activities (flying a kite) is what life is all about.

Guess Who's Coming to Dinner (1967) and *Love Story* (1970) were more pointedly celebrations of youth's virtue and passion and a judgment against the older generation's shallow hypocrisy.[50] Both movies challenged parental attitudes and celebrated the love and acceptance expressed by the younger generation. But no movie so overtly exposed youth's new spirituality, with its elevation of golden rule behavior to sublime heights, as the musical *Jesus Christ Superstar* (1973), which furnished the poignant hit song "I Don't Know How to Love Him."[51]

Freedom and Spirituality

Just as there was a certain idealistic spirituality expressed in many pop culture articulations of love and the golden rule ethic, so too did the theme of spirituality coalesce with the harder-edged elements of the counterculture, with the pursuit of freedom and the rebellion against the norms of the parental establishment. We find in the songs and films of the era a vibrant protest against the "outmoded" older generation. In 1965, The Who, one of the most popular of the rock bands that emerged from England to conquer America's youth with their trenchant vibes, asked spitefully of their elders in "My Generation," "Why don't you all f-fade away?"[52] In November of the same year, The Rolling Stones warned the killjoys menacing youthful desires to "Get Off of My Cloud."[53] By 1968 the group Steppenwolf had announced they were "Born to Be Wild"; and they sang on behalf of their contemporaries, "Like a true nature's child, we were born, born to be wild. We can climb so high, I never wanna die."[54] The Rascals hit number one when they pleaded, "People Got to Be Free," and called out to the world, "Listen, please listen, that's the way it should be. Deep in the valley, people got to be free."[55]

Few cinematic productions expounded this message more inspiringly than the astoundingly successful movie *The Graduate* in 1967.[56] In the film, the upper middle-class father asks his son, Ben, played by Dustin Hoffman, who has just returned from college, what he wants out of life. "Something different" is the simple but important response. By the end of the movie, Ben has convinced his heartthrob Elaine (Katharine Ross) to abandon her middle-class destiny as well. She hesitates, however, and it does seem to the viewer that she might marry someone other than Ben, another man approved for her by her parents. But at the last minute she flees the church, the ultimate symbol of the establishment's ritualistic and therefore nonsensical conformity, and in her flight escapes social convention and runs toward an undefined but sure freedom with Ben. The relatively low-budget movie connected powerfully with America's youth, surpassing its competitors in box office income and coming in fourth amongst the top grossing films released within two years of its distribution.

One should not think this movie deprecated spirituality; rather its spite was aimed more at hypocrisy and mindless ritualism. Indeed its famous soundtrack, by Simon and Garfunkel, includes the song "Mrs. Robinson," which alludes to faith in a cryptic way, but in a way nonetheless charged with Christian terms and symbols. "Jesus loves you more than you will know," the folk-rocker sings, "God bless you please, Mrs. Robinson, Heaven holds a place for those who pray."[57]

In the superb counterculture film *Easy Rider* (1969), the theme of freedom courses through every frame.[58] The two footloose heroes, Wyatt (Peter Fonda) and Billy (Dennis Hopper), move across America's landscape on their chopper motorcycles heading for a good time in New Orleans. On the way, they encounter a rancher-farmer, a hippie commune, a small town southern lawyer (an alcoholic but perceptive man), and crass rednecks. By the time they meet their doom at the end of a redneck gun blast, it seems Wyatt and perhaps Billy have discovered something about life. Life is about freedom and authentic love.

The introspective hero Wyatt admires the life of the rancher-farmer—as opposed to the urbanite caught up in the technocratic rat race—who can "do his own thing in his own time." He also understands the spirit of the commune, wherein men and women live off their own labor, are beholden to none, are at peace in a mystical way with the environment, and are willing to share themselves with those of like mind. But it is the small time lawyer, George Hanson (Jack Nicholson), who reveals to them the dire nature of the American establishment that they live in. Real America is not free like they are, and real America therefore feels threatened by them. In the end, all three will be murdered because of their insistence on freedom and their refusal to be conformists.

Easy Rider, however, is not just about being free; it also locks into religious imagery: by the prayer said at the rancher-farmer's house, in the mystical moments in the commune setting, in the Jesus graffiti scribbled on the wall of a jail, and in the religious imagery displayed in the New Orleans cemetery, the viewer is bombarded with an authentication of things spiritual. Reinforcing the imagery is the Byrd's soundtrack "Jesus Is Just Alright." Whether it is *Easy Rider, The Graduate* or even the grittier countercultural flick *Midnight Cowboy* (1969), or later *M*A*S*H* (1970), religion always seems to edge its way in, and it did so because countercultural youth could relate to it, and wanted it included, no matter how ambivalent their feelings about their old Sunday school lessons.[59] At one point in *Midnight Cowboy* a fundamentalist-styled preacher hounds the would-be stud Joe Buck (John Voigt), whose empty mind holds no moral distinctions congruent with traditional Christianity. What is significant is that the director of the film expected his young audience to understand the preacher's religious jargon and gesticulations, just as he expected it to be repulsed by and to mock such anachronistic dogmatism. The director understood the spiritual quest of the sixties' youth.

In *M*A*S*H*, we find the same phenomenon. To save a despondent dentist from killing himself, Hawkeye (Donald Sutherland) and his cohorts engineer a salutary religious experience for their friend. At the conclusion of a last supper, which is in imitation of the Last Supper as depicted by Leonardo da Vinci, the dentist swallows his fatal dose of poison, which turns out to be a sleeping potion. He awakens to a heavenly sexual encounter, made possible by a compassionate and compliant nurse.

The countercultural audience understood spirituality and appreciated the inclusion of spiritual motifs in film because many of them were seeking out a spirituality for their own lives. And many of these spiritual "seekers" of the sixties wanted a spirituality that went beyond the religious restrictions established by the older generation and mainstream society. This meant that they not only wanted to venture beyond the stereotypical religiosity of fundamentalism, but beyond the spirituality of mainstream religion as well. They wanted a spirituality that encompassed an authentic golden rule and defied the white, middle-class technocracy.

Conclusion

In sum, the youth of the sixties counterculture possessed a remarkable sensitivity to things spiritual. The spirituality that they were drawn to accommodated certain passions that they inherited from the otherwise despised older generation; passion for freedom (expressive individualism) and the golden rule ideal would be two of the most prominent. In the songs and films patronized by young people, these two themes, along with that of a renegade spirituality, often shared the limelight. The problem for writers, filmmakers, songsters, and for many of the young people themselves was to rationalize, or bring into a logical harmonious relationship, expressive individualism, the golden rule ideal, and an acceptable type of spirituality.

The spiritual solution had to be authentic and self-consistent—that is, bereft of hypocrisy and shorn of the constraints of time or place—because youth demanded it; being middle class and educated, they responded best to messages framed with a measure of intellectual sophistication. True, they swayed to music with innocent lyrics, like "I Want to Hold Your Hand," and watched superficial but fun movies like *Beach Blanket Bingo*, but they also found depth of meaning in "We Shall Overcome" and "Blowin' in the Wind," and they probed their own worldview and spiritual consciousness in *The Graduate*, *Easy Rider*, and *M*A*S*H*.[60]

A spirituality that would support and validate both a passion for the golden rule and the imperative of expressive individualism was not easy to come by. The golden rule ideal demanded an ethical lifestyle conforming to infinite love, and yet if ethics were validated spiritually, that is, by the supernatural, it would be hard to say ethics did not limit expressive individualism, because the moment the godhead stated that one thing was eternally good, its opposite became eternally evil. A clear-cut sense of right and wrong made expressive individualism uncomfortable. The balancing of the golden rule ideal and expressive individualism would demand some creative thinking on the part of countercultural youth.

Furthermore, countercultural youth also had to deal with their middle-class affluence. How would one rationalize affluence and the golden rule? Fortunately, the apparent contradiction between a life of affluence and a life of love (of living for others) was not as difficult to resolve as that between a spiritually validated system of ethics and an allowance for expressive individualism. In fact, countercultural baby boomers seemed to easily detach affluence from the technocracy. They spent, but they did not think it necessary to enslave themselves to the "rat race." They could live in plenty, welcoming dad and mom's monetary contributions to their lifestyle at college, or they could wander the streets, drop into a commune and get by with the minimum necessary for sustenance. Easy come and easy go, they could share and share alike. One could be loving and affluent, as long as one did not step onto the technocracy's corporate ladder and crush people on each rung as one climbed to the top. One could have money and things and yet love. And if one found the spiritual answer, one could undoubtedly continue to be affluent and loving, as long as one did not join the technocratic system which precluded authentic spirituality by making religion subservient to efficient productivity.[61]

In the end, as many of these countercultural youth embarked on the road to self-realization through a spiritual quest, they distanced themselves from their theologically liberal past and considered alternative routes to religious expression. One of these routes took them in the direction of biblically grounded Christianity.

3

Old-Time Religion and New-Time Youth

Biblically grounded Christianity in the mid-twentieth century was anything but a monolithic religious establishment; indeed, it had several expressions, which one could divide up into the following general groups: fundamentalist, Pentecostal, new evangelical, and charismatic.[1] Some of these expressions of biblically grounded Christianity would prove to be very enticing to countercultural youth, and some would not. Fundamentalism, for example, easily antagonized America's boomer generation. Yet if it were not for fundamentalism, it would be hard to explain the future success of biblically grounded Christianity amongst sixties' youth. To understand how fundamentalism furthered the cause of biblically grounded Christianity, we need to understand the social and political nature of fundamentalism and its relationship to America's middle-class youth.

The Bible Trumps Intellect, Love, and Pop Culture

First and foremost, fundamentalists had an unwavering faith in the veracity of the Bible. For them, the Bible communicated to humankind the realities of things supernatural and natural, spiritual and material. Confidently ensconced in this worldview, they pronounced sentence upon the world and the human condition, preaching that all men and women were sinful, youth not excepted, and were hell-bound unless they repented of their wickedness and accepted Jesus as their Savior, for such was the unadulterated message of the gospel.

The fundamentalist devotion to Scripture would be maintained up to and through the 1960s. In 1965, for example, a well-known fundamentalist minister, W. A. Criswell, devoted several sermons to the trustworthiness of the Bible and derided mainline Christians and others who shortchanged or mocked its accounts of miracles and claims about Jesus' divinity.[2] This single-minded commitment to the Bible certainly alienated most of America's middle-class youth who had been taught that open-mindedness and dialogue were prerequisites for living out the golden rule.

Furthermore, it seemed to many youth that fundamentalists, in their zeal to make religious converts, ignored the socioeconomic needs of the poor and oppressed. And it is true that from the inception of fundamentalism, its advocates had often ridiculed liberal Christian philanthropy. Billy Sunday, the popular Bible-thumping evangelist of the early 1900s, could not get enough of condemning liberals for preoccupying themselves with social work while dismissing the eternally important issues of repentance and conversion. Mainline ministers returned fire by charging that Sunday and his ilk, by limiting their own works to sermons on "judgment and hell," exhibited a visceral and chronic disregard for the golden rule.[3] Even after Billy Sunday passed away in 1935, this liberal criticism of fundamentalism was still common fare in sermons and Sunday school lessons served up to mainline parishioners both old and young.

The aversion that young people had to fundamentalism, however, was not entirely due to the persistent polemics of liberal clergy and secular humanist skeptics. The fundamentalists themselves helped their ideological enemies marginalize conservative faith. Soon after an especially incisive and withering critique of fundamentalism in 1922 by America's renowned liberal Christian orator, Harry Fosdick, biblically grounded Christians promoted ever more enthusiastically an ecclesiological strategy that surrendered mainstream culture to the liberal Christians and secular humanists. A year after Fosdick's "Shall the Fundamentalists Win?" the most erudite defender of fundamentalism, Princeton Seminary's J. Gresham Machen, published *Christianity and Liberalism*, and through its pages he made a clarion call to biblically grounded Christians to either eject liberals from their midst or withdraw from churches hopelessly fallen under liberal hegemony.

Separatism, of course, was already being practiced as a matter of course by many churches outside the middle-class Methodist, Presbyterian, Episcopalian, Baptist, and Lutheran churches. Nowhere were separatists more prevalent than in the South. In 1927, a popular southern preacher named Bob Jones, Sr., established a college to help propagate the doctrine, and as southern religion spread across the nation during the twentieth century, fundamentalist sectarianism would be reinforced with a southern accent.[4] For upscale youth who had grown up mocking southerners as hillbillies, this only created a deeper, broader chasm.

In separating themselves from liberal Christians and secular humanists who embraced urban life and modernism, fundamentalists also rejected much of popular culture, the heartbeat of the youth movement. Fundamentalists felt they had little choice: mainstream culture was driven by the despised new intellectual elite (liberal Christians and secular humanists) and by the new immigrants (Catholics, Greek Orthodox Christians, Jews, and socialists), who were known to be at odds with the Christ of fundamentalism. Fundamentalists therefore preferred to stick to the tried and true, the lifestyle created by the Victorian evangelicals of yesteryear. This is not to say that fundamentalism was static, but that fundamentalists were by nature cautious about change. The popular innovations of the twentieth century were viewed with suspicion, and many were rejected. Modern music, dance, clothing styles, and movies—along with the use of tobacco (in most areas) and alcohol—were anathema to fundamentalist Christianity.[5] In sum, fundamentalists came to define their religion not only by what the Bible allowed for but also by the standards of Victorian evangelicalism. America's youth, however, were not going to confine themselves to Ira Sankey songs and Christmas plays.

Fundamentalism and Old-Time Politics

As if they had not done enough to alienate America's youth by adhering to an anachronistic lifestyle and projecting an image of hillbilly "intellectualism," high profile fundamentalists went a step further by enthusiastically taking up a reactionary and ultimately repugnant political cause after World War II. Though most fundamentalists in the postwar era were fairly private about their political views, a few fundamentalist militants made loud public proclamations that communism, because it denounced religion, threatened Christian America. In describing the gravity of the situation in 1949, fundamentalist Carl McIntire went so far as to claim that the world was neatly divided into two warring camps, with biblically grounded Christians on one side battling against the communist forces of evil and their liberal Christian fellow-travelers on the other. To prosecute the war against communism, such fundamentalists as McIntire teamed up with an anticommunist Catholic senator by the name of Joseph McCarthy; in doing so, these biblically grounded activists identified fundamentalism with that part of the establishment—the anticommunist right wing—that countercultural youth would most despise.

For the most part, mainstream Americans believed fundamentalists exaggerated when they included mainline ministers in the infamous fifth column of communist conspirators. And many saw fundamentalists like Edgar Bundy, named executive director of the conservative Church League of America in 1956, as not only alarmists in denouncing the supposed subversive nature of UNESCO (the United Nations Educational, Scientific, and Cultural Organization), but also as laughable when warning Americans about the communist doctrines hidden within the *Girl Scout Handbook*.[6] Such claims young middle-class Americans scoffed at. Not so funny, however, was the fundamentalist position on Civil Rights. Segregation was deemed by many vocal fundamentalists, such as Bob Jones Sr., as sanctified by God.

Belligerently denouncing communism and desegregation, fundamentalist militants were clearly out of synch with the emerging political consensus of the 1960s. After the Lyndon Johnson landslide victory, fundamentalist activists rode out on Barry Goldwater's coattails, and grave problems soon beset them. Already in 1964, the bombastic fundamentalist activist Billy James Hargis lost tax-exempt status for his Christian Crusade ministry. According to the Internal Revenue Service, the organization preached more politics than religion. Fundamentalism as a political platform limped through the rest of the sixties. In 1970, the FCC shut down McIntire's massive radio ministry for violations of the "fairness doctrine." Fundamentalist author-activist John Stormer, whose 1964 book *None Dare Call It Treason* had been a sensation amongst conservatives, became despondent.

Stormer, a former Goldwater delegate and executive committee member of the International Council of Christian Churches (McIntire's brainchild to counter the liberal World Council of Churches), published *Death of a Nation* in 1968. In this book, Stormer complained about the changes taking place in America, especially the country's concessions to communism, and he expressed a lack of hope about the nation's future. "America tolerates court-ordered bans on prayer and Bible reading in the schools," he lamented, "while permitting communists to teach. America has ceased to be good. Will America soon cease to be great? Even if there were no communist threat, growing moral decay and spiritual bankruptcy will destroy America from within."[7]

The Fundamentalist Alienation of Youth

By practicing separatism and embracing McCarthyism and segregation during the fifties and sixties, fundamentalist activists marginalized themselves socially and politically. As evangelical religious observer Richard Quebedeaux wrote in 1974, in the midst of the Watergate scandal and just prior to the rise of the Religious Right, the fundamentalists continued "to fight for the status quo, the Protestant ethic and the morality implicit in Americanism, including militarism."[8] But the leading fundamentalist activists did not marginalize only themselves; they managed to make pariahs of other biblically grounded Christians as well. Wheaton's Walter Elwell, looking back on fundamentalism as a whole in 1984, succinctly described what had happened during the previous decades: people who were not fundamentalists took notice of some of the underlying theological similarities amongst all biblically grounded Christians and then lumped them all together as hardcore fundamentalists.[9]

With such a reputation, fundamentalism, and the biblically grounded denominations associated with it, had little hope of connecting with America's countercultural youth or of reenergizing biblically grounded politics. Radical collegians, or even "with it" high schoolers, could hardly be expected to give assent to a religion that lacked intellectual sophistication, an openness to expressive individualism, or a commitment to the golden rule ethic. But precisely because biblically grounded Christianity had become categorically identified with the fundamentalist stereotype, there was hope. There was hope because the stereotype was something of a straw-man that masked the true nature of biblically grounded Christianity. Biblically grounded Christianity had much more depth and flexibility than its detractors gave it credit for, and it was this miscalculation that gave biblically grounded Christians opportunity. An alternative expression of biblically grounded Christianity could slip past liberal Christian critics and catch youth unawares, introducing them to the common factors shared between the counterculture and biblically grounded belief.

A Youthful Alternative: New Evangelicalism

By the 1960s, a new form of biblically grounded Christianity was competing for the allegiance of America's youth. This new expression of Christian faith had been formulated in large measure by a collaborative effort between Presbyterian-trained Harold Ockenga and Pentecostal-raised J. Elwin Wright. These men encouraged Christians of different biblically grounded denominations to come together to present a united front for Christ.

At a convocation of biblically grounded leaders in 1942, Ockenga and Wright called for the creation of a new interdenominational organization that would present the gospel in a positive light. Hardliner Carl McIntire predictably objected and argued that fellow religionists need only join his American Council of Churches which had been organized to wage an aggressive war of polemics against the liberal Federal Council of Churches.[10] The majority of the conference participants were of a different mind and rejected McIntire's offer. Meeting in Chicago the following year, Ockenga's group established the National Association of Evangelicals (NAE).[11] By 1948, Ockenga was calling upon biblically grounded Christians to create a new evangelicalism that eschewed separatism and both engaged liberals in dialogue and battled against social injustice.

Working together in an interdenominational atmosphere, NAE members stripped down the gospel message so that it would be acceptable to the greatest number of new evangelical Christians, and thereupon created a number of effective parachurch ministries. These ministries proved to be more successful with youth than traditional ministries because they were free of denominational oversight and therefore able to experiment and more easily adapt the gospel message to popular culture.

The new evangelicals' preoccupation with youth is revealed in the titles of organizations largely staffed by or even created by NAE-type Christians: Inter-Varsity Christian Fellowship (1939 in the United States), Young Life (1940), Youth for Christ International (1945), Campus Crusade (1951), and Fellowship of Christian Athletes (1955).[12] The popular Youth for Christ evangelist Billy Graham identified with the NAE and became an influential spokesperson for new evangelicalism.

Addressing Youth Intellectually

For any socio-religious movement to have credibility amongst college-bound youth, it needed to have an intellectual framework supporting it that was relevant to their concerns. Fortunately for new evangelicalism, pioneering members of the NAE formulated, during the forties and fifties, both an intellectual apologetic and a popular presentation of their cause. In 1947, an important institution for the nascent evangelical position came into being, an institution established by the folksy radio evangelist Charles Fuller and largely shaped by the astute academic Harold Ockenga, its first president. True to the NAE spirit, the professors of Fuller Theological Seminary carried on the intellectual tradition of Machen, but without the master's petulant militancy.[13]

It is significant that the new evangelicals chose to found their academic institution in the future heart of the counterculture, California; the west coast location demonstrated the founders' aspirations for a new biblically grounded intellectual endeavor. Their goal was nothing less than the creation of a fresh and dynamic clergy capable of renewing American religious life and saving Western civilization. At the seminary's first convocation, President Ockenga asked provocatively, why "should the west forever look to the east for its preachers?"[14] He recognized the creative energy bound up in Californian culture and its potential to serve the evangelical cause.

Invigorated by Ockenga's winning spirit, the new evangelicals eagerly sought out gaps in the liberal worldview and carefully planted signs designed to redirect spiritual pilgrims toward a biblically grounded worldview. As stated in 1949 by Fuller professor Carl F. H. Henry, the new evangelicals would respond with candor and effectiveness to the hard questions put to them by their theological and philosophical opponents. In its Foreword, Henry's *Giving a Reason for Our Hope* made the claim that "the Christian philosophy of creation, revelation and redemption leaves a smaller residue of unsolved problems than any other world and life view and that, rather than converting life into an enigma, it alone avoids that reduction of history and experience into inexplicabilities."[15]

The NAE-inspired strategy, however, frustrated and enraged the separatist McIntire, who attacked Fuller and the NAE viciously in his *Christian Beacon* publication. In the late 1950s, then, the fracture between separatists and new evangelicals snapped into a clean break.[16] Ironically, the new evangelicals profited from the spate of fundamentalist attacks. McIntire's diatribe made it apparent to those theologically conservative Christians who were discontented with traditional fundamentalism that the Fuller seminary, the NAE, and the new evangelicals had abandoned the vitriolic polemics of the past.

Many of the theologically conservative Christians favorably impressed were actually found within mainline denominations where hierarchies had become or were becoming decidedly liberal.[17] In 1967 Pastor Charles W. Keysor of the liberal Methodist Church published the biblically grounded magazine *Good News*, eliciting a positive response from Carl F. H. Henry, who wrote, "A mighty fine beginning—congratulations!"[18] With ministries like Keysor's, new evangelicals not only spread their outsider rendition of Christianity amongst reactionary adults within mainstream denominations, but they also reached the liberally raised youth who still resided, albeit reluctantly, within those denominations.

It is clear that from the beginning, new evangelicals had drawn certain conclusions about young people and religion, and these conclusions formed the foundation of their outreach. New evangelicals determined that youth were equally dissatisfied with the allegedly watered-down spirituality of liberalism and the obscurantism of fundamentalism. The challenge, then, was to demonstrate not only that youth had a right to be dissatisfied with both liberalism and fundamentalism, but also that they had a compelling reason to be satisfied with new evangelicalism. More to the point, new evangelicals had to validate the supernatural in the modern world without appearing anti-intellectual. If they succeeded, they might just provide the right grail for disillusioned youth pursuing a spiritual quest.

Billy Graham and Fuller Theological Seminary came together on this issue in a concrete way in 1956 when they established a new forward-looking and biblically grounded intellectual journal entitled *Christianity Today*, with Carl F. H. Henry as editor.[19] Graham expected the journal to be theologically conservative but liberal on social issues, a beacon of truth and mercy.[20] Henry obliged him, writing in a 1957 issue of the journal, "The real bankruptcy of fundamentalism has resulted

. . . from a harsh temperament, a spirit of lovelessness and strife. . . ."[21] At a time when middle-class youth were beginning to question their parents' views on religion and civil rights, new evangelicals positioned themselves favorably.

In spite of Graham's popularity in the sixties, his suit-and-tie, preacherly style and pointing finger still appeared old-fashioned and "square" to a good number of university students. The new evangelicalism needed evangelists who identified more effectively with the collegiate youth culture. In January of 1960, Henry introduced to the greater evangelical world through the pages of *Christianity Today* a new personality that would fit the bill.

Francis Schaeffer, who graduated from Machen's seminary in 1938 and had followed McIntire until the latter's negativism turned him away, had established his own mission to young people in the Swiss Alps in the mid-1950s.[22] During the sixties, Schaeffer expanded his ministry to more effectively reach England and America. In 1966, armed with a well-polished presentation of the gospel, he conducted a six-week tour of the United States and spoke at a number of churches, Bible colleges, seminaries, and, more importantly, at secular institutions.[23] In 1968, he toured again and delivered his final lecture at Harvard.[24] Out of his lectures came his books *Escape from Reason* and *The God Who Is There*, both well received by the younger crowd.

Schaeffer's message was not new, but it appeared new to students reared on liberalism. As a faithful follower of J. Gresham Machen's intellectual tradition, Schaeffer presented the biblically grounded gospel through the logic of Scottish Common Sense philosophy.[25] Because of the popularity and success of Schaeffer among college students and even high schoolers, who in the sixties were more precocious than their elder siblings in investigating innovative spiritual propositions, it behooves us to review his sixties' rendition of evangelical Common Sense philosophy and to come to grips with how his arguments neutralized the liberal and humanist skepticism that had obscured the biblically grounded worldview for most of the twentieth century.[26]

In sum, Schaeffer argued that behavior, as well as thought, determined what was real. And if one behaved as if the world and its objects actually existed, then one ought to adopt a worldview that posited first off the concrete existence of material objects that were both distinct from the mind and capable of being truly comprehended by the mind. And since the world, then, existed "out there" and could be truly seized upon by the mind, the world's data, including its history, could be objectively investigated, and its nature and meaning defined; therefore, investigating the claims of the Bible was a legitimate endeavor, as would be the investigation of any data supporting any other worldview. And when one did investigate biblical claims, and when one did understand the biblical propositions, one would see, Schaeffer insisted, that the biblical worldview outshined all the other competing philosophies and theologies, including the most recent, such as that of modern existentialism or liberal Christianity.[27]

According to Schaeffer, the worldview of the liberal and secular-minded person, the technocratic person, did not fully explain the human experience. It was a closed system based upon an arbitrary presupposition that only natural events could occur. Perforce it excluded the possibility of a supernatural revelation, but such a system, objected Schaeffer, unfairly precludes the consideration of a biblically grounded worldview. "It is obvious that propositional, verbalized revelation is not possible on the basis of the uniformity of natural causes. But the argument stands or falls upon the question: Is the presupposition of the uniformity of natural causes really acceptable?"[28] It is interesting to see here the apparent convergence of Schaeffer's and Marcuse's, and even Roszak's, arguments: true science would allow for all dimensions of phenomena, something denied in modernist scientism.[29] Schaeffer's critique of the modernist worldview confirmed many in his young audience in their conviction that the older generation of liberal Christians and secular humanists were indeed guilty of obscurantism and close-mindedness.

Schaeffer salted his arguments with an impressive number of illustrations drawn from history, art, and philosophy, which gave his whole message, for young students especially, a certain scholarly aura. He was later to be criticized by detractors as less than a philosopher, as a man who manipulated history to prove a point, but this did not diminish his evangelical effectiveness in the sixties.[30] His undisputed strength lay in identifying the spiritual malaise of youth and in presenting an apparently fresh and certainly alternative worldview that suggested, with due intellectual sophistication, solid and eternal answers to their problems.

A New Spirituality for Freedom

Schaeffer proposed to America's youth an antitechnocratic, noncompartmentalized spirituality; his was a faith for all seasons that allowed for the supernatural in the quotidian and in all aspects of the human experience.[31] Modern naturalism, Schaeffer argued in *True Spirituality* (1971), disguised the full reality that humankind was meant to live in and enjoy. According to Schaeffer, "There is to be an experiential reality, moment by moment. And the glory of the experiential reality of the Christian, as opposed to the bare existential experience or the religious experiences of the East, is that we can do it with all the intellectual doors and windows open. We do not need a dark room; we do not need to be under the influence of a hallucinatory drug; we do not need to be listening to a certain kind of music; we can know the reality of the supernatural here and now."[32]

Schaeffer did not deny the need for expressive individualism, but he did insist on an intellectually responsible spiritual basis for its practice. He contended that his apologetic embodied a common sensical belief in the supernatural and not a "leap of faith."[33] It was, therefore, a rejection of the latest liberal claims to spirituality, which called for a commitment to faith even though there was no intellectually satisfying reason for believing in the supernatural.

In sum, Schaeffer's God was a God that middle-class youth could both have feeling for and be intellectually proud of; and, not least in importance, he was a God who opened up infinite possibilities for human creativity by liberating the individual from naturalistic philosophy and the technocratic lifestyle that naturalistic philosophy had imposed upon society. Freed from the machine and connected to the infinite, the human experience became a never-ending adventure. This was full-fledged expressive individualism.

In contrast to most members of the older generation, who typically criticized the younger generation for its music, drugs, long hair, and other forms of expression that were out of synch with mainstream behavior, Schaeffer embraced creative behavior and encouraged youth to find liberation and fulfillment in it. Certainly he waved away drug use, but not because it was out of synch with mainstream behavior but because mind-altering drugs limited a person's authentic view of the infinite and eternal creativity that resided in God. Many countercultural youth could relate to this argument.

A Sixties' Gold Rule

As pointed out above, youth looked skeptically upon fundamentalists because of their religious and social separatism, their radical anticommunist stance, and their support of racial segregation. These faults betrayed a disregard for the golden rule and new evangelicals did not want that stigma. In an open break with the anti-Catholic bigotry of the fundamentalists, Billy Graham cultivated positive relationships with certain leaders in the Catholic hierarchy in the 1950s, with the result that even the archdiocesan newspaper of Boston celebrated his preaching.[34] As Graham explained in 1956, "most people were not going to take us seriously if we spent all our time debating our differences instead of uniting at the Cross."[35]

There was something both ironic and significant in the new evangelical-Catholic convergence on evangelism. Ironic because liberals made much fanfare and worked long and hard to settle differences between mainline Protestantism and Catholicism, but the pace toward institutional ecumenicism seemed to be slow and halting. Meanwhile, the emerging new evangelicals, who derided the mainline ecumenical movement for giving up Protestant doctrines for the sake of unity, actually practiced a good measure of interfaith cooperation through nondenominational parachurch organizations, such as Graham's.[36] This cooperation was even extended, under certain conditions, to liberal Christians as well. Graham was more than willing to work with liberal Christians to organize an evangelistic crusade.

No doubt the emerging new evangelical openness toward Catholics matched youthful expectations better than did fundamentalist intransigence. Particularly important for the future, though, were two features of the Catholic experience of the time. In the first place, many second- and third-generation Catholics were moving up in the socioeconomic scale and were proving to be modern middle-class citizens indistinguishable in behavior and thought from other suburbanites. Secondly, liberal theology also had a foothold in Catholicism, and the affluent and educated Catholics tended to be attracted to it. Their college-bound children, however, were just as suspicious of this mainstream technocratic mentality as their Protestant co-eds. The upshot of this development was that middle-class youth of a theologically liberal Catholic background were as susceptible to new evangelical apologetics as liberal Christians from a Protestant background.

The willingness of new evangelicals to work with liberal Protestants and Catholics on evangelistic campaigns no doubt left a better impression upon America's youth than did the fundamentalists' sectarianism, but what about the new evangelical attitude toward communists? Could new evangelicals show themselves less attached to McCarthy than McIntire had been, or would they be just as uncritically pro-capitalist and hateful of socialist ideals? The process was slow, but there was, over time, less of a commitment to McCarthyism.

Graham, to be sure, had scathingly condemned Marxism more than once; in 1953 he described Soviet communism as "the greatest enemy we have ever known." In time, however, he came to see Russia as a mission field.[37] In 1959, he visited Moscow as a tourist, and in 1967 he went into communist Yugoslavia as a preacher; ten years later he traveled as an evangelist into the Soviet satellite of Hungary.[38] More poignantly, in the late 1960s Carl F. H. Henry came to question America's fight against communism in Vietnam. New evangelicals, of course, would not abide the tyranny of communist dictatorship or the communist diatribe against religion, but some could agree with at least part of the communist critique of America's greedy materialism.

The most critical issue relative to the golden rule ethic in the 1950s, however, was not religious bigotry or McCarthyism; the most critical issue was racial prejudice. To the consternation of most southern fundamentalists, Graham challenged the well-honed custom of racial segregation. Convinced that all humans were equal before God, he desegregated his audiences even before *Brown v Board of Education*. Later in the fifties, President Eisenhower, struggling with the integration issue as Arkansas Governor Orval Faubus openly defied the *Brown v Board of Education* decision, telephoned Graham for his opinion on the subject. Graham recalled telling him, "I think you've got no alternative. The discrimination must be stopped."[39] That same year in New York, Graham invited Martin Luther King, Jr. to a retreat to explain America's racial situation to his Team.[40] Then in 1959, Graham went to Little Rock and held an integrated meeting, in large measure to drive home a point; Governor Faubus attended, but with such a large integrated crowd, he was unable to locate a seat and ultimately found himself sitting in the back, on some steps.[41]

Graham carried his golden rule ideal abroad as well and was once again ahead of the curve (with respect to U.S. foreign policy) in defying racism. In 1960, he refused to conduct an evangelistic crusade in South Africa because the ruling whites in that country refused to integrate his meetings. Against the wishes of the whites in Rhodesia, he made sure his message was translated into the local African languages so that more blacks might attend his meetings. He returned from Africa, he claimed, ever more opposed to racial discrimination.[42] In 1962, in an effort to unite black and white Christians, he invited white Southern Baptist leaders, who were attending the Baptist World Alliance in Rio de Janeiro with him, to attend a dinner there in honor of Martin Luther King Jr.'s father.[43]

By 1960, unbeknownst to many liberals, the new evangelicals shared a perception of the golden rule not very different from that of most young middle-class Americans.[44] As Carl Henry would write in 1972, "The test of our Christian commitment is whether we really love those who are given over to other life-styles and who are strangers to the love of God in Christ—whether we love them both for themselves and for what they are as fellow human beings bearing God's image, whether we love them also for the sake of Christ, who offers authentic life and hope."[45]

Conclusion

In the final analysis, new evangelicalism answered some of the questions that youth posed as they quested for a new worldview without the perceived weaknesses in their parents' liberal religion. The new worldview that countercultural youth sought, as evidenced by the themes found in their music, songs, and protests, had to meet several criteria. It had to offer a spirituality that was not compartmentalized. It had to respect the golden rule ideal, and it had to allow for expressive individualism. Moreover, it had to do all these things with a measure of intellectual sophistication that a middle-class college or college-bound student could endorse. Better than most forms of biblically grounded Christianity, new evangelicalism provided that measure of intellectual sophistication.[46]

Most importantly, new evangelicalism had free access to young people because it entered America's streets and campuses unrecognized as a biblically grounded religious expression. While liberals continued to launch their diatribes against McIntire and his kind, the new evangelicals like Francis Schaeffer and Bill Bright of Campus Crusade for Christ met little effective resistance as they proselytized America's youth. Liberal accusations of obscurantism and separatism missed their mark as youth saw for themselves that these newcomers were intelligent and fully engaged in American culture.

4

A Radical Spirituality for a Radical Generation

Though new evangelicals produced appealing apologetics and sensitive polemics, some countercultural youth were questing for something more than a spirituality deliberately tied to intellectual propositions. They desired a more intense spirituality that recognized the value of apologetics and polemics but was less preoccupied with them. It happened that there was a biblically grounded tradition that was unashamedly spiritual; unfortunately, it not only shared some of the same limitations as fundamentalism, but also had its own set of religious peculiarities. Prior to the 1950s, most informed Protestants, whether theologically conservative or liberal, considered these Christians, the Pentecostals, as Protestantism's illegitimate offspring at best; theological conservatives suspected them of superseding the Bible with newly received revelations while liberals accused them of replacing modern reason with irrational emotionalism.[1]

Although the accusation of antiscriptural revelations was largely unearned, it is true that from a doctrinal perspective, Pentecostalism differed significantly from fundamentalism and early new evangelicalism, both of which drew upon the Calvinist tradition, which posited that a person once saved could never lose his or her salvation. Pentecostalism, on the other hand, was an offspring of Arminianism, a Protestant theology developed during the seventeenth century that countered the predestination doctrines of Reformation theology. Arminianism argued that though salvation is a gift from God it does not nullify free will; therefore, salvation ultimately depends upon a believer's willingness to persevere in the faith.

In regards to how salvation was attained, this meant that Pentecostalism expressed a view more akin to the Catholic concept of "faith and works" than to the Reformation dictum "faith alone." In other words, Pentecostalism would have an inside track compared to Reformation derived denominations when proselytizing Catholics. At the same time, however, this theological affinity would allow for effective dialogue and cooperation between Pentecostals and Catholics; discussion about this development and the impact upon countercultural youth will follow later.

For the moment, more needs to be said about the nature of Pentecostal belief. The Pentecostal premise about salvation demanded of the believer constant vigilance, which meant that an emotional confirmation of one's faith and position with God became a perpetual concern. This concern, however, was tempered by the fact that Pentecostals believed that the Holy Spirit bestowed upon them, after the initial acceptance of Jesus as Savior, a second blessing, recognized experientially, that not only comforted them but also empowered them to live Christ-like lives.

The key element denoting a second blessing was a spiritual gift known as glossolalia or speaking in tongues. To receive the gift of tongues, the spiritual seeker prayed for the power to speak in tongues and had others praying for him (or her) until, after a prayer, or a long series of prayers, or perhaps a laying on of hands, the seeker would open his mouth and release his vocal cords, and out would come sounds like unto a foreign language. At this moment he knew that he had received the Spirit.[2] At this second baptism, a quest was consummated and a more fulfilling life began. Baptized by the Spirit like the apostles at Pentecost, the believer might also be empowered with the gift of interpreting what was said by others in tongues, the ability to prophesy directly to a gathering of believers, or the power to heal the sick.

Fundamentalists could not abide Pentecostals for several reasons, most notably because of their view of salvation, which according to fundamentalists turned faith and hence salvation into a work, that is, a human rather than divine accomplishment. This was, for fundamentalists, heresy; the very crime Catholics were guilty of. According to fundamentalists, the Bible unequivocally stated that sinners were justified by faith alone: the biblical proof text was Ephesians 2:8-9, "For by grace are ye saved through faith; and that not of yourselves: it is the gift of God: Not of works, lest any man should boast" [AV].

But there were other complaints as well. The Pentecostals rejected a dispensational teaching of the fundmentalists that relegated the gift of tongues to the age of the apostles. Also disconcerting was the Pentecostals' claim that God verbally revealed his will through them. Fundamentalists understood this as an open door for extra-biblical revelations, and thus for further heresy. Most irritating, however, was the Pentecostals' spiritual arrogance. Uniquely blessed with the evidence of the Spirit, Pentecostals projected the view that other Christians were less enlightened, spiritually deficient.

Though Pentecostals worshipped apart from people whom they deemed less spiritual, one must not lose sight of the fact that they did not perceive other Christians as pagans in disguise, as did fundamentalists viewing liberals, Catholics, or even Pentecostals.[3] Because the difference between Pentecostals and other Christians was simply a matter of spiritual depth, there was always the possibility for rapprochement. In spite of their spiritual elitism, then, Pentecostals demonstrated a certain openness that was absent in fundamentalism.[4]

Pentecostal Potential

Pentecostals proved to be broadminded in other ways as well. They were, for the most part, poor and under-educated and therefore free from some of the technocratic prejudices of mainline denominations. Women and minorities figured prominently in the movement from the outset. The first known person to speak in tongues was a woman, and one of the most visible interwar evangelists was the Pentecostal Aimee Semple McPherson. During the Depression, McPherson impressed even mainstream Americans with her compassion for the disinherited as she provided what she could for the material needs of some one and a half million impoverished souls, regardless of religion or race. Her tolerance of other churches, of lower social classes, of other races, and her natural openness to women in ministry made Pentecostalism in some ways an avant-garde religious expression.

In its early days, Pentecostalism was remarkably multiracial. McPherson, for example, was ordained by a minister who had received the baptism of the Spirit at Azusa Street in California. The Azusa Street revival, a magnet for men and women of all ethnicities seeking a higher spiritual experience, was spearheaded by African-American evangelist William Seymour.[5]

Although racial segregation did eventually settle into the Pentecostal movement, there were, nevertheless, white Pentecostal preachers who remained open to the participation of women and non-whites in their ministries. And any religious movement that included ethnic minorities, women, and the poor in its midst (as opposed to providing arms-length donations at certain festive times, like Christmas, which was the practice of many mainstream churches) had potential to draw postwar youth sensitive to civil rights issues and the plight of the indigent.

Equally important for America's baby boomers would be Pentecostalism's leniency toward new expressions of spirituality. Because of its doctrine of the Spirit, Pentecostalism invited change and self-expression in a way that fundamentalism could not. In Pentecostalism, a person under the power of the Spirit could rise up in an assembly and speak forth the word of God. True, that man or woman might call upon a sinner to repent of his drunkenness, his movie-going, or his night life, and such recriminations would ring hollow to affluent middle-class collegians, but the divinely inspired Pentecostal might just as well call upon the assembled to love the sick, the poor, or the downtrodden of another race. In social and spiritual terms, Pentecostalism had the potential to initiate a dialogue with young Americans; what held it back was its blind condemnation of popular culture and its lack of intellectual sophistication.

Beyond Pentecostalism

If only Pentecostalism could work alongside non-Pentecostal denominations, such as the new evangelicals, it would not only distance itself from sectarianism, it would also move Pentecostalism closer to popular culture and to respectable apologetics and polemics. The first move toward a more generous and inclusive mindset was made in 1943 when Ernest Williams, superintendent of the Assemblies of God, America's largest Pentecostal denomination, extended the hand of fellowship to the NAE. By 1960, the Assemblies of God was fully integrated into the NAE, as evidenced by the election of Assemblies of God leader Thomas Zimmerman to its presidency.[6]

Meanwhile, evangelist David Du Plessis preached glossolalia with a difference; unlike most zealous Pentecostals, he encouraged those baptized in the Spirit to remain within their non-Pentecostal churches. Furthermore, he reached out beyond the Protestant community, and at Vatican II (1962–1965) he met, during the third session, with the Catholic hierarchy, eventually establishing the Roman Catholic-Pentecostal Dialogue.[7]

While Du Plessis and Zimmerman endeavored to unite Pentecostals and other Christians at the top, other Pentecostals wooed people at the grassroots level. Pentecostal evangelist Oral Roberts is a case in point. Driven by an order given him directly by God not to "be like any denomination," Roberts ministered to all comers and eventually became a Methodist himself.[8]

Another example of outreach was afforded by Demos Shakarian, who in 1951 established the Full Gospel Business Men's Fellowship International (FGBMFI), which penetrated into America's middle class. Though Shakarian had no intention of stealing parishioners from others, his organization did become a second home for non-Pentecostal Christians who had undergone the baptism of the Spirit. The FGBMFI impact on converts within liberal circles was extraordinary and would even shake up some mainline denominations.

Harald Bredesen, a Lutheran minister, underwent the baptism of the Spirit in 1946, and in spite of the fact that the baptism and glossolalia ran contrary to Lutheran practice, he remained in mainline churches while attending FGBMFI meetings. Bredesen used the organization not only as a support group for himself, he also used it as a means to mentor other non-Pentecostal Christians who had experienced Holy Spirit baptism. Some of those he inspired and guided would become prominent in the late sixties and seventies; Pat Boone and Pat Robertson are two of Bredesen's better known spiritual protégés.[9]

Pentecostalism for Youth

By the 1950s, Pentecostals found that their message resonated with outsider youth. David Wilkerson is a case in point. With deep compassion for down-and-out teenagers caught up in gang and drug life, Wilkerson took the Pentecostal message into New York's rugged quarters and created a message tailored to the social rebels.

The youth Wilkerson succeeded with were not satisfied with their drug addiction and relationless lives, but neither were they seeking to become part of the establishment. These were fifties inner city youth who, not unlike the rebellious young of the next decade, wanted something different out of life; Wilkerson's Pentecostalism, adjusted to street culture, provided that something different, a radical supernatural connection. This was to be the most important Pentecostal contribution to biblically grounded Christianity, opening up a supernatural dimension that other biblically grounded traditions only teased with, and that the liberal tradition had to reject if it hoped to remain in harmony with scientism.[10]

Because inner-city culture and the popular culture of middle-class American youth were in symbiosis during the modern era, Wilkerson's work did not remain confined to gang members and drug addicts. He created a nationwide ministry for youth, Teen

Challenge, that spread to cities across the nation and penetrated streets with roving evangelists. Even at his early Teen Challenge center in Brooklyn, in 1961, the potential of Wilkerson's message to connect with middle-class youngsters became evident as his meetings attracted a number of college students.[11]

Wilkerson also reached the middle class in a more indirect way. His book recounting his New York ministry, entitled *The Cross and the Switchblade,* became a nationwide sensation, even prompting the production of a film version starring Pat Boone (1970). For many middle-class people, Wilkerson's book constituted the first acceptable medium for learning about Pentecostalism that they had encountered; readers did not have to risk their reputation by attending a holy roller tent meeting to find out what the message was all about, they could inconspicuously consider it in the seclusion of their own homes. At least one Pentecostal minister, Ralph Moore, had his youth group give away copies of Wilkerson's book.[12] Once inside a middle-class home, Wilkerson's book could affect the entire household. Indeed, the book's matter-of-fact endorsement of a supernatural participation in the seemingly mundane minutiae of life caught the attention of spiritually inquisitive youth who had become disillusioned with their parents' theological liberalism. Besides, Wilkerson's story dealt with the contemporary issues of interest to countercultural youth, namely gangs, drugs, and violence. Pastor Moore's church, Hope Chapel, would one day number its membership in the thousands, mostly because of its charismatic appeal to the younger generation.

Neo-Pentecostalism

Protestants were not the only Christians to read *The Cross and the Switchblade.* Some students and faculty at Duquesne University, a Catholic institution, read Wilkerson's work and subsequently attended Pentecostal-inspired prayer services; by 1967, these people had undergone the baptism of the Spirit and yet remained fervently, even more fervently, Catholic.

The success of Pentecostal-style worship in the Catholic Church, however, owed as much to the Catholics themselves as it did to outsiders. The groundwork for this spiritual renewal within the Church had been laid down prior to the Duquesne phenomenon. Toward the end of Vatican II, Belgian Cardinal Leon-Joseph Suenens insisted that the Church include a statement in its Dogmatic Constitution allowing for charismatic gifts. Although the Cardinal was not thinking of Pentecostalism at the time, this provision gave the Catholics who underwent the baptism of the Spirit in 1967 a doctrinal mooring within the Church. Later, recognizing the importance of the movement, Suenens proved to be a valuable advocate for Pentecostal-style renewal and helped make the constitutional statement apply to it.[13]

By the 1960s, Pentecostal practice outside of the official or traditional Pentecostal churches was increasingly being seen as something original and dynamic. Initially, some called the new phenomenon neo-Pentecostalism, but in time it would become known as the charismatic movement.

The main difference between the charismatic Christian and the traditional Pentecostal was the charismatic's greater measure of tolerance for Christian doctrines and practices that did not specifically emanate from the initial turn-of-the-century Pentecostal movement. The charismatic Christian, for example, often refused to make tongues a requisite mark of the Spirit-filled life, and quite often the charismatic Christian allowed non-Pentecostal denominational doctrines to be facilitators for Spirit-filled worship.[14] During the 1970s, charismatic ministries continued to shed the habits of Pentecostal sectarianism and became increasingly ecumenical as well as better attuned to popular culture, which made them attractive to members of America's younger generation.[15] There was something of a snowballing effect by this time as well. That is to say that as more young converts from liberal Christianity stepped into charismatic churches, with guitar in hand and dancing in their feet, the forces of change were bound to accelerate.

Charismatic Success

One might define charismatic Christianity as new evangelicalism with a Pentecostal spirit, and this would not be far off the mark. Like Pentecostals, charismatics focused on the experiential, and therefore could be more broadminded doctrinally than many new evangelicals; but on the other hand, charismatics were generally middle-class citizens with a definite respect for intellectual pursuit, and in this they resembled the new evangelicals more than traditional Pentecostals.

Charismatic Christianity experienced tremendous success among baby boomers, who by the 1960s and especially 1970s were leaving mainline denominations—United Methodist, American Baptist, Presbyterian, Episcopal, and United Church of Christ—in record numbers.[16] For some of those departing, charismatic Christianity was a viable alternative; it categorically rejected a religious life either limited or regulated by scientism, and it suffused the individual with an awareness of his or her relationship with the supernatural.

Donald Miller, a liberal Christian who wrote a sensitive and insightful analysis of the charismatic movement in the 1990s, well understood why the new charismatic churches succeeded when the mainline ones failed after 1960. His analysis reveals that it was the antitechnocratic nature of charismatic belief that won over people's hearts. In his book *Reinventing American Protestantism*, Miller admits that he had previously assumed, erroneously, that "mainline Protestant denominations were losing members because of the dissonance between their faith and culture. Now I realized that part of the problem was the focus on rationalized beliefs." What he had not understood previously was "the emotional and bodily dimension of religion."[17] What Miller termed rationalized beliefs I have referred to as liberalism's accommodation with the technocratic viewpoint, and specifically with scientism.

Charismatic Christianity offered Americans a new worldview that ministered to their antitechnocratic spiritual aspirations, without radically abandoning American popular culture. Even more than new evangelicalism, charismatics allowed many aspects of the affluent American lifestyle to persist in their expression of biblically grounded Christianity. This is not to say that there were no scriptural limits to charismatic behavior, but many charismatics stretched the Scriptures as far as they could while still maintaining a biblical grounding. Some in the 1980s, especially the high profile televangelists, like Jim Bakker, went too far and were openly condemned, even excommunicated, by fellow charismatics.

Defying the Older Generation's Liberal Christianity

Stolid liberals found it difficult to deal with charismatics within their ranks because the charismatics were not, on the whole, openly belligerent as were fundamentalists, even though charismatics held to ideas that reflected a biblically grounded worldview. To oppose the charismatics formally or to excommunicate them would make the liberals themselves appear sectarian and intolerant and unfaithful to the golden rule ideal, worthy of the very invective they habitually leveled at the fundamentalists. According to religious historian Peter Hocken, "the majority of denominations adopted positions of cautious openness, neither welcoming [charismatic renewal] with enthusiasm nor rejecting it as inauthentic."[18]

In spite of their caution, most mainline denominations eventually wrote up statements in the early 1970s that allowed for charismatic practice.[19] By 1974 national conferences on charismatic practice had been held by the Catholic, Presbyterian, Lutheran, Mennonite, Episcopalian, Orthodox, and Methodist denominations, and each of them had charismatic newsletters in circulation, the Presbyterian charismatic bulletin having been published as early as 1966.[20]

Mainline charismatic parishioners succeeded in making themselves at home inside the liberal denominations in part because charismatic practice illuminated for them the long obscured biblically grounded heritage of the mainline churches. Many charismatics combined commitment to an interactive God, communion with his indwelling Spirit, and faith in his supernatural Word with a recommitment to their denominational origins. Pat Robertson, who worked for a time in a Methodist Church, read John Wesley's writings from a charismatic perspective and discovered an eighteenth-century soul mate, whereupon he declared a new spiritual understanding began to open up to him.[21] Robertson was not originally a Methodist and worked within a liberal denomination for only a little while, but other charismatics, particularly those who hailed from liberal denominations, did continue work within them. The Episcopalian priest Dennis Bennett, for example, began introducing charismatic practice into his denomination in 1960.

Mainline Christians of all stripes who were now baptized in the Spirit adopted a worldview half blind to the modernist landscape that had been shaped and colored by scientism. Born anew through the baptism of the Spirit and confirmed by the gift of tongues or some other manifestation of the Spirit, charismatic believers turned the liberal doctrine of tolerance against its champions, as they obliged liberals to live up to their oft-proclaimed broadmindedness and to allow for a biblically grounded faith to grow up within the precincts of liberal churches. They created, in a sense, a church within the church, a place where biblically grounded Christians could gather and live out a new type of religious life; charismatic insiders provided a new hope and a haven for youth who had remained associated with their parents' mainline church even though they had grown disenchanted with liberal doctrines.

The charismatic renewal was so pervasive that it affected more conservative Protestant churches as well. The official statements produced by conservative Nazarenes, Lutherans, and Baptists denouncing it were evidence of the inroads the charismatic renewal was making or threatening to make within their respective denominations. In the 1980s, Don LeMaster, senior pastor of West Lauderdale Baptist Church, helped organize charismatic Southern Baptist churches and with them sought to maintain affiliation with the Southern Baptist Convention.[22] Some suggest that by the 1990s over two hundred charismatic Southern Baptist congregations had come into existence, which is possible, given the leeway permitted to member churches by the congregationalist governance of the SBC.

Conclusion

Although the charismatic renewal prompted some mainline churchgoers to reach back to their denominational origins, it moved other converts to abandon the liberal hearth. Finding a new mode of spirituality shorn of scientism prompted some to question the necessity, or even the usefulness, of remaining within what they viewed as accommodationist churches. Many of these Christians wandered off, not toward denominations full of alternative doctrines and traditions hammered out through the past century, but toward assemblies that were somewhat undefined and still in the process of becoming, churches that called themselves nondenominational precisely to reflect the individualistic spirituality and emotional vitality that young footloose middle-class pilgrims felt was inherent in apostolic Christianity.

The flexible ecclesiology of the charismatic movement had definite ties to the counterculture.[23] By the time the religious right had arisen and made its entrance into American politics, these ecclesiastically unconventional charismatics outnumbered mainline charismatics. Although by the end of Ronald Reagan's second term over six million charismatics attended traditional churches in North America, more than twice as many fellowshipped within nondenominational assemblies.[24]

These novel nondenominational churches merit our attention because of their role in providing a refuge for baby-boomer Christians who had abandoned their theologically liberal upbringing. Although initially many of the new churches made it a point not to become a denomination, they nonetheless spawned daughter churches throughout the United States and beyond, and kept connected with one another in spirit, if not in polity. After the seventies, some of these churches did decide to go ahead and officially constitute denominations, but even these still possessed something distinctively countercultural and antimainline in their comportment.

The importance of charismatic spirituality within traditional denominations, in nondenominational assemblies or in its new denominational expressions, is that it provided a warm biblically grounded environment for many rebellious sixties' youth nurtured in American affluence and antitechnocratic ideals. While the fundamentalists housed some rebellious youth, they were reputedly too rigid and dull-witted to appeal to many. The new evangelicals, who otherwise garnished a good number of young countercultural converts, were enticing but lacked a daringly radical spirituality; for some, the traditional Pentecostals were hobbled by anachronistic traditions and an insufferable spiritual elitism. And so, for those youth who found fault with these aforementioned churches—fundamentalist, new evangelical, and Pentecostal—there was, as far as "organized" religion went, the charismatic renewal, whether located within a traditional denomination or, more often, found in a novel nondenominational setting.

5

The Evangelical Lifestyle

So far, we have discussed biblically grounded Christianity under four major subheadings: fundamentalist, new evangelical, Pentecostal, and charismatic. We have noted that fundamentalists tended to emphasize fire and brimstone, new evangelicals intellectualism, Pentecostals experiential spirituality, and charismatics a mixture of intellectualism and experiential spirituality. We also observed that emergent forms of new evangelical and charismatic Christianity shared some important traits with liberalism as all three not only endorsed American affluence and, to varying degrees, expressive individualism, but also upheld the importance of sound intellectual apologetics and polemics while reverencing the golden rule ethic.[1]

The resemblance comes as little surprise if one considers that new evangelical and charismatic Christianity were, for the most part, postwar religious developments, originating largely within America's middle class. Indeed, important members within the leadership of both new evangelical and charismatic Christianity consisted of men and women from liberal upbringings who had converted over to biblically grounded Christianity. It is small wonder, then, that these biblically grounded religious movements reflected some of the liberal values that America's middle-class youth, predominantly raised in a mainline religious setting, found meaningful. In the final analysis, while fundamentalism and Pentecostalism appeared more obscurantist and sectarian than new evangelical and charismatic Christianity, the latter modes of religious expression had broad appeal for those who came out of a liberal religious upbringing.

The new evangelicals and charismatics, when considered collectively, can be referred to simply as *evangelicals*. This can be confusing as the term new evangelicals is already in use, but many historians, and most journalists, refer to these new styled biblically grounded Christians as evangelicals.[2]

For the moment, then, we put aside the diehard separatist fundamentalists and Pentecostals and focus upon the new evangelicals and charismatics, "the evangelicals," in order to consider their lifestyle and its correlation to the counterculture. This examination is important because it was the lifestyle of evangelicals, as much as evangelical discourse, that revealed to countercultural youth the evangelical alternative to mainstream belief and behavior.

Evangelical Love

As previously pointed out, expressive individualism and the golden rule ethic went hand-in-hand. Nowhere have these two concerns come together so intimately in American thought as in the civil rights movement of the fifties and sixties. If the progressive-minded wanted to determine if a white person upheld the golden rule ethic and the right for all Americans to live free, they only needed to know how that white individual interacted with "people of color."

How did America's evangelicals behave in this regard? A good example is found in the life of Pat Robertson, who, though a southerner, had few qualms about ministering to or working with non-whites. On one occasion, Robertson went with Harald Bredesen to call on the wife of Norman Vincent Peal, Ruth, to talk with her about speaking in tongues. While there, a cleaning lady openly admitted to Bredesen that she herself had the Holy Ghost and that she had prayed for twenty years that the Peals might experience the baptism.[3] In spite of the fact that Robertson refers to the cleaning lady as "the Negro maid," one senses that for this southerner there was but one family of God in the Spirit. Living out this egalitarian perception of humanity, Robertson moved into a parsonage in a Brooklyn slum. Robertson's mother was horrified that he lived "in the midst of one of the largest black ghettos in America," but he made the slum his home and ministered to many blacks who had been evicted from their homes and had nowhere to stay.[4]

Later, as a rising television owner and manager, Robertson had to face up to opponents of his racial open-mindedness. When informed that one of his employees was married to a black woman, he admitted, "Here I was, dependent on the conservative Christians of the Tidewater area for our support, and getting ready to bring in a hippie-type disc jockey with a black wife." He writes that he was willing to have his ministry destroyed rather than refuse a man whose marriage had been approved by God. (Robertson also admitted that her light skin color played in her favor during those days when racism was rampant, overt, and aggressive).[5] It is noteworthy, however, that in the South, a high profile evangelical leader was living out the golden rule ethic where it counted most for countercultural youth, in the area of race relations.

Robertson was not an isolated case. In the late 1950s, David Wilkerson moved into crime-ridden urban America to address the suffering caused by teenage violence: drug addiction; one of those he helped out of a life of crime was the Puerto Rican gang leader Nicky Cruz. Also in the 1950s, Francis Schaeffer and his wife Edith lived in a community environment, sharing their time and resources with spiritually troubled youth from across the globe. Oral Roberts, himself partly Native American, reached out to America's lower class and outsider ethnic groups with his integrated healing lines. Billy Graham went beyond integrating his evangelistic meetings when, joining with R. Sargeant Shriver, he spent time and money to develop a film documentary to draw attention to some of the social problems of the impoverished of Appalachia.[6]

The practice of the golden rule ideal among evangelicals went further than race relations and poverty issues in the

United States, however. Many evangelicals empathized with the poor of non-white nations, and thousands of such evangelicals went overseas to serve as missionaries in the Third World. There, they worked selflessly to alleviate what they perceived to be both spiritual and economic hardships.

Middle-class American youth who encountered Robertson, Wilkerson, Schaeffer, and the like, could see with their own eyes that these biblically inspired people did not just preach a high-minded sermon about love and then line up at the church door to shake hands and exchange compliments with high society parishioners. They practiced love in the nitty-gritty of everyday life, interacting empathetically with young people from all walks of life, from all ethnicities, and from all cultural traditions.

Evangelical Rebels

When one looks at the lives of evangelical leaders, it does not take long to realize that these leaders rebelled against many of the institutions that the sixties' youth would also reject. Billy Graham, for example, had to defy the accepted lifestyle of his high school peers in order to become a biblically grounded Christian himself. Such a decision put him at odds with mainstream churches, the school, and even public opinion—what we would now call the "politically correct" opinion—maturing after the Scopes Trial.

The difference between Billy Graham and countercultural youth, of course, is that Billy Graham was raised in a biblically grounded home, and his youthful disaffection did not last long before he returned to the fold. Sixties' youth, on the other hand, rejected their parents' liberal Christian background without remorse. Nonetheless, Graham and many evangelical leaders had themselves rebelled against the modern society that they had at one point embraced. This integration into and disengagement from modernism gave them insight into the countercultural mind; the experience furnished these evangelicals an understanding of what the younger generation objected to.

Some evangelicals, however, had in their youth an experience in defiance that more directly corresponded to the sixties rebellion. Francis Schaeffer is a case in point. This sixties' spokesman for the evangelical cause had to reject his parents' worldview and lifestyle when he became a Christian back in 1929. He grew up in a blue collar and secular household, and the church he attended was, according to him, a very liberal one.[7] He found the liberal message unsatisfying; for him, it provided no satisfactory answers to important questions, as to why man existed or why suffering occurred in the world. For him, the scientism to which liberalism acquiesced made human life only as meaningful as the life of a plant, or a rock, or some other object tossed and turned by the unmitigated laws of nature. It had no answers for human needs.[8]

So when Schaeffer became a biblically grounded Christian and decided to believe in the presence of a personal and interactive God who had, in Schaeffer's language, "explained himself" and the meaning of life truly and sufficiently to humankind in a book, the Bible, the young convert had to reject his parents' view of things. Schaeffer's pursuit of theological studies seemed nothing more than a waste of time to parents who expected him to study electrical engineering.[9]

A similar parent-child disconnect is disclosed in the life of Pat Robertson. When Robertson set out blindly for Tidewater, Virginia, taking only seventy dollars with which to set up a television station, expecting only God to meet any further needs, his father, who was chairman of the Senate's Banking and Currency Commission, considered his son's endeavor ridiculous.[10] For such evangelicals, the generation gap existed before the sixties, and, because of their experience, they could relate to rebellious young people in a way most modernists could not.

Living Without Scientism

Although spiritual experiences were not foreign to liberals, the evangelical spiritual experience differed somewhat. As it was for liberals, the evangelical believer felt the presence of a divine Person touching and informing the heart, but the evangelical also believed that God would readily suspend the physical laws of nature and intervene in the world in miraculous ways. In sum, evangelical belief allowed for God to intervene supernaturally anywhere and at any time. The intervention might be to miraculously bestow a vision on a believer, or it might be simply to provide the money necessary to pay the rent. Evangelical spirituality was distinct from mainstream spirituality; it was outside the mainstream where countercultural youth would be searching for new modes of spirituality.

In the creation of Fuller Theological Seminary, one easily spots a decidedly antitechnocratic spirituality. To see if God personally sanctioned the effort to create a seminary, the exploratory board for the proposed seminary summoned the support of the president of Club Aluminum Company, Herbert Taylor. If he agreed with the project, surmised the board, then God had spoken, and Fuller and Ockenga could proceed with it.[11] Taylor joined the team, and Ockenga and Fuller organized the seminary. Again, for student recruitment, although the arrival of students was problematic, the founders would trust God simply to utilize Charles Fuller's announcements on his radio program.

Although optimistic about the prospects for a new seminary, Henry and Ockenga thought the institution would not be prepared to open its doors until after 1947; Charles Fuller, however, surprised the other visionaries by boldly declaring that classes would begin in the fall of 1947. His reasoning was based on faith rather than rational projection. He submitted a bid for the purchase of what seemed to be the necessary school property, a mansion; there were to be competitors for the estate, but they did not show up for the sale, and his low bid carried the day. As Fuller understood things, God himself had intervened in the matter and had acted in favor of a new seminary on the west coast.[12] There would therefore be both building and students. So, without having everything lined up in the way one would expect an institution of higher learning to be planned, these men launched their institution by faith, a faith that knew God would tie up the loose ends.

Miracles related to evangelical ministries were not always on such a grand scale. The Schaeffers, for example, considered asking God to provide for them a normal way of life that would satisfy their simplest needs. Their conviction ran somewhat against the grain of traditional Presbyterianism, and when the Schaeffers were young and at Westminster Theological Seminary, Edith Schaeffer was rebuked by a faculty member's wife for praying for material blessings.[13] The Schaeffers refused to kowtow to what they considered theological determinism, which they no doubt judged to be ominously similar to the liberal worldview. In the same way, David Wilkerson tackled mundane and trivial problems by including God in the answers to them. When being considered for a pastorate position by a small church, he prayed that God might give him and his wife a sign as to whether he was to accept the position or not. In his prayer he said that a unanimous decision by the church committee would be part of the sign, but also God's answer ought to include a decent refrigerator and a thorough fumigation of the parsonage for pests. According to Wilkerson, each sign was given, and he began his pastorate.

The founder of Campus Crusade for Christ, Bill Bright, exhibited a similar habit of living by faith. When his young ministry was in dire need of $485, he candidly turned the matter over to God in prayer. As he prayed, recounts his biographer, the mailman came to the door and delivered an unexpected $500 gift from a couple from Zurich.[14] In Bright's ministry, and in the ministries of other evangelicals under consideration here, these were nearly quotidian events, and the expectation of such divine intervention was constant.

All evangelicals were expected to share in this openness to miracles and signs. Lee Braxton, a businessman who owned over twenty corporations and associated with authors like Dale Carnegie (*How to Win Friends and Influence People*), Frank Bettger (*How I Raised Myself from Failure to Success in Selling*), and Napoleon Hill (*Think and Grow Rich*), was also a good friend and supporter of Oral Roberts and worked for him as a dollar-a-year man. Like other biblically grounded businessmen,

Braxton could see a miracle in what other more materialistically minded business people might have deemed a financial disaster. When Roberts lost his tent, which seated seven thousand, to a storm, Braxton interpreted the fact that no casualties were incurred in its collapse as a message from God to obtain another tent, seating ten thousand.[15]

Traditional businessmen may have come to the same conclusion as Braxton, calculating that a successful ministry ought to try to profit from such a disaster by increasing its capacity, but such an analysis would be imputing a secular modus operandi into a spiritual worldview. As the evangelical president of Raytheon Company, Tom Philips, who in August of 1973 would lead Charles Colson to Jesus Christ, stated, "All the material things in life are meaningless if a man hasn't discovered what's underneath them."[16]

A life of faith, of course, did not just apply to ministry-related business. Once, when Bill Bright lost out on an oil deal because of a business partner's slight of hand (illegally drilling an offset well in adjacent property), his reaction was, "When you're a slave of Jesus, it saves you a lot of heartache. This was the Lord's problem, not mine, because everything I now owned had been given to Him." Bright's evangelical biographer underscored how the Supernatural took care of such things when he commented that "later the partner's offset well was flooded with water and ruined."[17]

As one looks into the behavior of evangelicals, even amongst the least affluent of them, one observes an antitechnocratic spirituality wherein the laws of nature, or the laws of economics, are often trumped by the supernatural. For youth disenchanted with the modernist commitment to unrelenting cause and effect, this evangelical behavior seemed new, powerful, and adventurous. As a bonus, it even allowed for a certain nonchalance in regard to material things, something hippies found attractive. Indeed, one of the most radical ways to rebel against the establishment, against the technocracy, was to adopt an evangelical spirituality.

The Spirit Within

Although the most striking aspect of the evangelical faith may have been its willingness to allow God to intervene in the minutest of worldly affairs, we must not neglect the fact that evangelicals were primarily preoccupied with deep-seated spiritual issues. Billy Graham addressed one of these problems in 1949 when a good friend of his, a Princeton Theological Seminary student, derided Graham's faith. "You're fifty years out of date," this friend told him. "People no longer accept the Bible as being inspired the way you do."[18] The accusation, combined with Graham's reading of Barth and Niebuhr, drove the rising evangelist into a profound spiritual crisis.

After consulting with a respected Bible teacher, Henrietta Mears, Graham took a night walk into the woods and prayed in earnest. He told God that he could not understand all of the Bible, and that he knew it contradicted modern science. He recounts in his autobiography, "I was trying to be on the level with God, but something remained unspoken. At last the Holy Spirit freed me to say it. 'Father, I am going to accept this as Thy Word—by faith! I'm going to allow faith to go beyond my intellectual questions and doubts, and I will believe this to be Your Inspired Word.' When I got up from my knees . . . my eyes stung with tears. I sensed the presence and power of God as I had not sensed it in months. . . . I knew a spiritual battle in my soul had been fought and won."[19]

According to evangelical leader Bill Bright, his mother's prayers guided him, a hard-nosed and unreligious young man, toward an encounter with God. In 1944, he left the Midwest for Los Angeles to fulfill the American dream and make his fortune, but his first night there led to a spiritual encounter. A stranger invited him to the house of the founder of Navigators (a biblically grounded Bible study program) and then on to a birthday party for Dan Fuller, son of the famous radio evangelist Charles Fuller. The next year Bright committed his life to Jesus and studied under the influential Presbyterian Bible teacher, Henrietta Mears, the same person who would counsel Billy Graham during his spiritual crisis in 1949.[20]

During one session of Bible study, Henrietta Mears called upon Bright and other listeners to commit themselves totally to Christ, to be "expendables for Christ." This invitation provoked a spiritual experience that Bright would hang on to for the rest of his life. Taking up Mears's challenge, he and two other men began to pray together intensely, and then suddenly, he later recalled, "We knew the living God had come to take control. And we were so excited we were like intoxicated people."[21] As they prayed, they saw in their minds the nation's campuses ready for the harvest.[22]

After a short stint at Princeton Theological Seminary, Bright returned to southern California where he enrolled in Fuller Theological Seminary and studied under Carl Henry and others. In 1951, during another intimate encounter with the divine, he received a conviction, or, as he put it, "the Vision," to reach the world for Christ in his lifetime, and to start the process by evangelizing the nation's campuses. In that same year and to that end, Campus Crusade for Christ was founded.[23]

Also in 1951 Francis Schaeffer experienced a life-shaking spiritual revelation. Schaeffer, who had by then been a Christian for a number of years, felt that his spiritual life had lost the appeal it had had when he was a brash young convert. "Why," he asked himself, "is there so little reality among orthodox evangelical Christians? Why is there so little beauty in the way Christians deal with one another?" He pondered this question intensely for two months, and though praying, he even came to wonder if he had been right in becoming a Christian.

Schaeffer concluded that he had been right in becoming a Christian, but that he had been missing something vital in his biblical understanding, something that if not possessed would make it impossible for him to be at peace with himself. As Schaeffer recounts it, the something missing was this: "that the finished work of Christ on the cross, back there in time and space, has a moment-by-moment, present meaning. Christ meant his promise to be taken literally when he said that he would bear his fruit through us if we allowed him to do so, not only in our religious life but in all of our life."[24]

For Schaeffer and the other evangelicals there could be no compartmentalization of religious life; the supernatural inhabited daily life, with a constant willingness to break through the laws of nature and quicken the soul. In this aspect evangelical spirituality was akin to that all-encompassing spiritual realm sought out by countercultural youth who wished to be done with the perceived hypocrisy and contradictions emanating from a liberal and compartmentalized Christianity. Youth listened when these evangelicals spoke about an unfettered God, but more importantly youth watched these people pray and claim answers to their prayers. For those who wanted to believe in something, this was alluring; this spirituality was unlike anything they had seen before, and yet very much like something they had been reaching for all along.

Godly and Affluent

When one considers the spiritual undergirding evangelicals gave to life, one is understandably curious as to how the evangelical viewed the American way of life, with its acquisitive and hedonistic tendencies. Indeed, this question is especially important when one considers that many American youth from the 1950s onward came to fully endorse affluence and to live out their expressive individualism within the context of plenty. For the moment, of course, we are discounting the back-to-nature youth who were an important part of the counterculture and who sought their own reflection in evangelical primitivism and a revived agrarian movement. We will return to the environmentally sensitive wing of evangelicalism in a later chapter. Here, we are focusing on the greater part of rebellious middle-class youth who lived as if there were no tomorrow.

Most sixties' youth, despite their disgust with the capitalistic system and the establishment, accepted affluence and willingly indulged in the material niceties provided by American industry and technology. Most evangelical Christians were no different; they were not prepared to emulate Francis of Assisi . . . but neither were they grasping materialists.

Nearly all of the great evangelists of the twentieth century speak of their meager beginnings in the ministry.[25] They also speak of warding off any suspicion of financial impropriety by establishing oversight committees for their finances. Whether this was effective or not is debatable, but it is noteworthy that Oral Roberts, as early as 1948, established his nonprofit Oral Roberts Evangelistic Association, Incorporated, and created a board of trustees composed of five Christian businessmen and women, along with Roberts himself and his wife, to oversee finances.[26] Billy Graham established policies early in his career to counter potential improprieties.[27]

This careful and circumspect approach to collections does not mean the evangelists believed money to be evil. They had a use for it and a certain indifference toward it at the same time. For those evangelists who never did become wealthy, that indifference could more easily persist.

Pat Robertson gives us insight into the ambivalent attitude toward material things that many evangelicals shared. Robertson recounts the days when he was just on the verge of committing his life to Jesus Christ. While considering this decision, he went to meet a missionary-evangelist for dinner at a restaurant in Philadelphia, a man by the name of Cornelius Vanderbreggen. It was Vanderbreggen who would lead Robertson to accept Jesus as his Lord and Savior. But it was also Vanderbreggen who led Robertson to a typically American understanding of Christianity. As the two of them sat down to dinner and looked over the menu, Vanderbreggen told his dinner guest, "You are the Lord's guest. God is generous, not stingy. He wants you to have the best. Order anything you want."[28] With evangelists like this, it is no small wonder that Saint Francis had such a small following among American evangelicals. This form of Christianity is often disparaged as the gospel of prosperity or of health and wealth. It holds that God wants the believer to live in material as well as spiritual abundance

Accepting this American interpretation of Christianity, Robertson willingly accepted material things that came his way and fit in well with the middle-class economic aspirations of the fifties. But at the same time, Robertson willingly lived without. At the beginning of his Christian life, for example, Robertson demonstrated a capacity to detach himself from worldly things. In his autobiography, he recounts how the Lord told him to "Sell all you have and give alms," and, without conferring with his wife who at that time did not share his newborn spiritual convictions, he sold all their possessions except a few essentials.[29] When he went to Virginia in 1959 to set up a television station, he resolved, "I would not rely on human resources and would ask no funds whatsoever in establishing God's beachhead in Tidewater."[30] The following year, the Christian Broadcasting Network was founded.

This indifference toward material things foreshadowed the attitude of the carefree sixties. As one recalls in the movie *The Graduate*, Ben Braddock, the college grad hero, wanted something different from the singularly materialistic and acquisitive lifestyle of his parents, and yet he took no vow of poverty. In considering Robertson's attitude, one cannot help but think of middle-class youth freely accepting and using mom and dad's money but denouncing capitalism at the same time and willingly moving into a friend's "pad" when immediate resources periodically dried up. The idea that provisions would come one's way without having to work for them in subservience to the technocracy was an idea shared by both sixties' youth and certain biblically grounded Christians. Passing the hat and soliciting free-will donations were practices shared by both.

There were nuances that made the countercultural attitude toward affluence and the biblically grounded one differ. The evangelicals gave spiritual reasons for their material nonchalance, whereas hippies typically did not. Whether in or out of abundance, evangelicals felt obliged to live out a Christlike life and never to let their material blessings distract them from that goal. Most hippies lived carefree in conscious rebellion against the Establishment; evangelicals lived their lives as witnesses for Christ. Televangelist James Bakker, for example, looking back repentantly upon his ministry after having done time in prison, acknowledged that at some point he had lost that holy indifference and had become a true materialist, controlled by the desire to create and possess material things. He remorsefully recalled when a fellow evangelist, James Robison, warned him of his overweening love of the material. At the time Bakker was building Heritage USA, a theme park, and Robison told him bluntly, "Jim, you are committing fornication with brick and mortar."[31]

Despite the spiritual overtones, there was something oddly similar in the disregard both evangelicals and sixties' youth demonstrated toward material things. The something similar was their antitechnocratic expectations. Provision for one's needs was necessary, and it would come, but in a thoroughly antitechnocratic way and for a thoroughly antitechnocratic purpose. Evangelicals had that purpose confidently grounded in their spirituality; most sixties' youth, in their quest, longed for something similar.

Gospel Freedom

Having noted evangelicalism's accommodation to affluence, one is immediately pushed to consider the relationship between evangelicalism and expressive individualism. If affluence were allowed, then the question of lifestyle options required new thinking. In discussing the meaning of expressive individualism for evangelicals, it is helpful to turn to the *Four Spiritual Laws* booklet drafted by Bill Bright that was so successful in drawing middle-class high school and college students into the evangelical fold.

The first of the laws not only dove-tailed with the golden rule ethic, it also reached out to the middle-class sense of expressive individualism, that is, how important each individual is and how each individual has a divinely appointed and anointed role in the universe with infinite non-technocratic possibilities.[32] Law number one was "God **loves** you, and has a wonderful **plan** for your life." This law, once stated, was then supported by two Bible verses that emphasized God's love and the abundance God held out for each individual.

The "spiritual laws" did not suggest that the individual was swallowed up by God and lost all freedom and power of decision. On the contrary, they declared that the individual was connected to God and therefore capable of achieving goals that could not be achieved by the non-Christian. For the young reader, then, freedom and the power to do the impossible would be experienced through conversion. Before conversion, the individual was bound by sin, locked into the prison of the mainstream worldview and lifestyle. Conversion was emancipation; it was freedom from drugs, freedom from homosexuality, freedom from hate, and freedom to love God, friend, and foe.

The new lifestyle, according to the evangelicals, was an adventure into the miraculous.[33] The sixties' mantra, "If it feels good, do it," could only have eternal significance if the doing were connected to the infinite, almighty, and all-loving God. As Billy Graham announced to a crowd of 180,000 at a youth rally in Dallas in 1972, "You are young. You are fearless. The future is yours." And later, "Put your hand in the hand of the man from Galilee. When you do you'll have a supernatural power to put your hand in the hand of a person of another race. You'll have a new love in your heart that will drive you to do something about poverty, the ecology question, the racial tension, the family problems and, most of all, to do something about your own life."[34]

Although the freedom advocated would be experienced within scriptural bounds, it operated clearly outside the Victorian limits of yesteryear. By 1978 evangelical clergy would begin to demonstrate more tolerant views regarding consumption of alcohol and expressions of sexuality (within the bounds of marriage) as well as support for civil liberties, a change that Robert Wuthnow would define as more liberal.[35] The term "liberal," however, is misleading. The evangelical interpretation of Scripture, its hermeneutics, was anything but liberal. They sincerely believed they were authentically expounding the biblical authors' meaning when they said Jesus made and drank wine, alcohol content included.

The Activist Lifestyle

Young evangelical converts actively sought to dismantle and remake the whole of mainstream America in their image. Prior to the advent of the modern civil rights movement, feminism, and flower power, evangelicals walked door to door proselytizing neighborhoods, pointing out the shortcomings of liberal spirituality but extolling the golden rule. Denouncing crass materialism, but not affluence, and calling upon fellow Americans to accept freedom in Jesus, young evangelicals proved themselves to be capable activists. In the 1950s Bill Bright's Campus Crusade for Christ spread out across the nation evangelizing America's youth, and by 1961 it had a staff of over one hundred (each staff member living off gifts) and was an established presence on forty campuses in fifteen states.[36]

It would be hard to overestimate Bill Bright's influence on the future of countercultural Christianity in the coming decade. Bright's organization became the biggest parachurch youth organization ministering to high school and college youth, and it played a pivotal role in acclimating new converts (from both liberal and non-Christian backgrounds) to the evangelical culture. Of course, the first Jesus People had not necessarily come from a liberal Christian background. Many had been brought up in Jewish households or homes hostile to religion. However, they still carried out an act of rebellion in embracing Jesus. One young teen who converted during the Jesus movement felt proud when her atheist father lashed out at her, "You're just a Jesus Freak."[37] But no matter what kind of background they came from, given the importance of colleges during the counterculture, these Jesus enthusiasts would be ultimately influenced by ministries like Campus Crusade.

When the Jesus movement gained ground on college campuses, it flourished in a milieu dominated by children of liberal Christian households. It was in this academic setting that Bill Bright armed his young activists with the *Four Spiritual Laws* pamphlet, cleverly tapping into certain approved liberal values while skillfully capitalizing on the rebellious youth's dissatisfaction with other aspects of the liberal worldview.

After establishing in the first law that God was loving, the pamphlet's second law challenged the reader to reject his or her liberal upbringing. By living a compartmentalized life separated from God, one lived in sin. Laws three and four, however, quickly followed up to bring the reader's attention back to God's love. The separation existing between the perfect God and the sinful individual could be immediately closed by receiving the Christ of Scripture as one's personal and living Savior and Lord, a once and forever relationship.

The formula, if followed by the target audience, resulted in a new lifestyle that separated the convert from mainstream religion and culture and brought him or her into a personal spiritual relationship with a God who interacted with the individual and with the world. The pamphlet ended with several observations and recommendations for the convert. It reminded the neophyte that Christ had entered his life and that his sins (his mainstream thought and life) were forgiven; he was now a child of God, he possessed eternal life, and he was to begin the great adventure for which he had been created, a biblically grounded life. The pamphlet then exhorted the convert to evangelize others and to walk in the fullness of God. It told the reader: "trust God for every detail of **your** life," and "allow [the Holy Spirit] to control and empower **your** daily life and witness."[38]

Evangelization, when one stops to consider it, is a pure form of activism. The evangelist is pitted against an opposing worldview, denouncing it, arguing for his own worldview, and boldly trying to pull people away from the opposing worldview one by one.[39] Oral Roberts, Billy Graham, Bill Bright, Pat Robertson and Francis Schaeffer were all activists, and in this sense held something in common with the sixties' activists, whether a Mario Savio leading the Free Speech Movement, a Tom Hayden writing the Port Huron Statement, or a Timothy Leary (who, incidentally, had visited Schaeffer's L'Abri mission) advocating a drug-induced enlightenment: they all wanted to remake people's minds and remake the world.[40]

And just as the secular activists of the radical sixties met in cells in order to make group decisions about how to promote their agenda, so did the evangelicals meet and plan. Participatory democracy was indigenous to the evangelical Bible studies and prayer groups before Tom Hayden had drawn up his Port Huron Statement. Instead of imitating mainstream Bible studies, which normally took place as adult Sunday school, where the faithful met dressed for church, at church time, and in a church facility, evangelicals took bible study into homes during the workweek. In informal settings, casually dressed, they discussed biblical topics openly with fellow believers and shared their particular experiences of God's activity in their lives. Evangelicals also held home-based prayer meetings, much like the Bible studies, but here they emphasized the individual needs of each group member and spent time praying, one by one, for those needs, with the confidence that each person had a direct access to the godhead. Although they discussed and prayed about illnesses, heartaches, joys, frustrations, and financial needs, they also discussed and prayed about the radical changes they hoped would take place in American society. Fortified in spirit, they went forth to accomplish the task, out to the neighborhoods, down Main Street, and onto college campuses.

Conclusion

The evangelicals, such as Bill Bright and Francis Schaeffer, rejected the mainstream. All were rebels against scientism and willing to defy the status quo. They were vocal and behavioral activists, protesting societal norms in word and deed. They did not reject affluence outright, they did not reject the golden rule ideal, and they did not reject expressive individualism as did separatist fundamentalists, but they did reject the technocratic ideal. Their ideals shared an uncanny similarity with the emerging priorities of the younger generation.

Prior to the 1970s, the activism that evangelicals participated in touched but on the fringes of the political world, or if in depth, only at specific points, such as on the issue of school prayer. Countercultural activism, perhaps because of its connection with America's intelligentsia, struck hard at public institutions such as universities and the government, institutions that the biblically grounded outsiders had considered off-limits. Biblically grounded Christians had learned to live as pariahs, and as such had shied away from aggressively attacking many middle-class and mainstream public establishments, focusing their attention on ecclesiastical organizations and individual believers. However, a significant number of countercultural youth, with their radical activism and rebellious individualism, were attracted to evangelicalism because it stood against the liberal establishment of their childhood.

Before we move on to examine the youth who were attracted to evangelicalism, however, a few important observations need to be made in reference to Francis Schaeffer. Schaeffer, as we have seen, not only rejected the mainstream, he also rejected his liberal or secular parents' worldview. He had also consciously and decidedly turned away from sectarianism and embraced the golden rule ideal for all seasons rather than a compartmentalized lifestyle.[41] Above all, and this was due no doubt to the intellectual nature of his conversion and his theological education with teachers well-versed in Machen's apologetics and polemics, he was obsessed with the intellectual debate. Schaeffer said things, and in such a way, that made him sound like one of the sixties' youth.

But not only did Schaeffer's language and gospel presentation sound harmonious to many young listeners, his lifestyle also was in tune with theirs. Francis Schaeffer was a tailor-made evangelist to countercultural youth. He was an eccentric who wore knickers, smoked a pipe, and, tucked away in the Alps, he exuded a hint of European avant-garde intellectualism in spite of his blue-collar childhood in Pennsylvania. Furthermore, L'Abri, Switzerland, where he lived and worked, was something of a commune; and although each family of L'Abri lived separately and with its own property, there were student visitors of mixed nationalities sleeping here and there, who gathered together during the day and into the night to discuss religious and philosophical questions in a relaxed, teach-in atmosphere.[42] As a *Time* magazine reporter wrote in an article on the Schaeffers in 1960, "Each weekend the Schaeffers are overrun by a crowd of young men and women mostly from the universities . . . professing every shade of belief and disbelief. There are existentialists and Catholics, Protestants, Jews and left-wing atheists. . . . The one thing they have in common is that they are intellectuals."[43] Schaeffer spoke a language young people could understand, or at least liked to hear, and he lived out a lifestyle they felt comfortable with, or perhaps envious of.

Schaeffer was more than just a forbearer of the countercultural Christianity that was to come in the mid-1960s out of the radical collegiate and hippie population; he was more than just a cutting-edge new evangelical. He was himself a countercultural Christian.[44] A *Newsweek* article published in 1982 hints at the role Schaeffer had had for biblically grounded Christianity during the sixties and seventies.[45] The author, in typical mainstream media fashion, referred to Schaeffer as a fundamentalist, and expected his readers to perhaps think of a fundamentalist philosopher as a "contradiction in terms," but the author also referred to Schaeffer as the "guru" of fundamentalism. In this the author caught something special about Schaeffer; and that is, that Schaeffer connected with middle-class youth, even rebellious youth, in a way that few biblically grounded leaders did. For this reason, the role Schaeffer played in the 1970s as a bridge between countercultural Christianity and the Christian Right can hardly be overstated.[46]

6

The Countercultural Christians

It comes as no surprise that all biblically grounded groups of Christians attempted to proselytize America's youth during the sixties; after all, each group hoped to remake America in its image, and where better to start than with the younger generation? But evangelistic success did not mean that the young converts conformed to conservative religion in all aspects. Indeed, those youngsters who came forward and opted for biblically grounded Christianity made their spiritual decisions for their own purposes. The original countercultural Christians were known specifically as "Jesus People" or "Jesus Freaks" precisely because they could not be called anything traditional, even though they tended toward biblically grounded Christianity.[1]

The first rumblings of a youthful swing toward biblically grounded Christianity came, quite appropriately, from the land of tremors and new beginnings, California. Fundamentalists, new evangelicals, Pentecostals, and eventually charismatics sent their laborers into the streets and onto college campuses and found fields ripe for harvest in the Golden State. But in going forth, the successful missionaries found that they had to adapt to the ways of their target audience, often dropping residual sectarian views and Victorian habits, and then they had to adjust their message so that it emphasized a revolutionary, hippie-like Jesus. In order to succeed, street evangelists had to recognize the authentic rebellion that youth were exercising against their parents' beliefs and lifestyles, and they had to match that rebellion with antiliberal polemics drawn from biblically grounded Christianity.[2]

Ministering in the Street

By the mid-1960s, while evangelical organizations such as Campus Crusade for Christ worked some of California's major campuses, such as UCLA, individual street evangelists, more or less freelance, distributed religious tracts on Sunset Strip and other major venues of hippiedom. Dispensing with suits and ties and donning hip clothing, these evangelists mingled, listened, and talked. The alienated street youth, who had abandoned family traditions for a liberated life of drugs and sex, and who now found drugs and sex had not quenched their spiritual thirst, discovered the evangelists' antitechnocratic message enticing, if not compelling. Many followed the evangelists home to see, learn, and experience more.[3]

The first significant sixties' street ministry (if one does not include Wilkerson's Teen Challenge), began in 1966 when Tony Alamo, an adult convert from Judaism, and his wife Susan, who had converted at a younger age, began evangelizing youth in Los Angeles. Before committing themselves to the street, Tony and Susan were young and popular Pentecostal evangelists who made a good living preaching from church to church, but one night, driving along Sunset Strip, they looked out from their car at the hippies walking alongside and came to the conclusion that the street youth were spiritual orphans who needed, wanted, a home . . . and they believed they could provide them that home in Jesus. They left their car, conversed with the young people, gathered a handful of them, took them to their own home, won them over to Christ, and bedded them down for the night. Because Tony had lived life fast and loose as an entertainer and talent agent prior to his conversion, his lifestyle and thinking fit in well with the counterculture crowd. He and Susan soon devoted themselves to the street, and in time the couple distanced itself from regular church ministry, and even became, to a degree, opposed to the traditional church.[4]

Another early street preacher was Arthur Blessitt, a young ordained Baptist minister who went to San Francisco to continue his religious education but became involved in witnessing to hippies instead. He and his wife moved to the Los Angeles area in 1967 where he went into secular coffeehouses, places where hippies met to "rap" and buy drugs, to carry on his witness. He finally secured a location for himself, one night a week, in a go-go bar where he could talk to youth. The venture was so successful that he went out to look for a permanent building and found one on Sunset Strip; he christened it "His Place."

One visitor to His Place was a certain Don Williams, college youth pastor at the First Presbyterian Church of Hollywood. Henrietta Mears, the lady who had counseled Billy Graham and mentored Bill Bright, hired Williams, but she passed away shortly before his arrival, leaving him on his own to seek out ways to connect with the countercultural generation. He soon discovered that music and the nightclub style would serve his purposes well. In 1968, with a sizeable donation from his well endowed church and with helping hands from its membership, he opened "The Salt Company"; in time thousands of youth from college, church, and street would flow through the establishment.[5]

Within a year, ministers and youth leaders descended upon Don Williams's operation to solicit advice on the best way to set up their own Christian nightclubs; by giving them vision, encouragement, and practical advice, Williams helped ignite an explosion of biblically grounded evangelism to countercultural youth. By 1970, over one hundred imitative nightclubs and coffeehouses populated southern California.[6] But they existed elsewhere in the country too, even as far north as Washington state. Here, the successful logger John Breithaupt had met Dennis Bennett, been baptized in the Spirit, and then abandoned his business to begin a ministry among hippies by opening up his House of Zaccheus in 1968.[7]

Also in Seattle, Linda Meissner, a former member of David Wilkerson's Brooklyn ministry, had a coffeehouse. Her operation, however, languished until she paid a visit to the House of Zaccheus and understood that she had to abandon her fifties' approach to evangelism. In 1969 she founded the Catacombs coffeehouse which, with its rock band and underground newspaper, would enjoy phenomenal success. By the early seventies, thousands of such countercultural Christian establishments sprung up within towns and cities from coast to coast, becoming especially prominent in the Great Lakes area.[8] Some of these places were tightly interconnected but most were independent enterprises, united simply in their rejection of establishment styles of worship and in their zeal for a hippie-friendly Jesus.[9]

Christian coffeehouses and storefront churches were meeting places set up by street evangelists for the spiritually inquisitive; they served as places to listen to music, get something to eat and drink, and sometimes find a pad to sleep on, but above all they served as places to share concerns and troubles. For those who warmed up to the gospel, they served as places to study with others about biblical solutions to emotional and material dilemmas, to pray over problems, and to wait over those problems with the confident expectation that divine resolution was in the offing. Christian coffeehouses played an important role in the early success of the Jesus movement, because they provided bases from which street evangelists could operate and into which they could draw prospects for conversion.

Just as important to the street was the literature published to get the message out and bring the youth in. Word of mouth was effective, but the printed page could reach behind doors and even beyond popular hippie gathering points. Several street ministries created, in addition to myriad tracts, substantial underground newspapers, many of which gained widespread circulation. By 1969, *The Hollywood Free Paper*, *Right On!*, and *Agape* had come into print, and the following year two more important papers, *Maranatha* and *Truth*, appeared. Four years after it began publication, *The Hollywood Free Paper* generated about half a million copies.[10]

The language used by these underground newspapers differed significantly from anything employed by denominational broadsheets. As the following excerpt from *The Hollywood Free Paper* demonstrates, the writers transformed biblical polemics and apologetics into the hip jargon attractive to countercultural youths.

> I know you can dig that almost everyone today is hung-up. Why? Because you have been sold a phony bill of goods concerning reality. You have let the 'system' pull the wool over your eyes regarding who Jesus Christ really is. I don't blame you for getting up-tight with the Christianity that most churches peddle. You get the idea that Jesus is some kind of a prejudiced, middle class materialist or else some kind of a milk-toast character that wants to spoil your bag with a bunch of rules and regulations. But, Jesus promises you life and liberty.[11]

The same kind of discourse could be found within the coffeehouses. Keith Green, who eventually became a well-known musician of countercultural Christianity, recorded in his diary his first visit to a Christian coffeehouse in Washington state.[12] Keith was typical of the kind of youth drawn into a Christian coffeehouse. He had experimented with drugs and Eastern mysticism, picking up religious impressions along the way. He felt that there was some important divine purpose to his life and that he needed to discover what the spirit world had to tell him about it. His brief account of his first coffeehouse visit gives the reader a sense of the type of conversation prevalent in these settings. Even though Green eventually became an advocate of countercultural Christianity, he was initially repulsed by the biblicism found there, an issue he, like many others, would eventually resolve. Keith reported in his diary, "We went to a 'Jesus Freak' coffeehouse and they tried the trip on me about believing the whole Bible, word for word, even the part that says God kills my brother and I just don't believe that. Not my wonderful Father!"[13] One notes that the language style of this diary entry differs little from that of *The Hollywood Free Paper*, and for good reason: both emanated from members of the counterculture.

The Christian coffeehouse was not all about spiritually seductive conversation; it had other attributes that lured in the young. Music figured prominently. Bob Dylan-styled folksingers, guitarists, drummers, and electric organists replaced surefooted pedal organists and choirs.[14] The music gave the coffeehouses a nightclub ambience (Blessitt referred to His Place as a Jesus nightclub), which drew youth in.[15] The novelty of singing Christian lyrics to rock 'n' roll or contemporary folk tunes sent the message home that this was a relevant form of religion. The songs were spliced together with individual testimonies by hippies who had just given their lives over to Jesus Christ. Lyrics, mini-sermons, and witnessing turned the coffeehouse into an evangelistic station more effective in some ways than even the Billy Graham-type crusade, mainly because the coffeehouse not only evangelized, it also provided a home for newborn Jesus People, and mentored them over time into committed Christians, who in their turn went out to seek more converts.

Sixties' Christianity, in its purest form, spread by way of the street. From Southern California to northern Washington the movement grew steadily and stretched out across the nation. By dressing casually, by confronting fellow youth one-on-one with a seemingly new spiritual message, by distributing tracts and newspapers presenting Jesus in popular style, by using the coffeehouse setting, with its rock 'n' roll music and standup sensational testimonies, street evangelists created a new type of biblically focused religion that is best described as countercultural Christianity.[16]

Street ministries, however, naturally led to college campuses, and from the beginning many students welcomed their music. The Christian band Exkursions from Chicago, for example, hooked up with an evangelist and toured dozens of colleges in the eastern United States, where they "broke down the stereotype views of Christianity . . . and presented Jesus to thousands" by intermixing contemporary secular songs with their own spiritually charged ones.[17] Once in the academic world, however, the Jesus movement would be obliged to present its case for faith in an intellectually respectable way.

Brother Jesus

In the beginning, countercultural Christianity was focused mostly on the experiential. The loving, hippie Jesus figured uppermost in the minds of these youth, fittingly known as "Jesus People." Jesus was human, he was God, he was living love itself; and so, he was the perfect friend and the true guide for a complete, authentic, and fulfilling life. Jesus was felt intimately in every moment as much as he was intellectually comprehended. Jesus made the soul cognizant of its eternal significance; he saved it from alienation and oblivion.[18] Countercultural Christianity was in essence relational. As one popular countercultural evangelist put it, "Accept Jesus Christ as the son of God, accept his deity, accept his love, and then you can accept yourself. Then when you pray to Jesus Christ for help, you know you will get it because you are praying to God and not some human being who lived two thousand years ago."[19]

Countercultural Christians drew their inspiration from the Jesus of the Bible, and they loved the Bible inasmuch as it described Jesus to them in terms that reflected their highest ideals, the golden rule ideal and the ideal of truth for all seasons, as well as the ideal of a humanity which encompassed non-technocratic spirituality. A thorough grounding in the Bible came slowly to some hippie converts, however. After all, many of these youth came from a secular or theologically liberal background. Devoted to the existential here-and-now, they were at first attracted to a spirituality that was experiential first, and scriptural second. But like some charismatics, who first found the Holy Spirit and later found the Bible, most of these youth would eventually end up committed to Scripture.[20]

Golden Rule Emphasis

The "golden rule Jesus" of countercultural Christianity is not hard to document, especially as this Jesus fit in well with the peace-loving mood of America's youth. As did all street evangelists, Arthur Blessitt emphasized the loving Jesus who would do anything for a friend, or for an enemy. When an acquaintance, who was a Hell's Angels member, came to visit Arthur, Arthur made it a point to tell the biker about Jesus' love. The biker, Tom, drew back at the sight of a huge wooden cross on the floor of His Place, and awkwardly left the Christian nightclub. But he returned later, explaining to Arthur that he could not keep the cross out of his mind. "It's not strange, Tom," Arthur told him. "Because God wants you. He is drawing you to Himself. He brought you to the cross, now He brought you back. Jesus loves you so much. He suffered and died for every sinful thing you've ever done."[21]

Of course the Jesus movement was more than just words. The compassion felt for others was genuine and brought out deep emotion manifested in tears and hugs. It also brought out concrete acts of charity. The Christian nightclub or coffeehouse, as noted above, provided free food, and sometimes a free bed. In the Jesus People communes, material things as well as emotions were shared.[22] The Alamos eventually created a Christian commune, covering some four hundred acres, that would have been the envy of Timothy Leary for its size and devotion to spirituality. There was a chapel and a twenty-four-hour-a-day prayer room, but there were also some fifteen hundred meals served each day. Everyone worked, many outside the commune, and these workers voluntarily gave ten percent of their earnings to it, and the commune took care of medical expenses for childbirth. It seemed to Glenn Kittler, who visited the commune, that happiness and love were everywhere in evidence there.[23]

David Wilkerson's Teen Challenge also ministered to youth, especially—but not exclusively—to youth in trouble with drugs, ghetto youth.[24] Wilkerson's mission was the same as with other Jesus People types: the organization took in young people who were destitute, emotionally or materially or both. Teen Challenge workers presented the gospel, but they also met the physical needs of these troubled youth. Many similar charities were carried out by Jesus People, some even reaching out to people of the Third World.[25]

Although Jesus People most often came from the white middle class, the coffeehouse ministries welcomed all races and ethnicities. There was no viable place for racism in their scheme of things.[26] Jesus the Jew had accepted them, they accepted others. They especially reached out to those hippies who at first seemed antagonistic, since many of them had at one time been just such enemies of the Jesus movement.

Jesus People accepted the risks involved, the ridicule, the threats. But taking their cue from the hippie Jesus, the ultimate peacenik, they refused to answer violence with violence. Like flower children they responded to accusations and fists with nonviolence. When Arthur Blessitt constructed his huge cross and began to take it across the country on foot, he was immediately confronted by a deranged man bent, apparently, on stopping him. The man rushed toward Blessitt and his ministry friends with a board fixed with a protruding nail and screamed "I'm going to kill you!" Blessitt told his friends, "Fellows, we can't touch him. I've never used violence, we can't begin now. If we live, we live . . . if you can't take it . . . run. If we die, we die . . . but we can't touch him." Blessitt and his team then knelt and prayed, saying, "Jesus, let this man know You love him, we love him." The man desisted.[27]

The golden rule figured prominently in countercultural Christianity. It was at the center of the gospel message—Christ's agony and death on the cross for the salvation of his enemies—and it was lived out in the witness of the street Christians.

A Seamless Life

The most important parts of Scripture for countercultural Christians, other than those gospel passages that made Jesus relevant and alive for them, were the Book of Acts and the epistles of the Apostle Paul.[28] Here, they believed, they found the necessary elements of the Christian lifestyle, and they discovered a continuum between what they read and the developing habits of the sixties. In their reading of the Scriptures, they found that primitive Christianity did not hold to the secular/spiritual dichotomy they detested in their parents' worldview. In the Book of Acts, believers' spirituality colored the whole of life. The belief that the gospel was relevant to every circumstance, rather than to just specific areas at specific times, marked countercultural Christians as distinct from Christians content with and subservient to the technocracy. It was their devotion to honesty and their abhorrence of hypocrisy, along with their recognition that the individual was an emotional and spiritual human being as opposed to a technocratic creature, that encouraged, if not forced, them to make all of life a spiritual enterprise.

This spiritual integrity, pervasive as it was, made countercultural Christians overbearing to some, because the hippie Christians insisted on making Christ the object of every action and every conversation, at every moment. This behavior stunned Glenn Kittler, contributing Catholic writer to the popular and religiously inspired *Guideposts Magazine*. Kittler wanted to investigate the Jesus People, so he placed a phone call to *The Hollywood Free Paper* and was greeted with a "Jesus loves you!" hello. "This greeting," he confessed in his book *The Jesus Kids*, "coming at me as it did, the first thing on an autumn Monday morning in 1971, startled me a bit. It was like unexpectedly stepping into a cold shower. It woke me up. This was, in a way, my first direct contact with what had become known as the Jesus People, and I wasn't prepared for such suddenness."[29]

At the height of the Jesus movement, Kittler traveled to California's Calvary Chapel to investigate first hand. Calvary Chapel was one of the first churches to enthusiastically embrace hippies and to not only accept them into its services but alter its worship style to match hippie tastes. Kittler recounted the sermon he heard when he attended there, a sermon he would subsequently discover accurately reiterated what the Jesus People believed without exception, that God was constantly present in the individual's life, speaking to the individual in the minutiae of daily living. "'Listen to the Lord,'" Kittler quoted the pastor, "'He's talking to you all the time.' This, I learned as I went along, is the general conviction of the Jesus People."[30] The stress on the infinite importance of each moment made countercultural Christianity into a religious reworking of Jean-Paul Sartre's existentialism.

In countercultural Christianity one did not have to shift gears from Saturday to Sunday, which meant countercultural Christians could gather informally, like in a teach-in, to share their thoughts, their joys, and their troubles. They found this approach to religion and life reflected in primitive Christianity. Christianity as lived out in the pages of Scripture was at one with the sixties' style: bare-boned, authentic, sharing, it was a *mélange* of the golden rule ideal and spiritual integrity applied to the whole of life. Here, the profane became swallowed up in the sacred.

Sixties Christianity was one coin of the counterculture; another projected the effigy of the Death of God movement, wherein the profane swallowed up the sacred. Both coins circulated in the countercultural marketplace of ideas. Both the Jesus movement and the Death of God movement dispensed with the dichotomous worldview of the technocracy that had compartmentalized the sacred and profane; liberal Christianity had become for members of both movements a religion discredited by its anachronistic view of humankind and by its inherent hypocrisy.[31]

Expressive Individualism

Authority in countercultural Christian groups, even though there were leaders or guides, was dispersed in accordance with the precepts of participatory democracy. Each individual possessed equal access to the truth, which lay in one's relationship with the biblical, yet living and personal, Jesus. A description of Teen Challenge meetings during this era demonstrates the popularity of participatory democracy amongst young converts to Jesus. To be sure, a team leader guided discussion, but it is evident that each participant could bring out his or her experience with, and knowledge of, spiritual truth. At one particular Teen Challenge meeting in Los Angeles, for example, an observer described a multiracial group of young men discussing Christ and how Christ lived in their lives. One young black man gave a long harangue about exorcizing the Devil from a man and physically battling with Satan.[32] No one in the room shut him off or curtailed his long and lively description. Each person, it appeared, who had an authentic spiritual life had a direct connection to ultimate reality and thus a right and freedom to share that truth with others.

Countercultural Christians wholeheartedly embraced Jesus and shifted their focus on life toward him without losing sight of their own radically individualistic nature, their own personal war against establishments, their own personal desire for freedom. Roger Bennett, a student of Bradley University, contributed an article on this subject to *Christianity Today* in 1972. Bennett defended young Christians' use of contemporary habits and styles. He admitted that while collegiate Christians did not practice free sex, "neither do they recoil in horror and set up a monastic counter-counterculture. No one should impose a guilt complex on the young." For Bennett, it was a matter of a *new propriety*, and the older generation needed to gain an understanding of the differences in propriety so that "a mutual tolerance bred of the Holy Spirit" might exist.[33]

The role of expressive individualism is perhaps the hardest element to fathom in countercultural Christianity because Jesus People loudly claimed to be liberated and free but did not promote sexual promiscuity or drugs; in other words, they did not promote things that most hippies identified with freedom. Countercultural Christians, the new Jesus People, most of whom had past experiences with drugs and promiscuous sex, claimed to experience a new freedom in abandoning those things.[34] It was not as if they were mindlessly clinging to a taboo that had been dinned into their conscience since birth, like so many Pentecostals and fundamentalists. This was their choice. They claimed that sex and drugs could be masters, oppressive masters that enslaved the individual, but that Jesus freed them from those masters. Again, they drew their inspiration from the New Testament and the Apostle Paul's explanation that there was freedom in Christ. As the Revised Standard Version of the Bible put it in Romans 8:1-2, "There is therefore now no condemnation for those who are in Christ Jesus. For the law of the Spirit of life in Christ Jesus has set me free from the law of sin and death." So at Blessitt's His Place, when a hippie accepted Jesus, the new convert went into the bathroom and ritualistically dumped his or her drugs into the toilet, symbolically replacing the dope high with the Jesus high.[35] Conversion was, it seems, a new freedom radically seized, a freedom from all addictions except that addiction to Jesus, who, as the street evangelist Duane Pederson had stated, "promises you life and liberty."[36]

Another noteworthy illustration of this conception of liberty comes from the example of a girl attending a Leighton Ford crusade. Ford, Billy Graham's brother-in-law, conducted a successful ten-day crusade in Rochester, New York, in May of 1972 that was attended by some 65,400 people. Of these, 3,293 inquired afterwards about the faith, half of whom were thought to be teenagers. In one of the collection buckets was found an ounce of marijuana with an accompanying letter: "Dear God, Please don't think me to be smart by putting grass in your offering plate. It means I am giving it up for your son, Jesus Christ. Your daughter, Debbie."[37]

The freedom that countercultural Christians embraced also made it possible for them to do, in Christ, things that churchgoing Christians often eschewed. If a thought, word, or action did not betray Jesus, they reasoned, that thought, word, or action could support Jesus. This is why rock 'n' roll music, so shunned by fundamentalists, hit a responsive chord with countercultural Christians, for nowhere had Jesus denounced music. All things—music, films, clothing, foods—could be used by the countercultural Christian if they were helpful in bringing another to Christ or strengthening another or oneself in the faith. As the Apostle Paul had written in 1 Corinthians 10:23-24: "'All things are lawful,' but not all things are beneficial. 'All things are lawful,' but not all things build up. Do not seek your own advantage, but that of the other."

Self-destructive behaviors such as drug abuse were not condoned in the Jesus movement. This did not mean, however, that the religious experiences hippies underwent with drug use were always discounted. For the countercultural Christians, even the LSD trips were interpreted as having opened up many a mind to things spiritual. Melody Green described one drug-provoked spiritual experience she had as a countercultural youth. She took some LSD with a friend and then walked down a side street in Santa Monica, California. "I saw a huge glowing cross hanging in the heavens. I blinked, but it didn't go away. It was a fiery, radiant gold. And it was beautiful. I stared at it in awe, and felt a peace wash into my heart." Later, she returned to the spot where she had had the vision. She could not resolve whether or not a drug-induced vision was valid, but, she wrote, "the peace that came with it puzzled me. I knew Jesus died on a cross, but I'd never thought of looking to him for any answers."[38] She eventually became a Christian, a countercultural Christian, and the vision had played no small role in orienting her toward Jesus. In fact, the emotional peace she experienced on the Santa Monica street returned to her during prayer meetings later. Once converted, the countercultural Christian usually came to understand, through the guidance of street evangelists, that the biblical way to spiritual experience was through fasting, vigil, and prayer.

Understandably, much traditional church music, which had seemed up-tempo in the nineteenth century when the organ was the only instrument capable of filling a sanctuary with music, made little impression on countercultural Christians armed with guitars, microphones, and amplifiers. The traditional sanctuary itself, with its wooden pews, seemed similarly quaint and irrelevant. What emerged, then, was the home church, where countercultural "parishioners" sat on beanbags and couches to sing, pray, and worship. The relaxed countercultural church gathering turned out to be more of a spiritual get-together than a religious "service," but it created the spiritual intimacy and a sense of spiritual authenticity that countercultural youth thought necessary.[39]

It is not surprising then that the idea of relevancy, uppermost in the younger minds of the sixties, also permeated the thoughts of the Jesus People. Things had to be hip to be authentic. And so, many of the successful street evangelists and coffeehouse managers were musicians, in short, entertainers; indeed, some of the best had been professional entertainers before their conversion (Duane Pederson and Tony Alamo, for example). Popular culture moved the Jesus People, bringing freedoms never considered appropriate in the old technocratic world of the 1950s.

Rebellious Activism

The countercultural Christians believed they possessed a Christ-centered freedom. And they believed in this freedom so fervently that they assailed those people and ideas that stood against it. They denounced alcohol, drugs, cigarettes, sex, or anything they believed threatened their liberty in Christ. These things were not evil in and of themselves, but inasmuch as they dominated a person or dictated that person's behavior they were evil. And the activism with which countercultural Christians promoted their brand of freedom and opposed anything that threatened it was consistent with other forms of countercultural activism. It was rebellious, aggressive and vocal.

The man who coined the phrase "Jesus People," because he didn't like the sobriquet "Jesus Freaks," Duane Pederson, was an early activist for countercultural Christianity; and his disdain for the establishment, including the church establishment, was often provocative. Like Tony Alamo, Pederson had gone into show business in California and lived in the fast lane prior to his conversion.[40] He gave himself over to alcohol, and then to drugs, before finally giving himself over to the Christian faith. After accepting Jesus, he went forth to evangelize the downtrodden, the outsiders, just as he understood Jesus had done, despite the disapproval of the church establishment. Finally, when the pastor of his church asked him to stop bringing in riffraff, Pederson realized that his Christianity differed from that of the establishment. He went back out to California and began an aggressive street ministry. Much like a political activist, he campaigned for his cause and denounced his opponents.

Arthur Blessitt also set up a street ministry that exhibited similar elements of countercultural activism.[41] His Christian center on Sunset Strip was immensely popular, entertaining some nights over one thousand youth. It was so popular, in fact, that it drew business away from the local bars and secular coffeehouses. In addition, some of Blessitt's enthusiasts plastered neighboring establishments with Jesus stickers, which probably did not help their business either; and the establishment reacted.[42] Gangs and police alike harassed Blessitt and his Jesus People. But in this instance, the police were not dealing with traditional evangelicals who would respect police authority at any cost and keep their radical witness to quiet one-on-one evangelism or at least within the confines of an organized evangelistic crusade. Blessitt, who himself had been arrested three times for blocking traffic as he witnessed, led over a hundred Jesus People through the night streets and marched them up to police headquarters in protest. He put the police, who periodically crashed into His Place without a warrant to find and seize people with drugs, on notice, warning of further demonstrations to denounce their infringement of his rights. This was the type of Christianity that the dynamic, daring, and rebellious sixties' youth could identify with.

Blessitt's radical style did not remain confined to Los Angeles; he himself made it into the major news networks more than once, and thus spread the new type of Christianity into America's homes via television. After his lease was up for the Sunset building that he rented, Blessitt set up shop elsewhere but was evicted once the owner found out he was an evangelist catering to hippies. At this, Blessitt took a large cross outside and chained himself to it for four weeks, with news crews milling around to film and report. Before he unchained himself, once a new location had been secured, his vigil had become a national and even international curiosity.[43]

The grassroots activism present in the countercultural Christians is poignantly depicted in Kittler's description of street evangelism. On Hollywood Boulevard, he reported, "Many times I saw [Jesus People] come running across the street to join an assault on a group of prospects. And then the questions: 'Have you had your experience with the Lord yet? Have you given your life to Christ? Do you know Jesus died for your sins? How are you getting along with your parents? . . .

The Jesus People would tell their story. So often it presented the same pattern. Trouble at home. Trouble at school. Drugs. Drinking. Sex. Running away. . . . Then suddenly Jesus. The Baptism. And peace and love and freedom from the Establishment."[44] For these Jesus People who knew no boundaries separating their world from their spirituality, this activism, religious as it was, had political potential.

From Spirituality to Politics

As one investigates the different aspects of countercultural Christianity—whether its activism or its countercultural ideals—one is continually reminded of the spiritual undergirding supporting these different aspects. Like the young Teen Challenge man who had physically battled with Satan, these countercultural Christians believed that the supernatural intervened in their lives and in tangible ways. Pastor Chuck Smith of Costa Mesa, California, confirmed this conviction in the thousands of hippie converts flooding into his church when he preached that God spoke to each individual and at all moments.[45] The Bible, then, became the countercultural Christians' guide as to how God spoke to them.

Countercultural Christians, experienced in mind trips, readily absorbed the prophetic passages of the Bible. These passages, as interpreted by evangelicals, often described Jesus' second coming, and the here-and-now generation assumed the coming was at hand.[46] The biblical prophecies of Daniel and the book of Revelation particularly spoke to the young radicals and inspired them to get out into the street to warn people of impending disasters and Christ's imminent return. They found they could readily support their arguments by pointing to recent world events that they claimed had been foretold in the Bible.

In 1970 Hal Lindsey's amazingly successful book on the coming age of the Antichrist, *The Late Great Planet Earth*, hit the bookstores. Lindsey's book described God's intervening hand in world events and argued that long-forgotten prophecies were being fulfilled with the sixties' generation. The "now generation" seized upon the arguments with unbridled enthusiasm.

The book's message clearly challenged the technocratic world and the idea of infinite technocratic progress by announcing not only that all events were subjugated to the divine in the present but also that a spiritual conquest of the world, a consummation of all things by the Spirit, was at hand. No longer did the past or future "accomplishments" of mankind matter, since current events demonstrated that in the present generation all things were being fulfilled.

God had foretold through his prophets that Israel must be restored as a nation, and this had happened.[47] He also foretold that the Jews must possess Jerusalem, and in 1967 this came to pass. He also foretold that the Jews must rebuild the Temple: it was just a matter of time. But once this last element would be in place, the second coming of Christ would be more imminent than ever before. And the countercultural Christians prayed for God's designs, prayed for the Jews to come together, to be restored, and for Jesus to come and take the believers up into heaven.[48] The "rapture," the ultimate trip, was at hand, perhaps due in 1988, when the forty years (a generation) since the establishment of the state of Israel would come to a close.[49] Jesus People singer Larry Norman underscored the importance of the impending event with his song "I Wish We'd All Been Ready." And though Jesus People held their breath, they also knew that for the moment, it was incumbent upon them to support the Jews in Israel. This was perhaps the first shepherding of Jesus Freaks toward a political position.

Conclusion

By 1971 journalists and news commentators who reported on religion recognized that America was experiencing a spiritual revival, but they also noted that in some significant ways this one differed from previous "awakenings." This awakening had a special place for youth, and especially rebellious youth.[50] The phenomenon was so striking and out of character that a spate of books flowed out of the publishing houses to explain it to the American people: *The Jesus Movement* by Edward Plowman; *Jesus People Come Alive* by Walker Knight; *House of Acts* by

John MacDonald; *Turned On to Jesus* by Arthur Blessitt; *The Jesus People Are Coming* by Pat King; *Jesus People* by Duane Pederson; *The Jesus Trip* by Lowell Streiker; *The Jesus Kids* by Roger Palms; *It's Happening with Youth* by Janice Corbett and C. E. Johnson; *The Jesus People* by Ronald Enroth, Edward Ericson, and C. B. Peters; *Berkeley Journal* by Clay Ford; *Spaced Out and Gathered In* by Jerry Halliday; *The Jesus People Speak Out* compiled by Ruben Ortega; *The Far-Out Saints of the Jesus Communes* by Hiley Ward; and *Call to the Streets* by Don Williams.[51] Billy Graham's *The Jesus Generation* joined the book parade and recorded sales of over half a million. Supplementing this book-writing spree, *Time* magazine's June 21, 1971 issue devoted a dozen pages of narrative and pictures to the Jesus movement. With all of this, the Religion Newswriters Association was rather obliged to declare the Jesus People story as the top religious news item of the year.[52]

The movement was having not only a religious impact but a sociological one as well. In opting for a biblically grounded religious expression, most Jesus youth had rejected their parents' worldview, which had been framed either by secular humanist agnosticism, liberal Christian theology, or in some cases by Judaism or Catholicism.[53] With the Jesus movement in full swing, the World Council of Churches, the brainchild of liberalism, seemed unable to deal with the exodus of youth from their member churches as the youth-centered religious revival continued. As Edward Plowman noted at the World Council of Churches' Central Committee meeting in 1972, "What the Central Committee left unsaid evoked comments among reporters and observers. There was no mention of the surging revival movements around the globe or of the growing charismatic phenomenon, and there was only an oblique reference to the Jesus movement among youth. Young people were absent from sessions, even in Sunday ecumenical church services."[54]

Like unto their fellow sixties' compatriots, the countercultural Christians were rebellious and decided activists. And in this they differed from the traditional evangelical in that they easily took their activism into all facets of life. They offered to biblically grounded Christianity an activist and rebellious expressive individualism. All that was left, as a prelude to the rise of the religious right, was that the two, countercultural Christianity and evangelicalism, merge.

7

The Merging of Countercultural and Evangelical Christianity

In a sense countercultural Christianity and evangelicalism never had to merge, because from the outset, countercultural Christianity had its roots in the *avant garde* of evangelicalism. Most of the pioneers of contemporary street evangelism were evangelicals who daringly took certain aspects of twentieth-century evangelicalism to the next level. Billy Sunday, Charles Fuller, and Billy Graham had already used contemporary media to communicate with Americans, including America's youth. Microphones, loudspeakers, radio, television, films, and comic books: for the cutting edge evangelists, the artifacts of popular culture were tools that God had put into their hands in order to reach the lost with the good news of salvation. The Graham generation of evangelists, those who had reached adulthood prior to the end of World War II, had made it acceptable to use mass communication to get out the biblically grounded gospel message.[1]

Popular culture, however, underwent drastic change in the late fifties, sixties, and seventies. Elvis, the Beats, and James Dean helped create, through the same media used by the great evangelists, a new sensuous, boisterous, and rebellious middle-class teenage subculture that no longer supported multigenerational events. By the 1960s, youth had consciously, deliberately, and defiantly gathered unto themselves, concluding that entertainment and ideas could only be experienced within their own subculture. Although youth continued to be a part of Graham's crusades, many sixties' youth could not bring themselves to attend a function that had such obvious affiliation with the older generation and especially with old-time religion.[2]

Because the evangelical methods of the fifties, although not old and not yet wholly outdated, would not work for a significant portion of America's sixties' youth evangelicals such as the Alamos became concerned. These evangelists, recognizing that America's youth was increasingly untouched by the gospel, decided to make themselves ministers to America's youth by venturing into the streets, into coffeehouses, and onto campuses to reach young rebels with the gospel message. From such efforts came not only the creation of countercultural Christianity but also the merger of countercultural Christianity and evangelicalism.

Ministers to the Street

There were three types of people intimately involved in street evangelism in the sixties. Some of these evangelists were mentioned in the previous chapter, but to understand how they all worked together in mediating countercultural and evangelical Christianity it is best to classify them. To begin with, it should be noted that there were the promoters of street evangelism, usually local church pastors, who spent little time in the street themselves but who encouraged and supported fulltime street evangelism. Secondly, of course, there were evangelicals, usually heading up a parachruch ministry, who did devote themselves to the street and who are properly called street evangelists because they evangelized youth directly. Third, there were the street youth themselves who had been converted to Jesus Christ within the counterculture and who accepted the responsibility to evangelize their peers. Now, it should be made clear that by referring to the *street*, I am denoting evangelization that took place outside of the regular churched context and in places frequented by youth. In its largest sense, then, the street might also refer to a campus setting as well.

A fourth group of people was also connected to street evangelism. These men and women were evangelists or ministers of national stature, such as Billy Graham, who were not intimately involved in the day-to-day work, but whose stamp of approval was nevertheless necessary in making street evangelism palpable for the greater population of traditional evangelicals. For the moment, however, we will focus on the local personalities to better understand the link, sometimes strained, that existed between countercultural Christians and evangelicals at the grassroots level.

The first two groups—the promoters of street evangelism (pastors) and the actual street evangelists themselves (parachurch ministers)—performed a function in the development of countercultural Christianity that was similar to the Beats' contribution to the development of the counterculture in general. Looming somewhere between Graham's World War II generation and the sixties' generation, they, like Allen Ginsberg and the Beat generation, could speak to and interact with the younger sixties' generation. And just as Ginsberg had a link with older generation outsiders or leftists, so too did the pioneers of street evangelism have a connection with the older evangelical outsiders. They were the bridge over which evangelicalism and countercultural Christianity could be joined.

The eventual unity and common purpose shared between countercultural Christianity and evangelicalism surpassed that shared by the Beats and the Old Left, however. So much so that whereas the Old Left and the New Left disagreed on the means and purpose of reaching a non-capitalistic manner of life, countercultural Christianity and evangelicalism eventually became unified both in goal and practice. And even though historians speak of evangelicalism in the latter 1970s without reference to the Jesus movement, it is the melding of these two initially somewhat distinct movements that explains why the "evangelicalism" of 1980 was radically different from the "evangelicalism" of 1965.

In examining the pioneers of street evangelism, one observes that evangelists of a variety of denominational backgrounds promoted and participated in the effort to take the biblically grounded gospel into the street. Fundamentalist, new evangelical, Pentecostal, and later, charismatic, were all represented. All of these who engaged youth within popular culture, however, can be referred to as evangelicals, because they all exhibited a great measure of tolerance for new forms of behavior and thought in order to work empathetically with hippies.

As to the background of the converts who became street evangelists themselves, some had known biblically grounded Christianity in their childhood before rejecting it for the counterculture. Many, however, had never experienced it and received only rudimentary instruction before hitting the streets as evangelists. Some, though, had a surprising reservoir of Bible knowledge left over from a liberal church upbringing. But whatever their background, the street evangelists and their converts tended to develop a unified countercultural Christian message shorn of denominationalism that greater evangelicalism would ultimately have to come to terms with.

The Street Evangelists

One of the first street converts to become an ardent evangelist of the Jesus movement was Ted Wise, who became a Christian in 1966.[3] Prior to his conversion, Ted had been a serious heroin addict while in the Navy and was eventually discharged because of problems related to his addiction. In San Francisco he experimented with LSD and marijuana. His wife Liz, although also into drugs, clung to her biblically grounded upbringing. Like so many young people who came to the Jesus movement, Ted believed, in keeping with some of the primal ideals of the counterculture, in the golden rule and spirituality. Although definitely not a churchgoer, he began reading the Bible because he believed it had inspirational things to say about love, even if it were not a wholly reliable source of religious truths.

In spite of his initial cynicism about the trustworthiness of the Bible itself, he became convinced that the New Testament's main character, Jesus, could save him from the anxieties of life. Drugs, he concluded, had been but a means of escaping the world; they had not helped him live within it. Jesus, on the other hand, he thought, could solve his problems in the world. All alone, he asked Christ to save him and thenceforth considered himself Christian. After this privately executed conversion, he believed that he had to make a public profession of his faith. Without telling Liz, he went to a hippie gathering to proclaim his newfound faith and, high on LSD, he took advantage of a lull in the conversation at the party to make his announcement; it silenced everyone. He and Liz went to their car and left, and as he drove, Ted said he heard Jesus speaking to him, and Jesus ordered him to go to church the next morning and announce, "He is back."[4] Ted obeyed, and thus began his career as a countercultural Christian with a ministry to hippies.

Ted did not come out of a biblically grounded background, but he would be mentored in evangelicalism by a promoter of street ministry, Pastor John MacDonald of the First Baptist Church, Mill Valley, California. Ted was a raw recruit, a true street evangelist; he proved an effective link between evangelicalism and the counterculture, because his life of drugs, rebellion, and audacity made him into a type of Christian who could translate the gospel effectively to hippies. He could tell his friends that they could replace the drugs with Jesus, for he had done so, but he could also tell them that they could continue to live an otherwise hippie lifestyle, because he did so.

Supported by Evangelical Concerns, Inc., a non-profit group organized by MacDonald, Ted and Liz opened up a hippie mission, the Living Room, in San Francisco's Haight-Ashbury district in 1967; it lasted for over a year and a half and ministered to perhaps twenty thousand.[5] Among the visitors to the Living Room were the successful Baptist street evangelist Kent Philpott and his hippie convert David Hoyt. In the fall of 1968, these two would establish Soul Inn, a place to minister to and shelter about twenty people at a time.[6] Later, the Wises joined with other couples to form a commune they christened the House of Acts, and in this environment they would continue to live out their Christianity without abandoning the expressive individualism and golden rule ethic so necessary to radical sixties' youth.

How Ted and Liz interfaced with their Baptist mentor is well described in MacDonald's 1970 book *House of Acts*.[7] The relationship between the minister and his church on the one hand and the hippies-become-Christian on the other was rough-and-ready and many disagreements came between them, mainly because the hippies regarded Jesus as himself a churchless hippie and the Holy Ghost as a free spirit who despised the fundamentalists' sectarian manners, "square" rituals, and restricted lifestyle. Nonetheless, MacDonald perceived that he and the countercultural Christians had something in common: their mutual desire to win others to a biblically grounded faith in Jesus.

Pastor MacDonald, although often shocked by Ted's maverick approach to propagating the gospel, took a trip into San Francisco with the street evangelist to size up the situation in hippiedom. It was there that MacDonald realized that Wise had potential that regular evangelicals did not possess. "I noted the ease with which he related to the citizens there," confessed MacDonald, "and the estrangement with respect to myself. By dress and appearance, he belonged. Clearly I did not." And as MacDonald observed Wise walk among the hippies, talk among them, and hand out money to those in need, he realized what lay before him. "Gradually an idea began to emerge. This was an unexplored field of evangelism."[8] In time, such a field would provide not only converts but also activists, missionaries of sorts in reverse, who merged their radical activism into evangelicalism.

MacDonald's and Wise's rough relationship was, of course, not unique. Even though evangelicals were outside the mainstream and shared some of the same concerns and beliefs of sixties' youth, evangelicals still had their own ways of doing things that were not always so far removed from the establishment. Most lived in homes, held jobs, and drove cars that were identical to those of their mainstream peers. Their clothing, haircuts, and mannerisms fit in with the larger society. One could not distinguish an evangelical in a crowd, although in any lengthy personal conversation his or her worldview would inevitably color the dialogue. It was precisely this worldview that connected with hippies. But the clothing, the job, the car and the like did not mesh well. Looking back, these differences may appear to be mere details, but it often seemed to street evangelists that the devil was truly in such details.

By challenging the acceptance of mainstream norms, whether in worshipstyle, politics, or economics, the street evangelists and their supporters ultimately would change biblically grounded attitudes and make possible a new type of evangelicalism, a type that incorporated a confrontational and activist spirit.

The kind of accommodation that evangelicals would have to make with countercultural Christians was demonstrated in the provocative ministry of Tony and Susan Alamo. The Alamos, mentioned in the previous chapter, worked as street evangelists in southern California. In their ministry they confronted the organized church with the obligation to take the gospel message to young people and to receive young converts into the family of Christ. Susan let churchgoers know in no uncertain terms how disappointed she was with them for shunning new Christians from off the streets. "We're doing your work, you know," she told them. "You should be taking these kids into your churches, you should be bringing them to the Lord, you should be helping them settle down and build new lives. Because you're not," she threatened, "don't be surprised when you find your churches empty."[9]

When the Full Gospel Business Men's Fellowship of Long Beach, California, invited the Alamos to come speak at a luncheon, the Alamos showed up with a busload of Jesus People and marched the young radicals with their hip clothing up to the front of the meeting. There, standing before a somewhat dumbfounded audience, Susan took the microphone and announced, "Ladies and gentlemen, if you, as Christians, consider yourselves to be brothers and sisters, I want you to meet some more of your brothers and sisters in Christ Jesus. As you listen to them, ask yourselves how you could ever turn them away. Tony and I could not." The youngsters then began to testify, one by one, how they had come to Jesus Christ.[10]

In the years to come, the Alamos' ministry, because it developed separatistic and dogmatic characteristics, would become ostracized by later street evangelists and evangelicals, but at the outset it demonstrated that youth were ripe for conversion, and soon other evangelists from other backgrounds would come onto the streets to bring evangelicalism to the counterculture and the counterculture to evangelicalism. Arthur Blessitt, for example, whose fundamentalist formation was quite distinct from the Pentecostal background of the Alamos, evangelized in southern California as well.

It could be that Blessitt's ability to engage the street was due in part to his relative youth, for he was nearly a baby boomer himself, being born just a little more than a year before America's entry into World War II, but undoubtedly his childhood experiences also prepared him for a ministry within the counterculture.[11] Though Blessitt's mother exhibited the traditional character of a biblically grounded woman, his father, in spite of his conservative faith, was controlled by alcohol. At the age of seven Arthur attended a revival meeting outside a Baptist church and gave his life to Christ. As a young adult, he attended Mississippi College, a Baptist institution, and then, after marrying, he matriculated at the Southern Baptists' Golden Gate Theological Seminary in California. He remained at Golden Gate for only a semester, however, because the nightclubs, bars, and streets lured him away, not because of the drink and drugs to be found there, but because such places abounded with troubled souls in need of Jesus.

What prepared Blessitt for his street ministry among drug addicts and down-and-out youth was actually his father's marginal lifestyle that was improbably mixed up with biblical principles. In his childhood, Blessitt had accompanied his father into bars and spent time passing out gospel tracts. He recalled, "I'd listen for hours as people would talk in the bars, what they were talking about, what they were thinking about." Six years after his conversion, he witnessed his father make a dramatic turnabout in life. In front of wife and child, his father prayed for Jesus to take away the bottle and take over his life. From that moment on, recalled Arthur, his father was a changed man who henceforth went into bars not to drink, but simply to share Jesus. At the age of 15, Arthur himself gave his life "to Jesus Christ to preach," a conviction that seemed to burn hotter within him as time went on and the sixties unfolded. As he noted some thirty years later, concerning his initial commitment to preach, "I have never had any desire to do anything else since that time."[12]

In Arthur Blessitt, then, we observe a relatively young minister—twenty-seven years old when he began dispensing the Jesus message to the hippies on LA's Sunset Boulevard—who had been raised and educated as a conservative Baptist. His fundamentalist upbringing made him an outsider to begin with, and an outsider with a worldview and spiritual message and lifestyle that definitely defied the technocracy. Career and money were of no consequence to him; on the other hand, living out a life dedicated to preaching, detached from the corporate ladder, and wholly devoted to helping the "hurting people of our time" (as opposed to stepping on others to get ahead) held an absolute significance.[13] And because of his practicing evangelism in bars as a child and his witnessing his father's life-changing exchange of alcohol for Jesus, Blessitt was able to connect with sixties' youth in ways a typical evangelical could not. He was not afraid to walk into secular coffeehouses and drinking establishments where promiscuous sex, drugs, and alcohol flourished; he knew that people disillusioned with sensual excess were to be found within and were prime candidates for Jesus. Blessitt understood that he did not have to bring prospects for Christ into a steepled church sanctuary in order to have them give their lives over to Jesus; he could meet them on their own turf, and this countercultural conception of church as casual, entertianing, and engaged would one day merge into greater evangelicalism.

Like Blessitt, other, often older, evangelicals also worked their way directly into the counterculture to win converts: not all street evangelists were young. Just as Timothy Leary, with his mind-bending credentials from the ethereal realm of LSD, was able to participate in the sixties' counterculture, so was another east coast professor who had evangelical credentials. Jack Sparks, a former Pennsylvania State University statistics professor and Campus Crusade worker, helped found the Christian World Liberation Front at the University of California at Berkeley in 1969.[14]

Sparks intended his organization to be as relevant to popular culture and open to contemporary intellectual debate as Schaeffer's L'Abri, which he visited. The Christian World Liberation Front sponsored marches, campus evangelism, and courses at the city's Free University. It produced an underground newspaper, *Right On!*, for sixties' youth, provided medical help, food, and clothing for street people, and supported an agricultural commune. Sparks and the Christian World Liberation Front represent the solid chain connecting street evangelism and campus evangelism. In all of the actions of the Christian World Liberation Front, one recognizes that the themes it pursued matched the needs and ideals of countercultural youth. It respected intellectual discourse, golden rule ethics, rebellious activism and expressive individualism. It also offered, of course, an antitechnocratic spirituality.[15] The flow of style and ideas between college students and hippies moved back and forth by its own synergy, but the creation of the Christian World Liberation Front highlighted how biblically grounded religion could also be a part of the reciprocal stream of thought and behavior, a stream that would eventually flow into greater evangelicalism.

In the early seventies, religious scholar Richard Quebedeaux, looking into phenomena such as Sparks's Christian World Liberation Front movement, recognized something dynamic and promising astir in evangelicalism. He even noted that liberal churches "find it refreshing to encounter completely changed students and street people who have kicked the drug habit, who are honestly trying to love their neighbor and bring the mandates of biblical faith to bear on the pressing social ills of the present day."[16] Perhaps, he suggested, liberals, whose ministries were dying out on campuses, ought to take a lesson from the new brand of Christians. Unfortunately for liberalism, the new brand was becoming decidedly evangelical.

Three years prior to Quebedeaux's 1974 statement, Carl Henry had noted that there were "bright signs" in the Jesus movement, and that "the Jesus-freak mood is yielding in many places to a Jesus-follower commitment." By this, Henry meant that the converts were becoming biblically grounded. "In ever larger numbers," he stated, "these young Christians are seeking a biblical understanding of the experience they have had."[17]

Nothing was more indicative of this confluence of countercultural and evangelical experience than the success of Campus Crusade's Explo '72 held in Dallas, Texas, where eighty thousand young people came from across the nation to worship, sing, and hone their skills in evangelism. For their grand finale, the organizers sponsored the "Jesus Music Festival," which drew in nearly two hundred thousand to celebrate the Lord with cheers and song. "Riding the wave of the Jesus revolution," wrote *Christianity Today*'s news editor Edward Plowman (also a longstanding board member for Evangelical Concerns), "Campus Crusade for Christ's International Student Congress on Evangelism—billed as Explo '72—turned out to be the largest youth training conference in church history."[18] This was the paramount manifestation of both the Jesus People movement as a phenomenon and its acceptance into evangelicalism. Symbolic of this union was the conversion of an evangelically churched kid by the name of Ted Haggard, who would go on to graduate from Oral Roberts University in 1978 and eventually pastor a fourteen-thousand- member church, become president of the National Association of Evangelicals, and be noted by the *Wall Street Journal* as one "of the nation's most politically influential clergy."[19]

Promoting Street Evangelists

Promoters of street evangelism, local pastors were as important as the street evangelists themselves for the success of countercultural Christianity. They provided a home base that housed the experience, knowledge, and resources of twentieth-century evangelicalism. Some of the more successful direct promoters were found, unsurprisingly, in southern California, notably the charismatics Chuck Smith and John Wimber.

One recalls that MacDonald gave moral support to the commune called House of Acts, whose hippie membership emulated primitive Christianity. In the House of Acts young people came dressed in their jeans, wearing beads, perhaps flowers in their hair, and they devoted themselves to Jesus and Jesus' family. And it is in such a setting that we witness the melding of evangelical and countercultural Christians. Solicited one day by the House of Acts to come to the commune and perform a wedding ceremony, MacDonald and his wife responded immediately.

MacDonald gives a vivid description of the House of Acts. Its inhabitants he identifies as "young people—usually from typical middle- and upper-middle-class young homes—who were breaking tradition."[21] The reader can easily imagine, from his account of the marriage ceremony, how strange such an event must have seemed to the more traditional evangelicals:

> The bride wore a gown which had been fashioned that day by her sisters in the commune. She stood barefoot, as did the groom, but her dress only barely covered her derriere. In fact, her long blonde hair reached almost to the bottom of her dress. Flowers laced her hair.
>
> The groom, with tousled curly black hair and a fiercely appearing black beard, grinned widely. He wore a multicolored embroidered blouse and denims which, curiously enough, also were decorated with flowers.
>
> But both were scrupulously clean and their clothes equally so.
>
> Rings? Of course, but made of Indian beads.[22]

In spite of the fact that Ted Wise could not digest the sectarian ways and restrained lifestyle of fundamentalists, there was a common ground. MacDonald wrote reflectively, "perhaps it was that night that I realized in a new way that I was seeing a new and different generation. With enlightened eyes I saw them as deeply concerned, committed, Spirit-filled men and women. . . . They had a vision and a capability for a type of ministry for which the institutional straight such as I was simply not prepared."[23]

The countercultural expression of Christianity would have a greater effect on evangelicals than Wise was probably willing to acknowledge. MacDonald confessed that he himself had to change religious habits that these young people were effectively exposing as superfluous or even counterproductive for living out the gospel in the twentieth century. "I look back with chagrin at my many blunders," wrote MacDonald. "Not only did I often err, but too frequently have I been thoughtless—even selfish and proud—in my unwillingness to comprehend the miracle of God which has opened before me."[24]

The interaction between Pastor MacDonald and the countercultural Christians had taken place because ultimately they shared something in common. Their rebellion against the mainstream and their antitechnocratic spirituality, though different in degree, had nonetheless drawn them together. And as MacDonald relates how other straight people (evangelicals) came to join in with the countercultural Christians and vice-versa, especially in Jack Spark's Christian World Liberation Front, one witnesses the leavening effect the countercultural spirit was beginning to have in evangelicalism as it inspired a rebellious and aggressive activism. Before long, MacDonald observes, the straights, alongside their countercultural brothers and sisters, "wear casual clothing, sport moderately long hair and trim beards. They take advantage of all the communications media available." And they proclaim their "true, unembarrassed, biblical Christian witness." The Baptist MacDonald himself is truly caught up in the spirit when he echoes a plea by the Christian World Liberation Front that sounds curiously like some Marxist call to action, "RADICALIZE THE REVOLUTIONARY MOVEMENT! GET INTO THE WORLD'S GREATEST REVOLUTION!"[25]

Countercultural Effects on a Local Church

Robert Girard, pastor of Our Heritage Wesleyan Church in Scottsdale, Arizona, welcomed the revolution into his staid congregation and turned his revitalized parish into a platform for spreading it. In reading his 1972 account of the "revolution," one recognizes the hippie theme as the church experiments with a Book of Acts form of Christianity. Three years after having exchanged a demure ministry for an enlivened one Girard wrote, "Whatever we are experiencing is no more than the *beginning* of renewal. 'The Acts of the Apostles' isn't yet being relived at Our Heritage Church. However . . . [w]e are beginning to smell its fragrance. Around the edges of our fellowship an occasional glimpse of New Testament life becomes visible."[26]

Girard's church growth experience demonstrates how aspects of countercultural Christianity came into an evangelical setting and remade evangelicalism into something more dynamic. The new Christians coming into his church were new to evangelicalism. "At the time we began preaching renewal," he wrote, "clearing superfluous meetings from the schedule, and forming small groups, *ninety percent* of the members of the church were *brand new Christians*, 'untainted' by experience with traditional evangelicalism."[27]

Like MacDonald, Girard wanted revolution; he wanted to take the new activism, the renewal, into churches as yet untouched by it. The older, more traditional churches, Girard warned his fellow travelers, "cannot just be 'written off!'" He would not accept the traditionalists' unwillingness to embrace a countercultural style. Christian zeal was not to be reserved just for the school prayer issue or some other specific agenda. Believers were to engage the culture for Christ at all times in all places. So he admonished the zealous not to be doting or to give in to their complacent brethren, but to revolutionize them. "We must not fit their mold, or pamper them in their immaturity, or back down in the face of their carnal outbursts. We must *not* stop seeking to bring renewal and revival to the church just because they don't like it."[28]

Not surprisingly, the renewal that Girard preached hit specifically upon the points that middle-class youth found important: non-technocratic spirituality, authentic, unhypocritical living and belief, intimate personal relationships, and the golden rule. To fulfill a Christlike ministry, he declared, "I would teach absolute dependence on the Spirit in all situations and for all needs. And I would seek to practice it. Honesty would become a keynote in my pulpit ministry. I would ask for courage and grace to admit my failures, my doubts, my struggle with the flesh. I would seek to be real and practical in my preaching and teaching. I would preach love and then admit that I did not have it myself and needed the help of other Christians in finding it. I would preach grace. I would seek to stop preaching law or trying to build the church on the basis of law. I would dare to dream of the ideal church, in the light of the New Testament."[29]

Countercultural Churching

The charismatic Chuck Smith, working in southern California, was one of the first ministers to successfully bring hippies into a church.[30] It took his wife Kay and their daughter some effort to convince him of the need to minister to the hippies congregating around the beaches, but once he had decided to do so, he in turn convinced his hesitant and somewhat reluctant congregation of the necessity as well. Unlike MacDonald, Smith, whose charismatic belief and praxis melded better with the counterculture than did fundamentalist traditions, was able to keep his church together and very few parishioners left.[31]

The importance of bringing sixties' youth into the sanctuary cannot be overemphasized, because it brought youth back into a multigenerational setting and fostered a reconciliation of generations born of give-and-take on both sides. Smith's type of ministry was instrumental in creating the robust evangelicalism of the late seventies.

Smith, one of the older pastors to become involved in countercultural Christianity, was born in 1927. He had been raised a Pentecostal and was educated at Aimee Semple McPherson's Lighthouse for International Foursquare Evangelism and ordained in McPherson's International Church of the Foursquare Gospel. The McPherson temerity for effective evangelism seems to have rubbed off on Smith. Not that he adopted her flamboyant lifestyle, because he did not, but that he was willing to adapt his church to the needs of people awash in popular culture. To expand the youth ministry, he even ventured to hire one of the beach hippies, a person who just happened to hail from Ted and Liz Wise's Living Room, the longhaired Lonnie Frisbee.[32]

Within two years Smith's church was inundated with youth, and his ministry had baptized some fifteen thousand converts in the nearby Pacific Ocean.[33] The swarm of young people into the sanctuary soon changed the nature and sound of worship for Calvary Chapel. In 1969 a rock musician, who had been won over to Jesus by a Campus Crusade for Christ worker, made his way to Calvary Chapel with his fellow bandmembers in tow, all of whom would eventually give their lives to Christ.[34] These professionals contributed greater quality to the church's hippie music, and Calvary Chapel soon became not only a magnet for born again musicians but the exporter of a new musical sound that would overtake the evangelical world. This brash and innovative style of music broke the establishment's hymnal mode and allowed young people to convey contemporary messages.[35] With it, evangelicals were able to express their ideas and emotions about one another, about God, about society, and even about socio-political issues. For the moment, however, they were content to express their joy in the Lord and their happiness in fulfilling the spiritual quest.

Under Smith's guidance, Lonnie Frisbee, along with John Higgins, expanded the ministry in a new direction by opening up a commune called The House of Miracles, where they helped young people with drug addictions. Higgins went on to create other such communities in the southwest before he moved north to Oregon to begin his own Shiloh Youth Revival Centers. Eventually, Higgins established some one hundred seventy-eight centers.[36]

Important to the evangelical-countercultural nexus was Smith's personable, unaffected, and simple approach to ministry and pulpit, which young people accepted as proper pastoral behavior. So when Smith encouraged young people to go out and begin their own ministries and their own churches, they went forth carrying Smith's plainspoken spirituality with them. A plethora of Calvary Chapel churches, sporting a laid-back and warm-hearted worship style, popped up in cities across the continent, usually attracting large numbers of baby boomers.

One of Smith's early associates, John Wimber, proved to be as effective as Smith in making evangelicalism relevant to sixties' youth and in bringing them into the church setting.[37] In 1980 Wimber would take on the services of Lonnie Frisbee, who had a falling out with Calvary Chapel and the two of them would initiate a controversial revival movement. But Wimber also brought to bear his own unique talents and insights, and a look into his past helps explain the innovative catalyst behind his successful ministry amongst Californian youth.

Wimber, born into a non-Christian home in 1934, became a pop musician who played with the Righteous Brothers; he indulged in alcohol and drugs before converting to Christ at a Quaker Bible study in 1963. By 1970 Wimber had proven his effectiveness as a Bible study leader and evangelist. Working as an adjunct instructor at Fuller, he continued an effective ministry that attracted young people. In 1977 he began a church, Calvary Chapel of Yorba Linda, California, associated with Smith's Calvary Chapel of Costa Mesa. Wimber's ministry emphasized the gifts of the spirit, speaking in tongues and healing and it also produced contemporary worship songs that emphasized the person-to-person relationship between God and believer.[38]

The expansion of Wimber's church movement would continue unabated through the late seventies and eighties. In 1982, Wimber's growing church would leave the Calvary Chapel group and join with some small congregations known as Vineyard churches that had their origin in the early seventies. These were churches inspired or planted by a friend of Lonnie Frisbee's, Kenn Gulliksen, a bearded, yellow-haired, surfer type who, in Melody Green's estimate, had a gentle and persuasive manner of presenting the Bible to young counterculture types like herself.[39]

In the 1980s the Vineyard churches, which would ultimately become a denomination, looked to Wimber for direction; and he provided it. Wimber made them the spiritual home not only for baby boomers, but also for the up and coming "generation X." When University of Southern California Professor of Religion Donald Miller visited Wimber's Church sometime in the 1990s, he noted that even though most of the congregants, some three thousand, appeared to be in their mid-twenties and early thirties, there were also "a surprising number of older people."[40] The enduring success of the Vineyard churches demonstrated that Wimber had connected profoundly with countercultural youth, deeply enough to keep baby boomers coming long after the sixties.

Why was Wimber so successful with this movement? The reasons are not hard to identify. Wimber had removed the ritualistic constraints found in traditional church services and turned worship time into something resembling a casual and pleasant "happening." At Wimber's church, comfortably dressed believers sang personal praises to God while their smaller children, perhaps even more casually dressed in pajamas, nodded off to sleep, or maybe amused themselves. Wimber's wife Carol recalled there was "No hype, no heavy prayers, no nothing. It was more like, 'Let's just relax here and see what God will do.'"[41] It worked. By the mid-nineties there were some four hundred Vineyard churches across the United States and two hundred abroad, and the median membership was about one hundred and fifty members.[42]

What was significant about Wimber's movement, however, was that his worship style, like Smith's, matched the needs not only of America's youth but also of many in the older evangelical generation as well. One could write about other similarly successful ministries in California and elsewhere during the seventies (Melodyland Christian Center and Hope Chapel for example), but suffice it to say that evangelicalism and countercultural Christianity became compatible in the late 1970s.[43]

Of course, not all evangelical communities were directly or significantly affected by countercultural Christianity. In order for countercultural Christianity and evangelicalism to merge at the national level, there needed to be national evangelical spokesmen with powerful influence who would turn a kind eye toward the radical religious youth movement.

In due course, several prominent evangelical leaders of the day began to endorse street evangelists and to give the Jesus movement serious attention. These influential personalities such as Carl Henry, Francis Schaeffer, Billy Graham, and Pat Robertson helped make the new expression of Christianity more understandable and even acceptable to the larger body of evangelicals. Their own spiritually inspired worldview and consequent outsider position had prepared them to welcome a countercultural expression of Christian faith.

Merging National Intellectuals

We noted earlier that Carl Henry, the Fuller theologian, looked favorably upon the Jesus People; more importantly, however, he sought to convince traditional evangelicals that they should also be receptive to this new expression of Christianity. To do this, he first pointed out that hippies sought the same answers to life's problems that had troubled all twentieth-century men and women ill at ease with the technocratic tilt of mainstream society. The similarity was so profound that Henry merely needed to update his 1949 work, *Giving a Reason for Our Hope,* and entitle it *Answers for the Now Generation* (1969) in order to provide an apologetic aimed at ministering to the needs of sixties' youth. Without deleting a word, Henry could include in his sixties' edition the same Machen-inspired critique of modern society that he had made in 1949: "The large universities are spiritually barren; the students themselves often discern, even when professors do not, that liberalism sold its spiritual birthright for a theological mess."[44] What Henry hoped to intimate to his audience, both countercultural and evangelical, was that the youth rebellion was not all wrongheaded.

In his revised work, Henry prefaced his 1949 statements with a positive commentary condoning the growing interest amongst sixties' youth in a primitive Christianity. "This generation of young intellectuals," he wrote approvingly, "is ready for a new look at the religious realities that sent the first Christians into a pagan world as confident bearers of truth and hope and of the moral fortunes of the human race."[45] Furthermore, Henry (returning to his 1949 text) pointed out that young people should not be condemned for seeking out "broader horizons than the confinements of the peculiarly modern outlook, with its frequent surrender to a philosophy of naturalism arbitrarily imposed upon a scientific age."[46] Sixties' youth had correctly perceived, maintained Henry, that the foundation of modern mainstream thought was not only wrong, it was also illogical and fundamentally hypocritical. Naturalism, and here Henry used Joseph Krutch's *The Modern Temper* arguments as proof, lead to a predicament where man "cannot feel what he believes, and cannot believe what he feels," leaving him frustrated and in despair.[47]

In the final analysis, according to Henry, youth were right to be searching for better answers to life's existential problems than those "answers" emanating from an ill-conceived worldview. Those youth who delved into primitive Christianity were on the right track, and evangelicals ought to encourage them to continue on, if not join them in their journey.

Francis Schaeffer reinforced Henry's message, and in the end was more successful in getting it out to the larger evangelical world. In the early 1960s, leading or informed evangelicals were aware of Schaeffer and his unique ministry to young intellectuals that thrived in the Swiss Alps; after all, it had been publicized not only by *Christianity Today* but also covered in a short article by *Time* magazine. With the turmoil in America by the mid-sixties, certain of these evangelicals appealed to Schaeffer to come to the United States, stating, "We need help in the effects of the twentieth century thinking upon our schools, churches, and families."[48] In 1966 Schaeffer answered the call and left his European home to conduct a six-week tour of American universities where his talks and question-and-answer periods aroused a great deal of interest.

Schaeffer's ministry, however, was not limited to students; he also met with church groups to keep the connection between sixties' youth and evangelicalism alive. In 1970, for example, on one of his return trips to the United States, he spoke at the Lutherans' Missouri Synod Congress in Chicago. Even after he was diagnosed with cancer in 1978, Francis and his wife, Edith, continued to tour universities and meet with religious organizations in the United States and beyond, publishing a score of books, with some three million copies selling before his death in 1984.[49]

How did Schaeffer identify with the sixties' generation and help bring countercultural Christians into evangelicalism? In the first place, Schaeffer explained to evangelicals that the gospel necessarily had to be presented in contemporary terms. "Every generation of Christians," he wrote in his first published work, "has this problem of learning how to speak meaningfully to its own age. It cannot be solved without an understanding of the changing existential situation which it faces. If we are to communicate the Christian faith effectively, therefore, we must know and understand the thought-forms of our own generation."[50] As he set about doing this, he endeavored to make sure sixties' youth converting to Christianity came to embrace a Christianity compatible with evangelicalism.

Schaeffer was highly suspicious of certain aspects of the Jesus movement, especially the Jesus Freaks' tendency to downplay Scripture and subjectivize religious experience. Hal Lindsey had noted, no doubt too enthusiastically for Schaeffer's taste, that after 1968, countercultural youth readily accepted the historicity of Christ if a friend or evangelist could give personal and convincing testimony about a miracle performed in the name of Jesus.[51] This feature of the Jesus movement, however, should not be interpreted as anti-intellectual, at least not in the sense that the term was applied to fundamentalists by liberal Christians. For Jesus People it was the technocratic or modernist denial of the spiritual that was illogical and obscurantist.

According to Schaeffer, however, if spiritually inclined youth were to find something eternal in which to ground themselves and their ethics, if they were to fulfill their spiritual quest, they needed a Bible-based historical Jesus. Otherwise they might end up adrift, such as one branch of the Jesus People would do in the mid-1970s, namely the Children of God.[52] "Trying to be modern," Schaeffer warned fellow evangelists, "we say something like this to young people, 'Drop out. Take a trip with Jesus.' What does that mean? Nothing. Gobbledygook. It's a contentless statement without meaning."[53]

Nonetheless, like Henry, Schaeffer exploited the disillusionment many sixties' youth had experienced with mainstream culture and coaxed them on in their rebellion. In his 1970 book, *The Church at the End of the Twentieth Century,* Schaeffer clearly understood the revolt as ultimately aimed at liberalism rather than evangelicalism. He therefore commiserated with the disgruntled youth and argued that they had reason to be disgusted with the older generation and liberal religion. Middle-class parents, Schaeffer pointed out disparagingly, "have no real basis whatsoever for their values." According to him, the middle class had given in to scientism and liberalism but had kept practicing Victorian values without any foundational reasons for doing so. There was no coherence between what the older generation purported to believe and the way they behaved; they were irrational and therefore prone to hypocrisy. As Schaeffer put it, "They just function on the 'memory.' This is why so many young people feel that the middle class is ugly. These people are plastic, ugly and plastic, because they try to tell others what to do on the basis of their own values, but with no ground for those values."[54]

Indeed, wrote Schaeffer, the student revolution was a revolution against what had become the modern and mainstream worldview. "Society has reaped the rewards of its escape from reason. From modern science to modern, modern science, from man made in the image of God to man the machine, from freedom within form, to determinism and autonomous freedom, from harmony with God to cosmic alienation, from reason to drugs and the new mysticism, from a biblically based theology to God-words—this is the flow of the stream of rationalistic history. Out of this stream comes the student revolution."[55]

Schaeffer excused youth, therefore, for not wanting to be a part of the system. Parents push their children toward college and on to a Ph.D., but the children rightly ask "Why?" The parents respond only by saying that it will give social status and a higher income, to which the children understandably ask "Why?" again. There is no answer to this question, Schaeffer informs his readers, in either drugs or modern theology, for both are equally "trips" devoid of real reason; reason takes into account both the objective and subjective worlds within which the individual operates. The students are right to be sick of empty promises and vapid answers to life's colossal problems, he argues. They are right because modern theologians have, in cutting themselves off from the Bible, disconnected themselves from meaningful words and a meaningful God. "They are cut off from any categories of absolute right and wrong and thus they are left with totally situational ethics. That is all. . . . There is no help here."[56]

Spiritually inclined countercultural youth delving into Christianity wanted a grounding for their existence, and Schaeffer knew this. Within the form of Scripture they would find, according to Schaeffer, the answers to their spiritual quest. All that was required, he often pointed out, was to reject the mainstream worldview and to replace it with a worldview founded upon the Christ of Scripture. In doing this, the countercultural Christian became a bona fide member of evangelicalism.

Schaeffer's admonitions did not just fall upon the young. As a mediator, he also demanded changes of traditional evangelicals so that they might receive the new believers. He upbraided the evangelical church for maintaining beliefs and customs that had no biblical warrant but were nevertheless given sacred status. "Mature Christians," he wrote, "must summon the courage to distinguish, under the Holy Spirit, between unchangeable biblical truth and the things which have only become comfortable for us. Often one hears people speak of 'the simple Gospel only,' when in reality they do not really care enough for those outside the churches, or their own children for that matter, to be willing to face what preaching the simple Gospel may mean in a changing and complex situation."[57] Extending this principle, Schaeffer recommended to churches that "nothing should be preached or taught in the general services and classes which will have to be unlearned when young people and others read and discuss the deeper problems or go away to university."[58]

Merging National Evangelists

While Schaeffer helped bring evangelicalism and countercultural Christianity closer together through talks, question-and-answer sessions, books, and, late in the seventies, through film, other leading evangelicals effected the same thing by other means. Pat Robertson is a case in point. His ministry, by 1969, operated six radio stations in North America, one in South America, and a color television station; and his ministry, the Christian Broadcast Network, could potentially reach millions of people twenty-four hours a day.[59]

In certain broadcasts, Robertson thought it important to lionize converts from the younger and wilder generation because he realized that "we were never going to reach today's youth with a bland diet of milk and crackers." It was for this reason that he hired a born-again hippie and gave him marching orders to "spice things up."[60] Scott Ross had a past that dipped into drugs, but his past had also made him a successful disc jockey in Long Island. He was familiar with the Rolling Stones, with whom he had smoked marijuana, and The Lost Souls, with whom he had dropped acid.

Once hired by CBN, Ross brought in earthy rock bands and used them as props for his gospel message. Regular staffers were at first repulsed as they saw these youngsters and witnessed them taking drugs backstage, but Ross persisted, calling out to one staffer, "You're living in the dark ages, honey. It's time to take a trip on Jesus and get turned on to the Holy Spirit. That's where it's at."[61] Ross's ministry in the South was cut short because he shocked white Southerners with his music while his wife shocked them because she was black; nevertheless, Robertson's openness to new modes of worship and evangelization persisted, and he sent the Ross couple into upstate New York where Scott would broadcast on CBN Northeast. With a free hand, he played the music he thought appropriate for America's younger generation, including an end-of-the-world tune by Barry McGuire called "Eve of Destruction." He also established, in 1969, a coffeehouse called Love Inn to supplement the radio ministry, which, by 1974 reached out across over one hundred and fifty stations.[62] Robertson was clearly endorsing countercultural Christianity.

Probably the most far-reaching and influential word of inclusion given by an evangelical for the countercultural Christian cause was spoken by the most recognizable evangelist of the sixties, Billy Graham. His endorsement of young people is not surprising, given that Graham had begun his nationally recognized ministry by preaching to youth back in the mid-forties. By the 1960s, Graham recognized that teenagers and college students needed very special spiritual attention. So, although Graham preached increasingly overseas during the sixties, he also spent time and effort communicating the gospel to American youth. As he later put it, "The rootlessness of the sixties generation burdened me greatly, and I was determined to do whatever I could to point young people to the One who alone gives lasting meaning and purpose to life."[63]

In this endeavor, Graham went straight to the nation's campuses and with Bill Bright of Campus Crusade spoke to thousands of students. In 1967 he was at the heart of the counterculture, appearing at UCLA and Berkeley. At UCLA some six thousand students came to hear him, at Berkeley, eight thousand. In the shadow of Woodstock, Graham decided to take his message to a rock concert, and three days after Christmas, he preached at the 1969 Miami Rock Music Festival. Graham understood that youth rejected the technocratic world imposed upon them and hoped for a spiritual reality. The message, he said, was in the music. "*We reject your materialism*, [youth music] seemed to proclaim, *and we want something of the soul*. Jesus was a nonconformist, I reminded them, and He could fill their souls and give them meaning and purpose in life. 'Tune in to God today, and let Him give you faith. Turn on to His power.'"

It was with joy that Grand Marshal Billy Graham saw Jesus youth brandishing the "one way" sign at him as he was driven down the circuit of the Tournament of Roses parade in early 1971. Indeed, nothing better symbolizes the coming together of countercultural Christians and evangelicalism than that image of the younger generation signaling the one way sign and the "Protestant Pope" responding in kind. Later that same year Graham suggested that young people coming to Christ were "solving the problem of materialism and the deification of technology by their commitment to one another."[64]

From Schaeffer to Graham the respected evangelicals had spoken, and their decision spread across the land as the evangelical press pumped out story after story "puffing" the Jesus Movement. The new Christians needed to be brought into the church. To do so evangelicals would have to drop some of their cultural prejudices and the countercultural Christians would have to anchor themselves in Scripture. It was a compromise that many thought reasonable and desirable.

Statistical Evidences

The movement of countercultural Christians into the evangelical fold during the 1970s is illustrated by statistics relative to America's religious life. Statistics indicate, for example, that individuals frequently changed religious affiliation during the seventies and eighties, especially those raised in a liberal mainline denomination. Nationally, sociologist Robert Wuthnow noted that of those Christians raised Presbyterian, 45 percent changed affiliation, 40 percent of those raised Methodist left their church, and 38 percent of those raised Episcopalian transferred. Even 15 percent of those raised Jewish switched religious affiliation.[65]

Apparently, a significant number of those moving about were moving from liberal churches to evangelical ones. While mainline denominations experienced over a 12 percent loss in membership in the West, for example, evangelical denominations grew by over 45 percent. The same shift in the religious population occurred in other parts of the country, but nowhere was it as spectacular as on the west coast, where countercultural Christianity had grown so phenomenally.[66]

It is also significant that although the number of college students going to church dropped from 1958 to 1968, the percentage of college-educated people in religious denominations actually rose during this period.[67] Regardless of the fact that universities became increasingly unfriendly to a biblically grounded worldview, the number of youth who had gone to liberal colleges but were within or joining biblically grounded denominations increased. In other words, many youth had either become biblically grounded Christians or retained their biblically grounded orientation in spite of their nonevangelical or anti-evangelical instruction.[68]

By the mid-1980s, 30 percent of college grads considered the Bible as true with absolutely no errors, and 25 percent claimed to be "born-again." The numbers are even more surprising among high schoolers, who had also been affected by the legacy of the counterculture and had attended secular public institutions. Of high schoolers, 66 percent believed the Bible absolutely true and 50 percent said they were "born-again."[69] For those who had not been raised in evangelical homes, this conscious embrace of the absolute supernatural character of the Bible was an aftershock of the sixties' rebellion against technocratic spirituality.[70] What would have seemed ludicrous for educated middle-class teenagers in the fifties had become fashionable for their younger siblings, or even their children, by the eighties.

Because a significant number of liberal parishioners shifted away from their childhood denominations, because the percentage of college-educated youth increased in evangelical denominations, and because evangelical denominations grew, especially where countercultural Christianity was prominent, it appears that a majority of countercultural Christians moved permanently into evangelicalism. Furthermore, given that college students participated in this shift, this phenomenon was in no small measure due to the influence, direct or indirect, of people such as Schaeffer, Bright, and Lindsey who had a primary interest in youth, as well as others who targeted all age groups, such as Robertson, Roberts, and Graham.

Conclusion

Around 1970, the Jesus movement had become a recognized religious phenomenon. At the national level men like Billy Graham, Bill Bright, Pat Robertson, and Francis Schaeffer had given countercultural Christian youth their blessing, and during the early 1970s the movement continued to grow. As early as 1971 Henry noted that Jesus People were starting to fall in line with evangelicalism. "While growing numbers of Jesus followers are shunning the pulpit ministry as a vocation," he observed, "they are eager nonetheless to master the logic of Christian belief and to wrestle the issues of theology and apologetics."[71] By the mid-seventies, evangelicals and countercultural Christians were openly working together at the grassroots level. In 1972, at Campus Crusade's Explo '72, over eighty thousand were in attendance. During the week of Explo '72, the Jesus People and evangelicals held their own version of Woodstock at which two hundred eighty thousand gathered to hear Graham and others and the latest in Christian musical talent.[72] At the local level, evangelical pastors applied aspects of countercultural Christianity to their church services and to their lifestyle.

By the late 1970s, the talk about "Jesus People" faded away with many other bright and colorful topics of the sixties, but the Jesus People themselves, the countercultural Christians, did not, of course, actually disappear. They continued to exist and continued to be "born," but since most of them merged into evangelicalism, there was no more reason to single them out as a specific subtype of biblically grounded Christianity.[73] Amongst the young middle-class street people and collegians who had joined the Jesus movement prior to the election of Jimmy Carter—including many of the fourteen thousand who attended InterVarsity Christian Fellowship's missionary convention in Urbana, Illinois, in 1976—were those who had come from liberal households and who had rebelled against their parents' ways.[74] By 1979, George Gallup, Jr., the pollster, concluded from his "surveys of teen-agers that they [were] more evangelical than their elders," and believed that the evangelical movement would therefore gain in strength.[75]

Jesus People were no doubt present in good number at the Jesus '76 rally at Orlando, Florida. Organized by Jesus Ministries and Calvary Assembly of God youth minister Alex Clattenburg, Jr., and attended by, among others, Pat Boone, Bill Bright, and Arizona congressman John Conlan, this event drew in twenty thousand people. But here, with a congressman and advertisements for Christian colleges and missionary organizations, there was something more sedate than the Jesus Freak communes and street evangelism of the late sixties and early seventies.[76] The young people were now considered evangelicals, not Jesus People, and the older ones had reached the dreaded age of thirty, married, had children, and applied their Christianity to their new non-campus and non-street lives.[77] They carried the countercultural commitment to the golden rule, intellectual sophistication, spirituality, and a seamless lifestyle into their new social context.

Also facilitating the movement of countercultural Christians into evangelicalism in the late 1970s was the conversion of important countercultural personalities to biblically grounded Christianity. These converts quickly associated with evangelicalism and thereby encouraged countercultural Christians to identify with the larger evangelical movement.

Perhaps one of the most radical born-again personalities was former Black Panther member Eldridge Cleaver. Soon after he had become a Christian and had left prison in 1976, he met in Washington D.C. with some important members of the evangelical community—Chuck Colson, Tommy Terrants, and former Senator Harold Hughes—two of whom, former Nixon aid Chuck Colson and former Alabama Ku Klux Klan leader Tommy Terrants, had been dramatic converts like himself. It was after this meeting that Cleaver spoke from Jerry Falwell's pulpit at the Thomas Road Baptist Church in Virginia.[78] Cleaver focused his life on a prison ministry, Eldridge Cleaver Crusades, and later criticized evangelicals for their "commercialized religion," but his meeting with evangelicals nonetheless linked an important countercultural figure with evangelicalism.[79]

Perhaps the final, if mostly symbolic, note played by the counterculture in its contribution to evangelicalism was the conversion of Bob Dylan in 1978 to biblically grounded Christianity.[80] Not surprisingly, Dylan's interest in Jesus Christ brought him into contact with The Vineyard Fellowship; it had a local church not too far from Dylan's California home in Malibu. Dylan spent over three months attending Vineyard pastor Kenn Gulliksen's School of Discipleship.[81] His conversion brought evangelicalism into the awareness of hundreds of thousands of baby boomers who had traversed the sixties. Those devotees of Dylan who had not become Christians had to confront this new Christianity.[82] And as Dylan publicized his conversion and echoed biblically grounded mores, one observes that he, like many of those countercultural youth who converted before him, also obliged traditional evangelicals to admit that radicals from the sixties could be a part of the evangelical faith.

This acceptance meant that evangelical churches were giving way to new practices. Folk-rock worship songs entered evangelical denominations and Sunday dress became more casual. Harvard faculty member Armand Nicholi II, M.D., had predicted this phenomenon in 1972. He analyzed the spiritual awakening at the time of the Jesus revolution and reminded his readers that youth set the standard in American society. "Adults, rather than taking the lead, anxiously try to imitate the young, adopting their dress, their language, their music. In films, on television, in books, plays and advertisements, one observes the indelible influence of youth."[83] And so it was to be as countercultural Christianity merged into evangelicalism.

The merging process, however, had begun in earnest a year before Nicholi II's prognostication. With the 1971 media blitz about the Jesus People and the open endorsement of them in that same year by Billy Graham, first at the Tournament of Roses parade and then with his best-selling book *The Jesus*

Generation, the convergence went into high speed. With the blessing of the "Protestant Pope," evangelical youth could now more easily join the Jesus People and appropriate their beliefs and style and contribute their own talents and knowledge to the movement.

For years young people in churches that identified with Billy Graham's form of Christianity felt awkward and frustrated: they admired many aspects of the counterculture but could not make the music, hair styles, and clothing square with parental and church expectations. Encountering the Jesus People made them realize that one could be Christian and hip at the same time; receiving the leadership's blessing made it easier to join the movement. Once a bona fide member, these new recruits in turn became extremely effective evangelists, especially amongst their secular humanist and liberal Christian friends who were in full rebellion against the establishment.

8

Awaiting the Religious Right

Prior to the advent of countercultural Christianity, evangelicalism, as has been noted, demonstrated an enormous amount of vitality but restricted itself, by and large, to the religious sphere.[1] The door-to-door evangelist peddled religion, not politics. The adage that "politics and religion don't mix" was generally respected by both the biblically grounded and the liberal Christian after World War II. The liberal appreciated the principle because mainstream institutions, including political ones, most often fit into his or her worldview anyway. And when radically left-leaning clergy did become politically active, in the sixties, conservatives within the liberal denominations employed the adage in order to dissuade their own zealous clergymen.[2]

Furthermore, biblically grounded Christians located outside the mainline denominations also disdained religiously charged political activism. The reasons differed, by and large, depending upon whether one resided in the northern and western states or in the South. In the South, fundamentalists still controlled their local culture and therefore had no reason to protest until the federal ban on prayer in school (1963) and the Civil Rights and Voting Rights Acts (1964 and 1965) brought the secular humanist and liberal Christian ethos into their midst.[3] In the northern and western states, the biblically grounded Christian avoided political grandstanding because the mainstream world, ever since the Scopes Trial and the end of Prohibition, had become increasingly hostile to him. Intimidated, most of these biblically grounded Christians reserved their politico-religious opinions to the confines of the home and left public politico-religious activism to a few zealots.[4]

The zealots who dared to publicly broach political issues were, for the most part, separatist fundamentalists. They heatedly denounced Soviet communism as an earthly manifestation of evil and believed that anything linked to it, however tenuously, was equally evil. In fact, it seemed that the harder it was to establish the link, the more pernicious and threatening the evil was to the American way. Other, comparatively minor, political judgments and pronouncements of fundamentalists often echoed the established Victorian mores of antimodern fundamentalism. They railed against card playing, movie theatres, drinking, modern music, mini skirts, longhaired men, etc. Fundamentalist politics, therefore, were easily associated with fundamentalist opposition to both popular culture and broadminded expressive individualism.

The style and tone these fundamentalists employed did not square with the less sectarian mode of dialogue new evangelicals were trying to cultivate during the fifties.[5] Nevertheless, if new evangelicals said anything of a political nature during the Eisenhower years, they tended to echo the statements made by these few outspoken fundamentalists. It must be admitted that it was difficult for anyone during that time, especially people with deep spiritual convictions, to be neutral about communist ideology which, it was understood, demanded the annihilation not only of private property and capitalism but of all religions as well, especially Christianity. In time, certainly by the 1970s, men such as Billy Graham and Carl Henry would develop their own voices; voices consonant with biblically grounded spirituality but not disengaged from the golden rule ideal. In spite of this mellowing by certain evangelical leaders, the movement as a whole showed little initiative in encouraging detente between the US and USSR; the anti-Christian ideology of communism remained just too foreboding a threat to ignore.

Furthermore, because evangelicals found themselves to be political outsiders, shunted off the public stage ever since the Scopes Trial, they suffered a psychological handicap.[6] They were not willing to compromise their spiritual principles that militated against certain aspects of the technocracy and social engineering, but they still wanted to belong to a country that had been founded as a "city upon a hill," an experiment of God. They thought their reputation as obscurantists and cold-hearted individualists unjust, but they were at a loss as to how to shake it off. They established Fuller Seminary, *Christianity Today,* tithed endlessly for church work, gave of their wealth and their lives to missions, and courted presidents, but still the opprobrious label stuck, and it sapped from them the self-esteem necessary to launch an activist political campaign.

The Evangelical Candidate

For evangelicals, the world took a turn for the better in 1976 when Jimmy Carter, the Democratic candidate for the presidency, announced that he was "born again." By that simple admission, he gave all biblically grounded Christians a renewed sense of belonging. The announcement, however, did not immediately result in a significant political movement within the Democratic Party by middle-class evangelicals or the countercultural Christians who now bolstered their ranks.

Nonetheless, 1976 was an important year. Carter not only unabashedly identified himself as "born again," he also unequivocally linked religion tightly to politics by making ethics a pillar of his campaign, promising never to lie to the American people. After Watergate, the old adage "religion and politics don't mix" just did not seem as clear-cut as it once had.[7] The argument for mixing did not need to be made for countercultural Christians within the evangelical churches because they had always refused to compartmentalize faith and had always stood against the mainstream; on the other hand, the willful mixing certainly liberated their more traditional brethren who through the decades had always felt bound and gagged by the liberal Christian and secular humanist establishment. Jimmy Carter had succeeded where Billy Graham could not.

As a result, evangelicals tendered 40 percent of their votes to Carter in 1976, a much better showing than George McGovern had posted amongst evangelicals in 1972. This meant that certain evangelicals were willing to vote for a candidate based on that candidate's religious identification rather than his party identification. The "reversal," reported *Christianity Today,* "in the ECP [evangelical-conservative Protestant] vote was the decisive factor in Carter's Missouri, Ohio, Tennessee, Kentucky, and Pennsylvania victories."[8]

Carter probably would have scored even more evangelical votes if he had not, toward the end of his campaign, clumsily alienated some important biblically grounded leaders. Just a month before the election, a Carter interview appeared in *Playboy,* a magazine that evangelicals accused of promoting free love and contributing to infidelity and broken homes. Baptist heavyweights Jerry Falwell and W. A. Criswell publicly criticized Carter on television.[9]

Furthermore, Carter equivocated on abortion, a hot button issue especially for Catholics, but something evangelicals objected to as well because they linked it to promiscuity, if not infanticide. A month before election night, John Warwick Montgomery, known in the evangelical world for his debates with the radical theologian Bishop James Pike and death-of-God theologian Thomas Altizer, openly questioned in the pages of *Christianity Today* how candidate Carter could say he was personally opposed to abortion and yet refuse to support a constitutional amendment against the practice.

Once elected, Carter continued to rankle evangelicals. Just a week after his inauguration, he committed a political gaff by snubbing fellow evangelicals, refusing to attend the annual convention of the tremendously influential and powerful National Religious Broadcasters (NRB) organization, an event other presidents had faithfully attended.[10] Furthermore, Carter appointed people to his administration who did not champion traditional evangelical values. *Christianity Today* found this hard to accept after having printed in a November editorial that Carter ought to name "cabinet members, ambassadors, judges, and White House staff members" who practiced "Judeo-Christian" ethics.[11] Even the outspoken Christian he did bring on board, Martin Luther King Jr.'s lieutenant Andrew Young, had worked for the liberal National Council of Churches.[12]

The cold shoulder given to the NRB, which along with the NAE was a doyen of evangelicalism, and Carter's refusal to name well-known evangelicals to positions of influence seemed to confirm the worst fears some evangelicals held just prior to the November election. Indeed, it appeared Carter was much more moderate theologically than initially supposed. John Warwick Montgomery must have been right. When he had questioned Carter's stand on abortion, he asked caustically, "does this remarkably irrational position stem from [Carter's] having had his head melted by the dialectic influence of his avowedly favorite (neo-orthodox and ontological) theologians—Niebuhr, Barth, Tillich and Kierkegaard?"[13]

Carter, then, holds the distinction both of encouraging biblically grounded Christians to vote for the Democratic ticket and of subsequently alienating them from the Democratic Party.[14] With Carter's failure to connect with biblically grounded voters, any hope for a new and massive left-leaning political movement by countercultural Christians and like-minded evangelicals during the 1970s withered.[15]

It must be admitted, however, that the creation of a sizeable evangelical movement within the Democratic Party would have been difficult for Carter to engineer even if he had not made any *faux pas*. In the first place, there were very strong anti-evangelical factions within the Democratic Party, such as the National Organization for Women. Secondly, evangelicals living outside of the South were mostly middle-class, educated, and politically conservative, if not Republican.[16] Indicative of this fact was *Christianity Today* magazine, which catered to these more affluent evangelicals; its pages had generally been supportive of Nixon and cool toward liberal Democrats. An editorial dealing with Vietnam in 1972 suggested that "all Americans, and especially Christians, should stand by the President, even if they think his policy is mistaken. Every Christian should pray that what is being done will lead to peace and justice."[17] On the same page was placed a laudatory piece on FBI director J. Edgar Hoover. Another editorial in the journal took a swipe at The Great Society when it informed readers that "The late primate of Sweden, Bishop Reuben Josefson of Uppsala, said that humanly speaking it is impossible for a free church to exist in a welfare state."[18]

Countercultural Christian Politics

If Carter could not easily have rallied traditional evangelicals in the northern and western states, one wonders if he might not have had some success amongst the newer members of the evangelical churches of those regions, the evangelicals of countercultural origins. Perhaps, but this too would have been a challenging undertaking.

Countercultural Christians, as most hippie types, lived in their own world, albeit fully engaged. And their own world was expected to come to a cataclysmic end in the not-too-distant future. So, they lived for the soon-returning Jesus, and for their brothers and sisters in Christ, and for the souls of the lost, but they were not politically savvy about precinct rules and delegate power. Besides, why would they affiliate with a political party that hobnobbed with the liberal churches from which they had only recently fled? And even if countercultural Christians had been interested in establishment politics, most would have been too young and inexperienced to create and sustain a focused political movement.

In spite of the fact that countercultural Christians were ill-suited to influencing national political parties in 1976, a careful observer would have nonetheless noticed that they had political potential. Countercultural Christians were old hands at shaking things up and selling ideas. Protests, tract distribution, and personal evangelism could all be translated into political activism.

Furthermore, countercultural Christians openly admitted that they hoped to transform the world. Echoing the countercultural rhetoric for change was Campus Crusade for Christ's director, Bill Bright. "As the head of a large, international movement," he proclaimed, "I am involved with thousands of others in a 'conspiracy to overthrow the world.' Each year we train tens of thousands of high school and college students from more than half of the major countries of the world in the art of revolution, and daily these 'revolutionists' are at work around the globe, spreading our philosophy and strengthening and broadening our influence."[19] In one sense, of course, Bright's proclamation was somewhat "tongue-in-cheek" since he did not mean his workers would execute a violent overthrow of established governments, but in another sense he was quite serious. His means for overturning the world would be different from those used by Maoists, but the objective of converting the world into a paradise of sorts for his own worldview was nonetheless declared in earnest.

By the late 1960s, certain evangelicals demonstrated an interest in tackling the political world. In 1969 a Graham official called upon believers to stop linking the gospel to anticommunism and to take up the cause of racial justice. An evangelical inner city pastor also pleaded with biblically grounded Christians "to engage in more 'political struggles with the establishment' in order to appeal more effectively to people in the ghetto."[20] It is no surprise, then, that at the height of the Jesus Movement, some countercultural Christians began engaging the political world.

At the New Hampshire presidential primary in 1972, for example, Senator and presidential candidate Edmund Muskie remarked that throughout the state young people had asked him repeatedly "Have you been born-again?"[21] Also during that campaign season, Arthur Blessitt held a press conference near the White House at which he presented a "Bill of Responsibilities" that called upon presidential candidates to adhere to. The bill was a mandate for candidates to pursue racial justice, peace, and morality. More explicitly, the new president would be expected to "call a national day of repentance, prayer, fasting, and brotherhood" and to be a Christian "who will openly share his personal commitment to Jesus Christ."[22]

When the National Democratic Convention convened in Florida in 1972, evangelicals converged on the city as well. Street preachers Sammy Pippitt from Chicago, Leo Humphrey from New Orleans, and Bob Phillips from Titusville, Florida, joined forces with Miami Baptist Richard Bryant to create "Demo 72."[23] At a park in Miami, about five hundred Jesus People moved onto ground occupied by the Students for a Democratic Society, Vietnam Veterans Against the War, the People's Coalition for Peace and Justice, the Southern Christian Leadership Conference, the Youth International Party, the Welfare Rights Organization, and the Gay Liberation Front.

Jerry Rubin of Chicago Seven fame was there to oppose the Jesus People, stating, "I don't believe in what they're saying. None of them has talked with me, and I wouldn't talk with them even if they tried. Jesus was a junkie. I don't want to be bothered by . . . those . . . questions."[24] The confrontation was not over which one of the two groups supported the establishment, but rather over why and how each sought to reshape the world. For Rubin, apparently, Jesus' solution was pie-in-the-sky; Jesus was different from the establishment but he could never prevail against it. A *junkie,* as presented in the pages of Jack Kerouac's *Tristessa,* was someone strung out on drugs and often incapable of doing anything.[25]

Not all was confrontation between countercultural Christians and the secular radicals in the Miami park. Jack Sparks and the Christian World Liberation Front were on hand too, handing out some five hundred tuna sandwiches and thirty-five hundred doughnuts. Sparks's organization claimed that fifteen radicals a day made a decision for Christ.[26] The CWLF, of course, would do more than hand out food and win people for Jesus. These Berkeley Christian youth also embraced certain political causes and published them in their underground newspaper, *Right On!*

More consistently radical, however, was Jim Wallis's *Post-American*. Wallis had grown up in a biblically grounded environment in the North but broke away from the religion of his youth because it failed to tackle the issue of racial discrimination. He became a part of the counterculture, an activist, and was named president of the radical leftwing Students for a Democratic Society at Michigan State University. Dissatisfied with the spiritual emptiness he experienced in leftist politics, he gave his life over to Jesus and went on to attend Trinity Evangelical Divinity School, an evangelical institution.

For most countercultural Christians who had been raised in what they perceived to be the ritualistic and lifeless liberal Christian church or in a spiritually indifferent secular home, any evangelical church, in spite of some establishment trappings, seemed to have something essentially dynamic and different about it. But for Wallis, who had not lived through and rejected a liberal Christian upbringing, the dynamism was compromised by what he perceived to be a pervasive accommodationist mentality. For this reason he vociferously and radically denounced any and all compromises evangelical churches made with the establishment and committed himself to live a Christlike life outside the purview of normative evangelicalism. This did not mean he dismissed the institutional church; rather he wanted to cleanse it and make it truly evangelical, using the first-century church, which had practiced Christian communalism, as its model. Wallis (and others), in sum, represented the countercultural Christians who advocated leftist evangelicalism.

It was perhaps because of young Christians like Wallis that certain left-leaning and reform-minded evangelicals held hopes for creating an evangelical political awareness and engagement. In 1972 the evangelical historian George Marsden, then teaching history at Calvin College, encouraged Christians to become socially involved. "In recent years many evangelicals," he wrote approvingly, "reflecting a variety of social philosophies, have been urging that charitable response to social problems should be made prominent in our preaching and practice."[27] Marsden's message, of course, was addressed to traditional evangelicals, but his reference to the "variety of social philosophies" cast a wide net that included evangelicals who were less than traditional.[28] Also in that election year, which matched up the politically liberal George McGovern against the incumbent Richard Nixon, the evangelical maverick Republican Senator Mark Hatfield, who deplored Nixon's Vietnam policy, exhorted American youth to become outspoken politically. "The prophetic voice which the church is called to speak in our age," he lectured theological students at Princeton, "is more likely to be heard and followed by those in political power when it is spoken by those who, in committed pastoral relationships, have shown their genuine concern and love."[29]

The left-leaning political potential of reform-minded evangelicals and young countercultural Christians inspired Richard Quebedeaux, director of the United Campus Ministry at the University of California at Santa Barbara, to write *The Young Evangelicals* (1974). In it, Quebedeaux expressed the hope that the new generation of Christians would, without giving up their biblically grounded theology, team up with liberal Christians for a revival of the social gospel. He pointed out that many "young evangelicals" believed in the Bible, in Jesus as Savior, and in evangelism, and they had not given up on the institutional church. If Quebedeaux, who counted himself among the young evangelicals at that time, could have had his way, the institutional church would have made allowance for the young evangelicals' biblically grounded worldview, whereupon young evangelicals would then have worked with mainstream Christians "in their fresh priorities which include . . . sexual love as a joyful experience, meaningful, interpersonal, and social relationships, the dignity of women, racial justice, peace and conscientious political involvement, the fight against poverty, a healthy natural environment, and a positive and happy participation in contemporary culture."[30]

In other words, Quebedeaux hoped to join liberal compassion with biblically grounded practice. Countercultural Christians and liberals would work together to help the poor and sponge away racism. It was a logical plan. The ecclesiastical institution was in place, a body of religionists and resources existed in number, all that was needed was to join forces, and who knows, perhaps quicken the whole with antitechnocratic spirituality.

Furthermore, there existed in the major political parties a few important evangelical personalities that could help implement a new Christian political agenda centering on social justice. Democratic Senator Harold Hughes of Iowa was an evangelical who championed liberal causes and, along with Hatfield, campaigned to bring an end to the war in Vietnam.[31] Supported by activists like Wallis and Ron Sider, who penned *Rich Christians in an Age of Hunger,* a strong, if numerically weak, leftist evangelical voice existed.[32] Its preaching and social involvement would survive the rise of the Religious Right, continue on into the next millennium, and preserve the hope of generating the next politically charged revival of evangelicalism. We are here concerned with the countercultural Christians who would work their way into the Religious Right rather than those who went Left, but it is important to mention the other side of the spectrum, because it demonstrates that countercultural Christians could be socio-politically minded and active in a variety of causes. It also shows that the trajectory to the right was not a given. The question we ask, then, is "Why did countercultural Christians generally move over into the greater evangelical movement that would underwrite the rise of the Religious Right?"

Prophetically Right

Part of the reason countercultural Christians would move gradually rightward in their political orientation had nothing to do with domestic politics but a great deal to do with world affairs. Already, before the apex of the countercultural and evangelical youth revival with Explo '72, young and new Christians had begun to formulate and voice opinions about world politics. The motive force in this movement was, as mentioned above, Hal Lindsey's book, *The Late Great Planet Earth,* which appeared in

1970 and had sold over a million copies by the time of the Dallas "Godstock" that had drawn a crowd of over 200,000.[33]

The explicit purpose of Lindsey's book was to provoke spiritual renewal. He wrote to convince nonbelievers that because biblical prophecy proved itself to be true and that the end of the world was at hand, they needed to immediately accept Jesus Christ as their personal Savior. Second, he hoped to demonstrate to all Christians that the end was coming and that they needed to make good use of the time left them on earth to spread the gospel as quickly and as effectively as possible.[34] But in addition to these spiritual messages, Lindsey also stated political opinions and positions that claimed to be in keeping with a biblically grounded interpretation of the Bible. Countercultural Christians generally found his assessment of international politics reflected their own opinions or suspicions about world affairs.[35]

Lindsey argued from the biblically grounded basis that politics, like all things, had a spiritual significance and provocatively applied this reasoning to one of the most politically volatile regions of the world, the Middle East. According to biblical prophecy, Lindsey informed his readers, the governments involved in the affairs of the Middle East had foreordained roles to play out: Israel, the Arab nations, the Soviet Union, Europe, and China were spirito-political entities, and the individual Christian needed to be aware of this.

According to Lindsey, God had a plan, revealed in the Bible, to reestablish the nation of Israel in Palestine in the latter days, a plan which had been put into execution shortly after World War II. As Lindsey had expalined it, "The same prophets who predicted the worldwide exile and persecution of the Jews also predicted their restoration as a nation."[36] With Israel in place, continued the author, God allowed for Arab antipathy toward the Jews to escalate so that in the near future an Arab-African confederacy headed by Egypt would attack Israel. When that came to pass, Lindsey warned, Russia would close upon the Middle East and conquer both Israel and the Arab-African confederacy.

The unfolding of events, Lindsey insisted, was not hard to decipher. The prophet Ezekiel had pinpointed the northern commander who would descend upon the Middle East as "Gog, of the land of Magog, the chief prince of Rosh, of Meschech and Tubal." As Lindsey explained it, Rosh was the root word for Russia; Meschech was the root word for Moscow; and Tubal was the root word for Tibereni, the name of an ethnic group living along the Soviet controlled Black Sea.[37]

Following the invasion of the Middle East by Russia, continued Lindsey, the revived Roman Empire (a united Europe), as an ally of Israel but led by the Antichrist, would intervene and destroy the Russian army. At this, Lindsey claimed, China, in accordance with Revelation 9:14-16, would invade with 200 million troops to clash with Europe's armies at the battle of Armageddon, and only then would Christ finally return and establish his reign of one thousand years. Here, Lindsey compared the biblical reference to an Oriental army of 200 million with the Chinese government's assertion that China could field 200 million militiamen. "In their own boast," wrote Lindsey emphatically, "they named the same number as the Biblical prediction. Coincidence?"[38]

Taking into account this end times scenario, biblically grounded Christians and especially the countercultural Christians with whom Lindsey had much to do, both when he had worked for Campus Crusade and when he directed the Jesus Christ Light and Power Company at UCLA, could position themselves politically. Christians were to support Israel, the country of the Jew whom the world despised and persecuted. The enemies of God had attempted to exterminate the Jews, but God had used the Holocaust to his own prophetic ends: because of it western nations had felt obliged to give the downtrodden Jew a homeland, and God's chosen people had been divinely reestablished in Palestine.[39]

The resultant political positioning meant that biblically grounded Christians stood against Arab nations bent on the destruction of the numerical underdog Israel, but such positioning also meant countercultural Christians opposed Russia, a united Western Europe (because it would be led by the Antichrist), and China. In other words, this meant that countercultural Christians, if politically engaged, would support U.S. policy that contained the Soviet Union and China and discouraged the transformation of the European Economic Community into a United States of Europe. Also, they would want to ensure Israel's military strength and to limit that of the Arab nations.

Countercultural Christian political opinions had nothing to do directly with economic or national interests, at least from a technocratic viewpoint, for surely economic and national security interests for the oil-hungry United States would have dictated otherwise, especially after the 1973 oil embargo. These political positions, as concerned the countercultural Christian warm to Lindsey's interpretations, had everything to do with a spiritual discernment of world events.[40] And so, the question of whether America should support or oppose a foreign nation ought no longer to be decided on the basis of whether that nation were communist or not, but on the basis of whether it supported Israel.[41]

9

Politically Right

The history of the countercultural Christian shift rightward is an interesting one. Hal Lindsey played a role; two other evangelical personalities, however, would have a much more important and decisive part to play. Bill Bright, who commanded the biggest parachurch evangelistic organization for youth, and Francis Schaeffer, who had most effectively translated evangelical apologetics and polemics for the countercultural mind, stood at the door as countercultural Christians entered the evangelical church; and these men ultimately ushered them in to sit on the right side of the aisle.[1]

Prior to the rise of the Religious Right, Bill Bright sensitized young Christians to the political world by encouraging them to evangelize politicians in Washington D.C. through the Christian Embassy organization and by supporting one of the first political groups of the new era whose purpose it was to enlist culturally conservative voters, the Christian Freedom Foundation. He also endorsed a politically conservative book for his staff, entitled *In the Spirit of '76*, that instructed readers on how to win elections. Bright's friendship with successful conservative businessmen such as Richard DeVos of Amway also created a conservative political atmosphere about him in which young Campus Crusade workers operated.[2] This is not to say that Bright imposed a rightwing political creed upon his organization or its activities, because he did not, but Campus Crusade definitely steered clear of the activist evangelical left, and that in itself is noteworthy.

More important for the future political direction of evangelicals, and the countercultural Christians amongst them, was Francis Schaeffer. As both a guide for countercultural Christians and a leading evangelical thinker, Schaeffer was uniquely placed to escort countercultural Christians toward a political expression.[3] He understood that any socio-political activism needed to be sensitive to the biblical virtues especially embraced by the baby boom generation. The golden rule ideal, the respect for intellectual sophistication and expressive individualism, and the commitment to an authentic and seamless lifestyle could not be ignored if one was to be taken seriously in the 1970s. Schaeffer, of course, had no trouble abiding by these ideals because he not only shared them, he also shared the younger generation's determination to employ such ideals to transform the world.[4]

Motivated by these principles, Schaeffer helped evangelicalism and countercultural Christianity develop a common polemic against liberalism. For his starting point, he used an argument, previously perfected by J. Gresham Machen, which stated that liberals used newspeak when talking religion. That is, they redefined Christian doctrines in order to replace the Christian worldview with their own non-biblical one. Though liberals said they believed in Christ, they actually redefined Jesus to the point that the Christ they really believed in never graced the pages of the New Testament. At the end of the day, the liberal Christian ethos could not be readily distinguished from that proclaimed in the 1933 *Humanist Manifesto*, a secular modernist document, signed by John Dewey, the leading light in modern educational theory, and thirty-three fellow humanists. In sum, Schaeffer attacked liberal spirituality for being inauthentic, a sham, for parading about in spiritual garb while being technocratic at heart.

Schaeffer also accused the older mainstream generation of glorifying the golden rule in word while denying it in thought and practice. Here, he hoped to tip the ethical scales in favor of evangelicals and fill biblically grounded Christians with moral confidence. The challenge, however, was daunting, because liberals had not limited themselves to delivering negative attacks against biblically grounded Christians. Ever since the early twentieth-century days of fundamentalist Billy Sunday's Bible-thumping, condemnatory, and extravagant evangelistic harangues, liberal Christians had progressively proven their own moral worth by championing ecumenism, peace, tolerance, and compassion. In practical terms they supported the World Council of Churches, the antiwar movement, human rights, and initiatives to end world hunger.[5]

Schaeffer, however, argued that the great misconception of the century was precisely the belief that liberals were tolerant and loving, and that biblically grounded Christians were not. Liberals, he insisted, shared a common starting point for ethics with Stalin's communists and even Hitler's Nazis. The pluralistic and love-everyone themes they preached were whitewash; underneath lay a human-based selfishness that threatened true freedom. The fact of the matter was that liberals curtailed liberties, especially the religious freedoms of biblically grounded Christians. Their political and social ridicule of fundamentalists and their liberally inspired judicial decisions, which forbade Christians to live out their faith in public classrooms, were not a testimony to freedom but rather a practice of intolerance and oppression.

Greater dangers threatened, according to Schaeffer. The tyranny of Christian liberals would soon overwhelm Western civilization because their morals, rooted only in fickle and capricious human nature, were adrift. He identified the opposing worldview responsible for the drift as "secular humanism," a calamitous ideology that fed the minds and hearts of liberal Christians as well as atheists and agnostics; furthermore, its reach was global and it sought dominion over both the communist East and capitalistic West.[6] In 1980, Schaeffer's alarmist but cogent arguments would be given even greater circulation by the fundamentalist preacher Tim LaHaye in his popular book *The Battle for the Mind*.[7] And this war between good and evil, defined in these terms and well understood by baby boomers nurtured in one way or another by Schaeffer's writings, would live on in LaHaye's later and more sensational bestsellers, the coauthored *Left Behind* series.

Given their basis in secular humanism, argued Schaeffer, mainstream ethics would continue to evolve, and behavior regarded as unethical today would be openly espoused and practiced tomorrow. The only thing bridling liberals and their secular soulmates at present, Schaeffer cautioned, was their transitory adherence to the traditions of a civilization that once acknowledged biblical norms. In time, however, the secular humanists' memory would fade and what is left of their biblically inspired customs would cease. With this peril looming, Schaeffer admonished biblically grounded Christians to participate in the public arena and avert an impending catastrophe. But in order to motivate evangelicals to act, Schaeffer needed to convince them that they held the moral high ground while liberal Christians and their secular friends were lost in a solipsistic swamp of moral incertitude and wrongheaded thinking deep enough to drown humanity.

Party Politics

In the early 1970s, Schaeffer refused to align himself with any particular political party. Christians, he instructed, should work politically with others to achieve a specific goal, but they should not submit themselves to an entangling alliance; they were to be cobelligerents, but not allies. "Christians must realize," he wrote, "that there is a difference between being a cobelligerent and an ally. At times you will seem to be saying exactly the same thing as the New Left elite or the Establishment elite. If there is social injustice, say there is social injustice. If we need order, say we need order. In these cases, and at these specific points, we would be cobelligerents. But do not align yourself as though you are in either of these camps: You are an ally of neither. The church of the Lord Jesus Christ is different from either—totally different."[8]

Why, then, did Schaeffer ultimately favor the Republican Party, and to the point that he came to seem more of an ally than a simple cobelligerent? It is true that he hailed from the North and that he had been religiously educated in the Presbyterian fundamentalist tradition, which reflected middle-class Republican values. But Schaeffer had long since dropped McIntire's brand of Christianity and dialogued with popular culture, which made his devotion to things Republican and conservative rather suspect.

Another significant factor, doubtless, is the fact that the Republican leadership was generally more receptive to Schaeffer and his message. In 1971 he traveled to Washington D.C. and spoke at a Press Club dinner and to lobbyists and Congressmen. He became friends with Jack Kemp, the future presidential hopeful (1988), and the Kemps began Bible studies based on Schaeffer's writings. President Ford's son, Mike, had spent time at Schaeffer's L'Abri, and the Schaeffers became acquainted with the parents, whom the Schaeffers later visited at the White House. And even if the Republicans did not share the Schaeffers' evangelical convictions, certain conservatives, of whom more will be said later, were willing to accommodate their worldview to that of the Schaeffers. The final upshot of all this was that, as Francis Schaeffer presented his biblically grounded message and his call for activism, he found more receptive ears in the Republican camp.

But there was a deeper and more important reason as well. Schaeffer knew that the socio-political reformation of Western civilization could not be accomplished without the enlistment of political institutions. However, Schaeffer shied away from the Democratic Party because he came to believe that committed and radical secular humanists, the diehard enemies of biblically grounded Christianity, had greater control over it. The American Civil Liberties Union, the organization that had defended John Scopes in the 1920s, was particularly active during this period and was supported by the Democratic Party's influential left wing. Moreover, during the late sixties and early seventies, other anti-evangelical organizations emerged, particularly the

National Organization for Women, and were universally welcomed by the Democratic Party leadership. Furthermore, the Democratic Party believed in the Great Society. For Schaeffer, this meant that the Democrats were accommodationists with the technocracy. Schaeffer came to the conclusion, then, that by positioning biblically grounded Christians more decidedly alongside Republicans, even secular humanist Republicans when biblically permissible, he could further the gospel cause in America and help to spiritually revolutionize Americans.

The Golden Rule Key

To energize evangelicals politically, however, Schaeffer needed a persuasive ethical argument to discredit the secular humanist mainstream. During the early seventies, he denounced American materialism, racism, and environmental pollution; he called Christians to a life of community, wherein they would live not only for one another but also for unbelievers.[9] What Christians needed to do, explained Schaeffer, was to repent of their sins, engage the world and, in a sense, prove the moral worth of their doctrine. To spread his message, Schaeffer put together a book and film series entitled *How Should We Then Live?* (1976). Starting in January of 1977, he and his wife toured North America with their program to conduct well-advertised three-day seminars in six major cities and one-day seminars in eleven others, including Winnipeg and Toronto in Canada.[10]

During the tour, Schaeffer delivered his well-honed themes. Liberals, he warned, might think that they could live in the world by resorting to majority ethics, but this should provide little comfort to the Christian or to humanity. "Let us remember," he wrote, "that on the basis of the absoluteness of the 51-percent vote, Hitler was perfectly entitled to do as he wished if he had the popular support. On this basis, law and morals become a matter of averages. And on this basis, if the majority vote supported it, it would become 'right' to kill the old, the incurably ill, the insane—and other groups could be declared non-persons."[11]

In true countercultural fashion, Schaeffer prodded evangelicals on toward activism against the secular humanist establishment. "As Christians, we are not only to *know* the right world view, the world view that tells us the truth of what *is*, but consciously to *act* upon that world view so as to influence society in all its parts and facets across the whole spectrum of life, as much as we can to the extent of our individual and collective ability."[12] If Christians did not act, government would be turned over to a technocratic elite who would promise personal peace and affluence to the masses as something of an opiate, while the fires of real human freedom and creativity would be slowly snuffed out.[13]

By 1977, Schaeffer realized that he could make an even more potent statement to discredit liberals and help launch a politically responsible evangelical movement if he joined forces with C. Everett Koop, an accomplished physician and founder/editor of the *Journal of Pediatric Surgery* (and future United States surgeon general under Ronald Reagan from 1982–1989). Their coauthored book, *Whatever Happened to the Human Race?*, was published in 1979, and it dovetailed smoothly with the rise of the Christian Right.[14] The first chapter was boldly entitled, "The Abortion of the Human Race," and in the opening paragraph the authors threw down the gauntlet, "Cultures can be judged in many ways," they wrote, "but eventually every nation in every age must be judged by this test: *how did it treat people?* Each generation, each wave of humanity, evaluates its predecessors on this basis. The final measure of mankind's humanity is how humanely people treat one another."[15] And in the accompanying film by the same title, Schaeffer turns to the audience and somberly announces that "the fate of the unborn is the fate of the human race."[16]

The 1973 *Roe v Wade* decision had provided Schaeffer with a golden opportunity to turn the tables on his opponents. Having issued his condemnation of mainstream ethics, Schaeffer proclaimed the authentic golden rule character of biblically grounded Christianity, a worldview that held dear the sanctity of all human beings, a worldview whose adherents would be willing to sacrifice position and reputation to protect even the smallest.[17]

Schaeffer and Koop met the liberal Christians on their own turf by acknowledging, indeed asserting, the primacy of the golden rule. And their argument that biblically based Christianity outclassed liberal theology, rooted as it was in secular humanism and, therefore, situation ethics, was convincing to evangelicals.[18] Schaeffer continued to sound the alarm during the ensuing years, highlighting the complicity between mainstream religion and infanticide. As Schaeffer stated in *A Christian Manifesto* (1981), in the midst of the Christian Right phenomenon, "It is significant to note that many of the denominations controlled by liberal theology have come out, publicly and strongly, in favor of abortion."[19] Because of abortion, politics and religion had become welded together, and no one was more influential in bringing evangelicals to a pro-life position, the position that made political activism not only possible but potent, than the guide of countercultural Christianity, Francis Schaeffer.[20]

Schaeffer gave traditional evangelicals and all the baby-boomer Christians in their midst a socio-political cause that directed them away from the Democratic hard core. A staunch, clear-cut ethical position, however, only created favorable conditions for a movement to develop. In and of itself, a belief, even if it suggests a socio-political agenda, does not necessarily result in votes. In order to create a voting bloc, one needs an organization to motivate citizens to participate in party politics and to go out and vote.

By the late seventies certain evangelicals took the initiative to get involved. Robert Grant, a Fuller Theological Seminary graduate, brought together like-minded people to form Christian Voice in 1978. The organization sought to guide the political power of the Christian community so that it might have "a massive impact on Washington, rather than dissipating aimlessly."[21] Although Christian Voice had roots in California, it was not a product of the Jesus Movement; nevertheless, it had indirect connections, because evangelical churches in California that listened to Christian Voice now included many of the former Jesus Freaks, and the attributes of the Jesus People had been injected into the life of those churches. In fact, on Christian Voice's policy committee would be a former Campus Crusade worker and founder of the Jesus Christ Power and Light Company, and author of *The Late Great Planet Earth*, Hal Lindsey.[22]

Christian Voice played a major role in laying down the groundwork for the future Christian Right, for sensitizing evangelicals through church networks to the religious implications of legislative decisions and initiatives. In order to launch a national political movement with numerical strength, however, the country's evangelical leadership needed to be mobilized.

The New Right and the Old Bible

In the late 1970s, political conservatives known collectively as the New Right helped evangelicals establish political institutions capable of swinging elections. Most of these New Right leaders, although they may have been religious, were not evangelical. The greatest early influences for the New Right included professor Leo Strauss, from the University of Chicago, who passed away in 1973, and the younger Irving Kristol, of New York University. Both were Jewish and supported social conservatism for pragmatic rather than religious reasons. Richard Viguerie, founder and publisher of *Conservative Digest* (1975), and Phyllis Schlafly, founder of the anti-Equal Rights Amendment organization Eagle Forum (1972), were both Catholic; Paul Weyrich, founder of the conservative Heritage Foundation (1973), was Eastern Rite Catholic, and Howard Phillips, founder of the Conservative Caucus (1974), was ethnically Jewish.[23]

The New Right was anticommunist, anti-union, and anti-big government; it attacked the programs and objectives of the Great Society and defended traditional individual rights, but it also criticized corporate executives.[24] The latter cause made the New Right atypical, at least in relation to the more traditional, "country club" elements of the Republican Party. This distinctiveness was due to the fact that some of its formative thinkers had been leftists. New Right luminary Irving Kristol, for example, had once been a Trotskyite.[25] Though not representative of all New Right participants, such intellectuals had an insider's perspective on liberal politics and demonstrated to others how to carry out an effective debate with the Left with a sixties-style flair. For this reason, the New Right, in its enthusiasm for traditional individual rights and, therefore, its opposition to busing and gun control, delivered a more relevant, incisive, and ultimately convincing message in the political arena than that traditionally expounded by the Republican leadership. Their own confidence communicated confidence to more traditional Republicans.

However, it must be remembered that the New Right protagonists influenced by Strauss objected to new individual rights sought by political liberals—such as abortion rights, women's rights, and gay rights—not because they believed these positions would destroy America spiritually per se, but because they believed such changes would destabilize society. There was a conviction amongst many of these neoconservatives that because religious morals had stood the test of time, they buttressed Western civilization.[26] Traditional Judeo-Christian mores, therefore, should be maintained for pragmatic reasons.

Ultimately, many New Right pundits sought to establish or confirm moral behavior and business-friendly economic practices for the purpose of making the technocracy itself function more efficiently. Even those with religious convictions delved into politics principally to reestablish America's lost social and economic order; for these, there still existed a compartmentalization of religious and public life. The problem was, especially in the case of *Roe v Wade*, that the government had launched a war against their religious life. Still, they did not intend to infuse government with religion; they wanted the *status quo ante bellum*. Unlike born-again baby boomers, the New Right activists did not instill a biblically grounded spirituality into their socio-political world through an intellectually sophisticated faith devoted to the golden rule. In short, New Right leaders had not been on an antitechnocratic spiritual quest during the sixties; the movement was, in fact, essentially reactionary.

The New Right leaders recognized, however, that they could gain support and votes for their conservative causes if they wooed evangelical leaders, with parishioners in tow, into their movement. On the surface, the challenge was tricky because a significant portion of biblically grounded Christians were located in the traditionally Democratic South.[27] Fortunately for the New Right, white southerners had become disgruntled with the Democratic party ever since the civil rights movement and the secularization of public schooling. Many southerners had even abandoned the Democtrats for George Wallace in 1968, a psychological breakthrough for some. But more importantly, as civil rights became a *fait accompli,* southerners could henceforth advance political ideas, such as private and home school advocacy, without having them automatically categorized as part of a racist conspiracy, although their political opponents continued to level the charge.[28] Finally, for southerners who were committed to a biblical worldview, Schaeffer and others handed them intellectually respectable arguments that justified a political realignment.

A Broader Evangelical Political Consciousness

For biblically grounded Christians, the political perspective, of course, differed from that of the New Right. Issues such as school prayer, pornography, abortion, and the like were not seen as "social issues" in the sense that most academics would use the term. To the biblically grounded, these issues were above all *spiritual* issues. The distinction is important. Historians may determine that biblically grounded legislation in favor of family values had consequences for society, or that abortion was a social issue, and they would be correct; but to think that the biblically grounded believers sought to restructure human behavior and relations simply to answer to the material needs facing the impoverished would be misleading.

Especially for traditional evangelicals, the restructuring of society would be a secondary effect, but certainly not the objective of their politics, because they simply did not think in terms of social restructuring as beneficial in and of itself. The traditional evangelical understood issues such as school prayer or the right to life as important primarily because they had an impact upon the human-divine relationship. The traditional evangelical considered *society* as significant chiefly because God dealt with people collectively as a nation, that is; God would punish a sinful nation and bless a good one. But here again, it was the human-divine relationship that was of greatest importance: whether or not social reformation promoted the maximum material wellbeing for the greatest number of citizens was of secondary concern at best. For traditional evangelicals, if society allowed the individual to live out his or her Christian faith, God would take care of the rest, including the question of daily bread. The important thing was to protect the individual from secular humanist constraints, from state control.

By the 1970s, however, the traditional evangelical perspective was changing, and largely because the new Christians, those born of the counterculture, and reform-minded evangelicals tended to look at these issues a little differently. Reformers and baby-boomer Christians understood that actions to help the poor, the sick, and the oppressed had important spiritual implications in and of themselves. Even interacting with the environment had spiritual ramifications. And the only way, sometimes, to help the environment or people, including non-Christians who were made in the image of God as well as anyone else, was through collective socio-political action. Francis Schaeffer brought this out, as did Jim Wallis.

With the coming together of countercultural Christians and traditional evangelicals during the 1970s, the latter came around to reordering their worldview with the authentic and seamless spiritual lifestyle of the former. Here the generation gap closed. This closure, which would be significant for an engaged political attitude, was facilitated by two things. In the first place, the younger generation, inspired by Jesus' admonition to "love thy enemy" was willing to accept the older generation even with its establishment trappings. To be sure, the countercultural Christians labored to dispense with those trappings, but they nonetheless joined the evangelical churches. Second, the older generation in many evangelical denominations humbly conceded that the younger generation had been correct. Christianity was not to be compartmentalized; one's spirituality was to infuse all of one's life, including the political, including the workplace.

There were difficulties of course. Many countercultural Christians formed their own churches, and many evangelical churches had "worship wars," which often meant an early morning church service geared toward the baby-boomer Christian style and a late morning service for the more traditional congregants. Certain churches, especially separatist fundamentalist ones, were less influenced by the countercultural Christianity. But overall, countercultural Christians and churched youth of the sixties who had endorsed countercultural spirituality and dispensed with many of the establishment trappings of traditional evangelicalism had injected into the greater evangelical movement a new mentality. This baby-boomer evangelicalism was committed to the seamless lifestyle wherein the Spirit of Christ breathed through everything they did, whether on Sunday or Monday, whether at church or at work, whether in the pew or the voting booth.

This was the Christian Right. In this movement, the government was no longer the "other"; on the contrary, through voting, participating in party politics as delegates, controlling party platforms, seeking appointments, and holding office, evangelicals engaged the political process in unprecedented ways. All issues now, such as abortion, Israel, taxes, and military expenditure, had to be approached from the perspective of a biblically grounded worldview.

Creating a Religious Movement

In sum then, whereas the New Right political operatives desired to reshape *society* so that it functioned better, and usually meaning in a *technocratic* manner, the evangelical politicians or activists desired to purify nation and individuals so that all might function better *spiritually*, meaning, firstly, in the human-divine relationship. Biblically grounded spiritual relationships, of course, simultaneously extended horizontally to link one individual with another, but it was always in a triangular relationship with God at the apex.[29] In the final analysis, then, the New Right and biblically grounded forces came together to pursue common, political goals for uncommon, ideological reasons.

In spite of the difference, the New Right was critical to the initial success of the Christian Right because it knew the ropes of the ship of state and could acquaint the evangelical newcomers with its riggings, and how best to go about getting control of it. New Right operatives Paul Weyrich and Howard Phillips recruited two Christian Right organizers, Robert Billings, founder of National Christian Action Coalition (1978), and Ed McAteer, a retired Colgate-Palmolive sales and marketing manager and a fundamentalist, to connect the New Right with the nation's leading evangelical ministers. To this end, Weyrich and McAteer traveled the country meeting with evangelical leaders to encourage them to get involved in America's political conversation. The ministers were at first reluctant.

After much coaxing, Weyrich finally convinced some of the nation's most influential evangelical pastors to help fund a survey of their followers to see if parishioners would support a move by ministers into politics.[30] The results of the survey showed that evangelicals were not only willing to lend moral support but monetary backing as well. With this revelation, Jerry Falwell, who had a huge radio and television audience and a bulging mailing list, agreed to become involved politically. Other well-known biblically grounded Christians, James Robison and James Kennedy, also showed interest, and the political movement known as the Religious Right, or Christian Right, was afoot.[31] The year was 1979.

Soon after the New Right introduced Falwell and other evangelicals to the political game, however, the New Right began losing control of its own movement. The Christian Right harbored more voters and accessed more money than the New

Right could ever hope to muster, and the recruits soon overshadowed their mentors.[32] As far as evangelicals were concerned, the New Right had completed its mission.

Adjusting to Baby-Boomer Christianity

When one looks at the political developments of the late 1970s and 1980s, as the Christian Right became firmly established upon the political landscape, one observes an evolution toward a political organization that could accommodate baby-boomer Christians, evangelicals who could be described as countercultural Christians, and churched youth who had adopted countercultural Christian thinking. Establishing the right type of organization was a process of trial and error, but through it evangelical leaders discovered that an effective political organization could not be too fundamentalist, nor too Pentecostal. In order to appeal to the greatest number of political conservatives across the country, whether evangelical or not, the organizers also had to respect, at least to the satisfaction of baby-boomer enlistees, the golden rule ideal, intellectual integrity, expressive individualism, and biblically grounded spirituality. The fact that the Christian Right moved progressively toward such ideals, as well as its increasingly activist style, is an indication that the baby boomers, brandishing their countercultural Christian ethos, exuded significant influence at the grassroots level

One of the early religio-political organizations to come out of the new coalition was the Religious Roundtable, created in 1979 by Ed McAteer who worked for the New Right Conservative Caucus. This organization hoped to mix together New Right and Christian Right leaders, and it proved successful in joining influential businessmen with the nation's top televangelists. In spite of its name, however, it failed to satisfy all evangelicals. Pat Robertson resigned in 1981, declaring that he preferred to see America change through spiritual means. His resignation, though, did not signal a decision to abandon politics. To accomplish his more spiritually motivated political objectives, he wanted an organization completely dominated by biblically grounded Christians. Adding to his already popular "700 Club" television show that promoted evangelically inspired political opinions, he soon established evangelical organizations to pursue his goals, most notably the Freedom Council (1981) to motivate conservative voters and the National Legal Foundation (1985) to counter what was deemed to be anti-evangelical legal actions and legislation.[33]

Other biblically grounded Christians joined the evangelical political movement as well in 1979. Tim LaHaye's wife Beverly founded Concerned Women for America, an evangelical response to the National Organization for Women, which it soon outstripped in membership and resources. Although Beverly and her husband were solid religious conservatives, they demonstrated that they had the acumen to adapt to their audience without giving up their biblically grounded convictions. From *The Act of Marriage* (1976), a manual on sexuality which they wrote together, through *The Battle for the Mind* (1980), to Tim LaHaye and Jerry Jenkins's blockbuster *Left Behind* series (1995–2006, ongoing) on end times, they always captured the interest of the baby-boomer generation.

The best-known political organization of the Christian Right during this formative era was the Moral Majority (1979–1989), established by Jerry Falwell, though the name was inadvertently suggested by Weyrich during a brainstorming session with Falwell.[34] When considering presidential candidates to support in the 1980 election, the Moral Majority settled upon Ronald Reagan. Reagan, raised by a fundamentalist mother, understood the evangelical perspective; and he won the resounding endorsement of leading evangelicals when he candidly admitted to them that he could do nothing more nor less than rely upon Jesus Christ for his eternal salvation. In November, Reagan defeated the incumbent born-again Jimmy Carter. Moral Majority judged that the evangelical vote, which they had roused, had given Reagan the election.

Of course, other important voting blocs contributed both to Ronald Reagan's and, later, to George H. W. Bush's presidential victories. Nevertheless, both presidents certainly owed a political debt to the Religious Right. Our purpose here, however, is not to give a detailed history of these Republican administrations; our concern is to identify baby boomers who experienced the counterculture of the sixties and ended up injecting evangelicalism with their ideals and voting with the Religious Right.

It is difficult to detect these countercultural baby boomers inside the Christian Right in its early phase because of the nature of the movement, dominated as it was at the upper echelons by the non-evangelical New Rightists and traditional evangelicals, which in 1979 featured fundamentalists like Falwell. Baby-boomer Christians were, for the most part, still too young or too new to evangelicalism to take leading roles. For our purposes, then, it is not profitable to give a lengthy and detailed history of the initial Religious Right organizations. In fact, because histories written about the rise of the Religious Right have, up until this time, focused primarily on the hierarchy of organizations, they have failed to accurately describe the true nature of the Christian Right phenomenon.

Despite their comparative lack of prominence in the early days, countercultural Christians, perhaps better denominated as baby-boomer evangelicals after the abeyance of the counterculture as a historical period, were nonetheless important to the Christian Right movement in a number of ways. Before addressing this issue, however, it is necessary to give a cursory overview of the Christian Right and its relationship to the Reagan presidency, because in their quest for political influence with the President, Christian Right organizations discovered that they were obligated to expand their power base. In order to do this, they needed the maximum number of members, and to reach that potential they needed to be careful not to offend the ideals of the postwar generation of evangelicals.

What alerted the Christian Right to their need for more numbers, more activists, and more clout was the negligible return they received for their campaign investment in Reagan. Reagan, though genuinely fond of evangelicals, generated few legislative proposals that were uniquely evangelical. There were a couple of reasons for this. For one thing, though Reagan did have a small number of bona fide evangelicals in his administration, such as Secretary of the Interior James Watt and Surgeon General C. Everett Koop, the circle of staffers surrounding him were at best neoconservatives who had little interest in religiously inspired politics. Deputy White House Chief of Staff Michael Deaver, reflecting back upon the Reagan presidency, admitted that he consistently obstructed evangelical access to the President. Obstructionism at the White House was supplemented by reticence on Capitol Hill, and Reagan no doubt knew he lacked the necessary congressional backing to push through an evangelical agenda. He did half-heartedly allow for some evangelical initiatives to leave his office and make their way to Congress. The bill for a school prayer amendment was one. It failed.

Nonetheless, evangelical issues made it into the headlines under Reagan, and most people in the Christian Right, especially those outside the beltway, were satisfied that the President was on their side. Indeed, Reagan gave moving speeches on behalf of the pro-life movement, which was most dear to evangelicals and most vociferously opposed by non-evangelicals. Moreover, the National Day of Prayer was officially declared for the first Thursday of May. Reagan also pushed through a tax and budget cut that weakened Great Society-styled projects. He fully backed Israel and bolstered the nation's defense in order to stand up to the threat of atheistic communists. National defense, tax relief, and a foreign policy sympathetic to Israel were not, of course, exclusively Christian Right concerns, but for most baby-boomer evangelicals they were non-negotiable priorities.

Why then did the most prominent Christian Right organization, the Moral Majority, prove ineffective and not survive the 1980s? The answer lies not only in its political naiveté and incompetence—its failure to threaten Congress and President alike with a voter boycott—but also in the religious outlook of the organization's leadership and its top-down structure. For one thing, Jerry Falwell's demeanor and provocative statements damaged the organization's image and effectiveness; more significantly, most leadership positions went to fellow fundamentalists who seconded their leader. Because of this heavy reliance upon fundamentalists, the organization, despite the many non-fundamentalists who followed its suggestions when voting, came to be associated with obscurantism and self-righteousness, and therefore became incapable of surviving as a viable national political organization for evangelicals at large.[35] In short, not only was the Moral Majority unsuccessful in pressuring the government to pass legislation, it also alienated its evangelical base.

The demise of the Moral Majority was thus, ironically, an indicator of the presence and strength of countercultural Christian thought in the greater evangelical movement. As the 1980s and 1990s unfolded, Christian Right political organizers came to realize that if they wanted to establish institutions that would have broad appeal, they needed to construe them so that they better reflected countercultural Christian values. Of course they did not say as much, and they were perhaps unaware that this was the group they had to take into consideration; not all evangelicals realized the extent to which biblically grounded Christianity had been reshaped by the Jesus People and the Jesus movement's legacy.

Pat Robertson, a charismatic, and Bill Bright, a non-charismatic, were two evangelical leaders who communicated with baby-boomer Christians better than Jerry Falwell. Bright continued to spend most of his efforts on directing new converts into the greater evangelical movement, but Robertson increasingly invested his time in developing a political consciousness among his listeners and viewers.

In 1980 both Bright and Robertson participated in the "Washington for Jesus" rally which drew over 200,000 participants, (some said half a million), to the capital city.[36] The event was ostensibly nonpolitical, but it was an election year and evangelical leaders had unequivocally identified themselves with the Christian Right. In any case, the gathering, which attracted as many participants as had the 1963 March on Washington with Martin Luther King Jr., had an impact upon evangelicals similar to the impact of the 1963 demonstration on the Civil Rights Movement. Robertson later said, "April 29, 1980 was the beginning of a spiritual revolution. And I joined with the 500,000 other people in the Mall and the millions watching on television in praying that one day this same spiritual revolution would sweep the nation."[37] This was indeed a movement that reflected the openness and activism of Christians who identified with America's postwar generation.

As the Moral Majority stalled and failed, the charismatics, led by Robertson, mounted a presidential campaign for 1988 with the hopes of spiritually transforming the country through politics. But just as Falwell depended too much on fundamentalists, so Robertson depended too heavily on his Pentecostal following, tapping into the support of nationally known televangelists Oral Roberts and Jimmy Swaggart. In some cases the support did more damage than good. Robertson's former connections with televangelist Jim Bakker, whose tryst with a secretary and racketeering through his ministry became public knowledge the year previous, certainly did not help his image; but Jimmy Swaggart's sexual misconduct and extravagant public apologies sullied and leveled ridicule at Robertson's campaign even more. It may have been guilt by association, distant association, but Robertson still had to spend precious sound bites on national television answering questions on the subject and refuting accusations.

Though Robertson had Pentecostals aplenty defending him, he failed to get the backing of important non-charismatics. Sensing the ultimate weakness that lay in Robertson's appeal, LaHaye, Falwell, McAteer, and others of the Christian Right threw their influence behind Congressman Jack Kemp's bid for the presidency instead. Kemp, who had been a friend to Francis Schaeffer (Schaeffer died in 1984) promised to come closer to what most baby-boomer Christians could endorse. He spoke highly of the golden rule ethic and was reputably a creative thinker; also, he was relatively young and even had a star quality about him, earned during his professional football days. All these qualities appealed to the baby-boomer generation. Unfortunately for countercultural Christians, Kemp failed to live up to his potential when he refused to match his campaign rhetoric to the hopes of his biblically grounded supporters and adopted instead a strategy of reaching out to nonevangelicals.[38] In any case, evangelicals failed to settle upon a single evangelical candidate and divided up their votes.

The significance of the 1988 election was not that Robertson and Kemp failed, but that no Republican candidate dared offend the Christian Right.[39] Bush, who once supported abortion rights, and Bob Dole, who once supported the ERA, now supported the pro-life movement and the Concerned Women for America constituency.[40] In other words, the major Republican candidates were forced to coopt Christian Right positions. Naturally, this development broke up the evangelical vote amongst the various candidates who echoed each other in their evangelically accented sound bites, but the issues of the Christian Right survived. And Christian Right organizations continued to refine their message in order to gain the largest activist biblically grounded following possible.

In 1989 Robertson, learning from his mistakes, organized the Christian Coalition which better matched the evangelical mindset that had by now been even more generally influenced by those who had matured within the counterculture.[41] By focusing on the grassroots, his Christian Coalition obviated the older traditional evangelical leadership and directly encouraged participation by baby-boomer Christians who were expected to be self-motivated activists willing to go door-to-door, deliver tracts, register voters, and demonstrate if necessary.[42] To head up this organization, Robertson employed the same strategy he had used back in the sixties when he hired the rock 'n' roll DJ Scott Ross to attract young listeners. This time he found a baby boomer named Ralph Reed.[43]

Reed was an interesting choice to head up a radical political organization, if Robertson hoped to communicate with and enlist baby-boomer Christians in the political cause of biblically grounded Christianity. In some ways Reed matched the countercultural Christian perfectly: he was a baby boomer and had been a radical, an activist, and a great partygoer while in college. Journalist and author Nina Easton wrote in her biographical sketch of Reed, "In every crowd of hard-drinking rowdy youth, there is one who pushes farther and harder, the lampshade guy. That was Ralph."[44] But Reed had a "born-again" experience in 1983 and rejected both his former religious notions and his former lifestyle.

In other ways, however, Reed definitely did not match the Jesus People profile. To begin with, he was a young baby boomer, born in 1961, and converted to biblically grounded Christianity after the Jesus movement. But most surprising, he had embraced many aspects of social conservatism prior to his conversion. He was a reactionary, a New Right activist. His 1983 conversion to biblically grounded Christianity did not result in an alteration of politics; he merely redefined the reasons he used to support certain political and legislative goals. When he converted, "he didn't change his views," according to one of his university classmates, "he just found out that God agreed with him."[45]

Reed's Christian Coalition reached its peak of power in the 1990s, helping conservative Republicans win the House. In an effort to broaden the Coalition's base by focusing on economic issues, Reed lost the organization's spiritual connection with many evangelical voters. The Coalition appeared healthy, however, as conservative Republicans, led by House Majority Leader Newt Gingrich, passed their Contract with America, which promised welfare reform and a balanced budget, among other things. When Gingrich fell into disfavor with American voters in 1996, though, and when Reed backed Bob Dole's failed candidacy for the presidency, the Coalition had spent itself. Reed left the organization.

An even better match with the ideals of countercultural Christianity than Reed's Christian Coalition came from another organization that, although it was not established as a political organization, had developed a political voice and very much influenced baby-boomer evangelicals. Focus on the Family was established in 1977 and headed up by James Dobson, a radio personality who held a Ph.D. in psychology.[46] He was to become the Dr. Spock for evangelical baby-boomer parents; his influential *Dare to Discipline* (1976) sold phenomenally.

His ministry combined the golden rule ethic with intellectual sophistication and promoted a biblically grounded spirituality; it thereby laid down the principles for family values that would guide Christians in the culture wars of the eighties and nineties.[47] His popularity and expertise were not ignored by Reagan. Dobson served on the National Advisory Commission to the Office of Juvenile Justice and Delinquency Prevention from 1982 to 1984, and then unofficially consulted the President on family issues. During Reagan's second term, Dobson served on various commissions for the Attorney General's Office as well as for the Department of Health and Human Services.

Though Dobson did not run for public office, he engaged the political world through his radio ministry and by forming, in 1981, the Family Research Council, which became incorporated two years later. This was a think tank and lobbying organization that advocated legislation in favor of family values and opposed legislation deemed inimical to family values. The organization would become independent in 1992 and directed by Gary Bauer, who would make his own bid for the presidency in 2000.

In the 1990s Focus on the Family demonstrated the best melding of countercultural Christian ideals and traditional evangelicalism. By the early 1990s, "Focus on the Family" would be the nation's second most popular radio show, a testament to Dobson's popularity among baby-boomer parents.[48] The organization had greater grassroots than the Moral Majority. And because it was not technically a political organization, it did not have to cut deals with cobelligerents as did the Christian Coalition. Dobson never wanted to be under a big tent. There were, of course, other organizations that appealed to a more radical countercultural constituency, such as Operation Rescue, an aggressive anti-abortion organization.

Conclusion

The development of a political consciousness within countercultural Christianity was not a priority during the 1960s and early 1970s. Most youth were simply interested in fulfilling a spiritual quest. But by definition, countercultural youth wanted an authentic and seamless life that was not compartmentalized, and this meant that they would inevitably apply their faith politically, especially after Watergate, as they aged, had children, and were necessarily drawn into school board and other community issues. When they became involved, they already possessed, as a consequence of their Scripture-based beliefs and their mentoring by people like Bright, Schaeffer, and Lindsey, an attraction to the pro-life movement and to the plight of the Jews that the Republican Party came to endorse.

As one analyzes the Christian Right, one realizes that the evangelical leaders eventually shaped their organizations to cater to the interests, ideals, and activism typical of countercultural Christians. This is not to say these operatives understood that their constituency had a countercultural background. It is to say, however, that they learned by trial and error to modify their platform so that it would accommodate the greater evangelical population, a population that had been heavily influenced by sixties' Christians. In the 1980s and 1990s, these newer Christians who now formed vibrant and fast-growing congregations, who attended services in jeans and T-shirts, and swayed to rock 'n' roll worship songs also went into the street to form human chains to protest abortion, registered like-minded believers for elections, and descended upon the voting booth with a mission to transform America.

10

The Christian Right and Its Sixties Inheritance

Francis Schaeffer had correctly perceived the importance of the abortion issue for galvanizing biblically grounded Christianity. Indeed, the abortion issue replaced communism as the jumping off point for evangelical political activism in the late 1970s. In the pro-life vs. pro-choice debate one finds some of the most radical political activists facing off.[1]

Indeed, it is here that some astute observers of the 1980s recognized the countercultural element in the anti-abortion movement. Tina Bell, for example, contributed an article to *Human Life Review* on Operation Rescue in 1988, and in it she readily identified anti-abortion activists as Christians with a countercultural twist. "The participants," she wrote, "are enthusiasts who've inherited the political legacies of the sixties. Many of the people I met both at rescues and evening rallies were young evangelical Christians who—with their blue-jeans, T-shirts and long hair—looked like the kind of people I saw when I went to Woodstock 20 years ago." And speaking of the leader of Operation Rescue, Randall Terry, she noted "he was only 14 when *Roe v Wade* legalized abortion. The claim cannot be made that the members of Operation Rescue—many of whom would have been undistinguishable in a crowd of '60s antiwar demonstrators—are protesting the demise of a *familiar* moral order. They grew up in the sixties and seventies!"[2]

As one investigates the background of anti-abortion activists in the Christian Right, one discovers many of them were very much a product of the sixties, although this is not to say they were all members of the early seventies' Jesus movement. For all of them, however, their coming of age in the counterculture shaped their activist character, even if they became evangelicals at a later date. Their battle against the pro-choice movement betrayed their countercultural origins as they formulated arguments in antitechnocratic terms, denouncing the minions of the "abortion industry" as heartless men and women of the medical establishment who lacked compassion and referred to human beings as mere "tissue" and to killing as a "medical procedure." At a "Meet the Abortion Providers" conference sponsored by the Pro-Life Action League in 1989, several abortionists who had become pro-life gave their testimonies and revealed as much.

Dr. Beverly McMillan, for example, was raised in a conservative Christian household but was not a fundamentalist or even a new evangelical by the late sixties. In Chicago, McMillan claimed to have been a radical feminist who in 1969 made her "decision to be an abortionist" in order to get involved and help women who chose abortion. She traveled to Mississippi to work with a group of concerned citizens and liberal clergy in running a clinic. While practicing there, she converted to biblically grounded Christianity and rejected the pro-choice position. Nonetheless, she maintained her spirit of activism. "In the fall of 1978," she said in 1989, "I was baptized and I resigned from the abortion mill. Today I am a sidewalk counselor and was the first ex-abortionist to be arrested and jailed for sitting in at an abortuary. I have been arrested three times for participating in rescue missions."[3]

There are, of course, other cases like McMillan's. Nita Whitten was not a physician, but she was an assistant who at one time worked in the Fairmount Center in Dallas, Texas, where abortions were performed. When she began her career there, she was "a radical feminist and completely pro-abortion," but as time went on, the abortion procedures troubled her.[4] In time, she used drugs and alcohol to get her through the day until she converted to biblically grounded Christianity, whereupon she then channeled her energies into the pro-life movement.

A countercultural Christian who had lived through the coffeehouse era and later became active in the pro-life movement was Melody Green, widow of musician Keith Green. Keith had originally encouraged Melody along this path by asking her to write an article for their Last Days Ministry magazine; the result was "Children, Things We Throw Away."[5] Three years after Keith's death in an airplane accident in 1982, Melody launched Americans Against Abortion "to educate the public, save babies' lives, and spare women the trauma of abortion." In 1987 Melody was received at the White House where she gave President Reagan a video she had made entitled "Baby Choice." Later that same year, she handed Reagan her part of the Petition for Life, the whole of which would be signed by nearly three million Americans. In 1988 she spoke at the Washington for Jesus rally that Pat Robertson also attended.[6]

Contemporary Christian music artists other than Keith Green supported the pro-life movement as well. Christian rocker Steve Taylor in his Meltdown album denounced the death of a downs syndrome newborn. "Respect A Woman's Choice," he sang defiantly, "I've heard that before; how can you ignore; this baby has a voice." He gave credit for his protest to Francis Schaeffer, stating that Schaeffer and Village Voice columnist Nat Hentoff had inspired him in developing "a foundational belief in the sanctity of human life."[7] Another contemporary Christian artist, Bruce Carroll, also condemned abortion when he sang that "sometimes miracles hide, and God will wrap some blessings in disguise."[8] Though handicapped at birth, his song narrates, a little girl's parents refuse the abortion option and let her live, and see her off to school one day. Without the Jesus movement, these politically charged songs—endorsed, bought, and played by the Christian Right—would not have been possible.

Other born-again countercultural youth became activists in Christian Right organizations. James Muffet who grew up as a non-Christian, though his family sporadically attended a

Southern Baptist Church, went, as he put it, "full-bore into the counter-culture as a hippie wanna-be, left-wing ideologue." He came to Christ at age twenty but said "I didn't discover my conservative political fire until I saw 'The Silent Scream' in 1980."[9] In the 1980s, Muffet entered the political arena, campaigning enthusiastically for Pat Robertson in Michigan. By 2006, he was director of the Foundation for Traditional Values, with its Student Statesmanship Institute, which trained young people so that biblically grounded values might live on into the next generation. As Muffet put it, "If we are successful in restoring values today, but neglect to teach them to our youth, we may have won the battle, but ultimately, we have lost the war." Also by 2006, Muffet was president of the Political Action Committee, Citizens for Traditional Values.[10]

Some of the pro-life organizations became extremist, using inflammatory rhetoric rejected by most evangelicals, suggesting even the use of force to transform America. Admittedly, Schaeffer had called for civil disobedience and rebellion, even stating that "the right of revolution is a part of the democratic process," but he stopped short of advocating violence against abortionists.[11] These younger radicals, however, went beyond Schaeffer. According to a 1998 article in the *Houston Chronicle*, pro-life militant Randall Terry stated that although he grieved for a Pensacola abortion doctor who had been murdered in 1993, he also grieved "for the thousands of children [the doctor had] murdered."[12] Another militant anti-abortion activist leader wrote, "Look closely at the pictures of the tortured dead babies. You will see there what motivates thousands of individuals in the United States today to think about blowing up abortion clinics and worse."[13]

This violent aspect of the Christian Right was beholden to the darker side of the counterculture. In the same way that certain sixties' youth could justify violence against those who advocated and practiced war or who denied civil rights to non-whites, some Christian Right activists justified violence against those who advocated and practiced, in their mind, murder.

Christian Right activist Neal Horsley was one of the most belligerent. But what was his background; was he a reactionary fundamentalist? In 1966, Horsley was discharged from the United States Air Force, and he moved to San Francisco where he became an enthusiastic participant in the counterculture. As he put it, "I thought by selling marijuana that I was helping construct a counterculture that would scare the people enough to move them to stop the war in Vietnam."[14] In due course, Neal was arrested and sent to prison, and it was there that he became a Christian. He then worked with Chuck Colson's Prison Fellowship from 1977 to 1985 and eventually graduated from Westminster Theological Seminary, the institution founded in the 1930s by J. Gresham Machen and attended by Francis Schaeffer.

In the 1980s Horsley became a vicious foe of abortion providers. According to journalist Marie McCullough, he admitted stating at Westminster, "The day will come when abortionists will be looking down the barrel of a gun. . . ."[15] Horsley's organization, The Creator's Rights Party, and his website Christian Gallery spoke admiringly of people who had committed violence against abortion providers.

Another activist who became a leader in the Christian Right was Flip Benham, director of Operation Save America, Randall's old Operation Rescue. Benham fits somewhere between Horsley's violent radicalism and Green's compassionate activism. After being discharged from the army in 1973, Benham moved to Florida where he ran the Mad Hatter Saloon. At that time, he was far removed from the pro-life movement, even encouraging his wife to terminate her pregnancy.[16] At the behest of a business acquaintance, however, Benham attended a religious service in a Free Methodist church. As a result of the sermon, Benham converted to biblically grounded Christianity. He attended Asbury Theological Seminary in Kentucky and then went to Dallas, in 1980, where he began his own Free Methodist church. Benham eventually shifted from being a biblically grounded Christian who was complacent about abortion to one viscerally opposed to it. "In seminary," Benham recalled, "we didn't talk much about abortion. We felt it was OK." In 1982, however, he changed his mind when he became convinced that human existence began at conception. The change of mind came when he was attending a Christian seminar. A speaker at the seminar had asked when the incarnation of Christ took place. "He said it was not with the birth of Jesus," remembered Benham, "but when the Holy Spirit visited Mary [and Jesus was conceived]. Instantly everything about abortion was changed for me."[17]

Benham took over Operation Rescue in 1994. This was the same year Benham yelled out to Norma McCorvey, the Jane Roe of *Roe v Wade*, who was signing copies of her autobiography at a bookstore, "Norma McCorvey, you are responsible for the deaths of over 33 million children." McCorvey herself eventually converted to biblically grounded Christianity and became another activist in the anti-abortion cause. She was baptized by Benham in 1995.[18]

The Anti-Gay Movement

Closely associated with the pro-life movement within the Christian Right was the anti-gay movement. Traditional evangelicals had made it an issue in 1977 when they walked out of President Carter's American Family Forum conference because liberal participants sought to include gay couples within the definition of family.[19] Countercultural Christians also joined the cause. In August of 1979 even Bob Dylan, who released an overtly Christian album *Slow Train*, blasted homosexuality in his concert at Tempe.[20] (Dylan's outspoken attachment to biblically grounded Christianity lasted into the rise of the Christian Right but faded in the mid-1980s.) In the 1980s another contemporary Christian singer, Scott Wesley Brown, in "This Little Child," also denounced homosexuality.

Other countercultural radicals who became Christians took an active role in opposing gay rights. Some of these proved to be quite vociferous and inflammatory in their denunciation of gays. In Oregon, for example, Lon Mabon became the campaign manager for Joe Lutz, a Baptist preacher, who unsuccessfully challenged Bob Packwood for his United States Senate seat in 1986. After the failed campaign, Mabon became the executive director of the anti-gay rights Oregon Citizens Alliance, created in early 1987. Mabon and his organization were considered by gay rights advocates to be a significant factor in convincing voters to support an initiative, Measure 8, which rescinded "an executive order banning discrimination in state employment on the basis of sexual orientation."[21] The initiative was later found to be unconstitutional by the Oregon Court of Appeals. Undaunted, Mabon, in 1992, presented Measure 9 to ban from public education anything "to promote, encourage, or facilitate homosexuality, pedophilia, sadism, or masochism." The voters rejected this measure 56 to 44 percent.[22] Mabon nevertheless continued to battle against gay rights during the 1990s and in 2002 made an unsuccessful bid for the United States Senate, stating in his campaign that "moral issues are the most important issues."[23]

But the question for us is, of course, from what milieu did Mabon hail? Was he a diehard fundamentalist from a fundamentalist past? The traditional histories of the Religious Right should lead us to think so. Such would be the wrong conclusion. Mabon was originally a Vietnam veteran turned hippie.[24] The same countercultural traits can be found in the background of other activists. Martin Mawyer, for example, who also opposed gay rights and in 1990 founded the Christian Action Network, had been an avid drug user in his youth.[25]

If these radical activists were products of the sixties, and had held countercultural values, one wonders how they balanced their virulent rhetoric with the countercultural golden rule ideal. In some cases one is tempted to conclude that they did not bother, just as Charles Manson did not bother. But we are not concerned with the Manson types, we are concerned with the Lennon types. Many of the radical activists who engaged in virulent rhetoric generally interpreted their passion as a passion not so much against abortionists or gays as much as a passion for the unborn and children, whom they feared gays would mislead and molest. But there were also those whose style was more in keeping with the Summer of Love, those who sought to dialogue with rather than abrasively confront women and men they deemed trapped in and bound by sin.

Countercultural Ideals in the Christian Right Era

Some Christians who had at one time been gay themselves became involved in ministries aimed at converting gays to a biblically grounded, and therefore straight, lifestyle. Obviously, inasmuch as their ministries supported biblically grounded values and endorsed Christian Right family values legislative proposals, these Christians can be considered part of the Christian Right even if their ministries were not political organizations. They are of interest to us because they demonstrate how baby-boomers-turned-evangelical-activists maintained the ideals of the counterculture; even though they denounced gay rights, they maintained that they held fast to the golden rule and expressive individualism, or freedom, as well as to an anti-technocratic spirituality.

David Kyle Foster is an example of the baby-boomer Christian who practiced, as he understood it, a respect for the golden rule ideal and expressive individualism even though he sought to undermine the gay and lesbian lifestyle. Before converting to biblically grounded Christianity in 1980, Foster had spent time in Hollywood and had a role in the teenage flick *Halloween* (1978). During his time in film, he lived a double life; a competitive actor during the day and a gay hustler by night. He also indulged in drugs and pursued a spiritual quest to make sense of his existence by studying under Guru Maharaj Ji.

Once converted to Christianity, Foster left Hollywood for ministerial training at Trinity Evangelical Divinity School and later at Trinity Episcopal School for Ministry for his doctorate. In 1987 he founded Mastering Life Ministries, an organization whose mission it was to deliver people from sexual sin. For Foster, homosexuality was an addiction, a lack of freedom. As he wrote in an autobiographical sketch some twenty years after his conversion, God "has healed those areas of sin and weakness that led me into bondage."[26] At the time of this writing, his ministry still pursues this mission, and the board of directors includes Pastor Jerry Bryant of Vineyard Christian Fellowship, a man who had been pastor to Melody and Keith Green's "Last Days" Community in the seventies.

Foster's understanding of homosexuality as a form of bondage was nothing new. It had been the position of countercultural Christians from the beginning. In 1972 street preacher Leo Humphrey prayed with a member of the Gay Liberation Front who had asked the evangelist to help get "the devil of homosexuality" off his back. The gay youth converted and began evangelizing others.[27] For the baby-boomer activists born of the counterculture, expressive individualism and the golden rule still figured prominently in their worldview.

Another group that opposed gay rights and upheld traditional marriage was Promise Keepers, which was endorsed and promoted in its early years by Focus on the Family. Detested by liberal organizations, Promise Keepers represented in the early 1990s the more widespread attitude of biblically grounded Christians toward the gay movement and family values. During that decade, the organization drew tens of thousands of evangelical men to mass meetings, claiming one million attended their 1997 Stand in the Gap gathering in Washington D.C.[28]

Promise Keepers, moreover, took a lead in bringing black and white evangelicals together. In 1997 the Promise Keepers publication *New Man*, for example, called upon whites to recognize their collective responsibility for racism and for blacks to respond to their repentance with forgiveness.[29] This golden rule message was preached and acted upon in their well-attended rallies.

It is also noteworthy that Promise Keepers chose as its first president Randy Phillips in 1991. Later, in 1997, Phillips became executive vice president of Promise Keepers' Global Ministry which had, as the name indicates, an international mission. The choice of Phillips is of interest here because the Promise Keepers' Web page of 2002 mentioned that he "came to know Christ during the 'Jesus Movement' of the 1970s."[30]

Countercultural Christians sincerely believed they were on a crusade to liberate people from a life of bondage, whether created by the shackles of drugs, sex, or prejudice, and to empower those set free to live out a meaningful life of expressive individualism.[31] And with these ideals and their activist dynamism, they had been, as shown by Melody Green and Phillips's examples, accepted into positions of influence in mainstream evangelicalism.

The Supernatural

But what of the commitment to the supernatural expressed during the sixties by so many youth; did it endure or become compartmentalized? To see if and how this ideal survived, it is best to investigate American society at the grassroots or local community level, where baby boomers, upon reaching middle age, found themselves increasingly empowered. The maturing baby-boomer generation was especially active in socio-political activism, and not just for the sake of opposing Planned Parenthood and abortion clinics. As parents, they attended school board meetings to voice their concerns about a variety of topics, not least of which were sex education and evolutionary theory. This latter topic is of special interest at the present.

Though baby boomers had been raised in public school to acknowledge evolutionary theory as fundamental to true science, they had in their conversion to biblically grounded Christianity rejected the scientism of the establishment that they believed underpinned the theory. Welcoming them into the world of evangelicalism were established creation scientists who shored up their grievances about scientism by providing them with well-honed arguments in favor of special creation and against the validity of the Darwinian model.

Unable to change the system, and confronted with legal challenges, parents often withdrew their children from public schools and contributed to the tremendous growth of homeschooling and private schooling, and ultimately to the growth of Christian colleges and universities. Many of those who sent their children into Christian schools lobbied government to help pay the cost of private schooling through tuition vouchers. As baby-boomer evangelicals, they wanted their children nurtured in a world where the supernatural was acknowledged in the whole of life and thought, the sciences not excepted. Their attitude, however, was not the one practiced by fundamentalists in the 1930s; these parents wanted their children well schooled both intellectually and spiritually so that they could enter worldly society to be active and influential representatives of Christ.

The struggle between the honest and godly few and the evil establishment, as exemplified in the battles fought in the field of education, was not a new one, nor was it one limited to local communities. It was an ongoing struggle, brought home most poignantly to the baby boomers by Hal Lindsey's *The Late Great Planet Earth*. But there were other writers too who quickened the sense of a supernatural face-off between good and evil in this world. C. S. Lewis, not an especially attractive author for the old-style fundamentalists and Pentecostals, connected with the college-educated baby-boomer Christians on this theme. His *Hideous Strength* and *Screwtape Letters* both revealed that the unseen but deadly forces of Satan strove to disempower the individual and overtake the world.

Writing along these lines, baby boomer Frank Peretti, who had grown up in an Assemblies of God church and been a Christian musician during the seventies, put his writing talents to work and penned *This Present Darkness*. Published in 1986, it was a phenomenal success. In this book, the supernatural, both evil and good, carried out battles affecting the actions of human beings in local politics and church life.[32] By the mid-1990s, when baby-boomers had reached middle age and hit the peak of their influence, Tim LaHaye and Jerry Jenkins released the *Left Behind* series, further emphasizing the role of the supernatural in national and international politics. Israel would not be abandoned.

Affluence

The supernatural ideal was not the only thing baby boomers, whether newly evangelical in the eighties or long-time evangelical since the sixties, valued. Whether of the counterculture or not, most baby boomers appreciated affluence. The plush auditorium churches with their high-dollar sound systems and professional quality entertainment were very much a product of this new membership in evangelicalism, and it all contrasted sharply with the sober meeting places and style of the pre-sixties era. By the 1980s, expenditures on God's place and God's people, including oneself, knew little bounds. On the other hand, to donate one's God-given wealth on public institutions deemed anti-evangelical was wasteful. The political conservatives found little difficulty in convincing this evangelical population, then, that smaller, less expensive government was better for all.

A focus on personal, individualistic spiritual fulfillment had always been the hippie quest, and it had survived. The "do your own thing" and "me" generations had made it into the church. The outgrowth of this mentality was evident not only in church architecture and interior design, it was also reflected in the songs, sermons, and prayers. The seeker-sensitive churches that gained strength in the nineties and early twenty-first century are reflective of this same bias. In 1992 these baby-boomer evangelicals created the Willow Creek Association, which, according to sociologist Kimon Sargeant, "stresses a subjectivist and therapeutic understanding of religious participation that is based less on duty or obligation and more on whether it meets people's needs."[33]

This is not to say these new arrivals to biblically grounded Christianity were selfish. They voluntarily gave to the needy, through missions usually, often traveling into less developed nations to participate in building projects or provide medical aid; and they donated time in their hometowns as well, perhaps counseling hesitant pregnant women to help them opt for a pro-life decision. However, to relegate this concern for others to the impersonal and ineffectual establishment, the government, would be poor judgment, if not sinful. The Great Society had been a secular humanist endeavor. The reason they could spend freely on themselves was the very same reason they could spend freely on the church and the impoverished of Central America. These were the same people who in their younger collegiate days could cash dad's check and live in a nice rental or, when money ran out, find a pad at a friend's place. As Christians, however, they perceived their affluence as part of God's grace, a blessing relegated to their management and enjoyment.

The Countercultural Christian Vote

Whether activists or simply voters, these affluent baby boomer evangelicals represented a double loss for the Democratic Party; that is, not only did the Democratic Party lose votes in its favor when baby boomers left the liberal church and the modernistic establishment it was identified with during the sixties and on through the nineties, but the competing Republican Party gained votes as well. To demonstrate this political shift, one need only compare the voting pattern among mainstream church members prior to the Jesus movement to the pattern in churches that had attracted baby boomers during and after the movement.

Larry Eskridge, who had been personally involved in the Jesus movement, did an in-depth historical study of the movement as associate director of Wheaton's Institute for the Study of American Evangelicals. From 1997 to 2004 he and David Di Sabatino, author of *The Jesus People Movement: An Annotated Bibliography and General Resource* (1999), conducted a survey of over eight hundred former Jesus People. A large majority of the respondents considered themselves to have been political moderates or liberals prior to their involvement with the Jesus movement, but at the time of the survey, over half considered themselves conservative. Very few considered themselves liberal. Once born again, these people changed their lifestyle, abandoning free sex and drugs for greater freedom, as they saw it, in Jesus. Such changes are unsurprising in people who had been raised in a secular humanist or liberal Christian household, but who later converted to biblically grounded Christianity as a rejection of their upbringing.

One notes that in three fast-growing congregations where there were a good number of countercultural Christians in attendance—at Calvary, Vineyard, and Hope—39 percent of the members claimed to have had either a liberal or Catholic upbringing and 25 percent had had either no church affiliation or something other than an evangelical or fundamentalist upbringing. By 1992, 70 percent of these congregants voted for George Bush and only 8 percent for Bill Clinton.[34] This voting pattern toward the right in large congregations is indicative of how the grassroots population of countercultural Christians voted.

The churches mentioned above were among some of the first megachurches to arise after the sixties. In his study of other megachurches, Scott Thumma, whose research was funded by the Louisville Institute Fellowship, noted some interesting characteristics associated with them. Though Baptists in the South had a number of such churches, he observed that "California had the highest concentration." Furthermore, and in keeping with results from the Eskridge-Sabatino survey, most of the membership came from other churches that had not measured up to the spiritual expectations of the postwar generation. On this point, Thumma quoted John Wimber, the founder of the Vineyard movement, who admitted that "God took us as he found us, broken-bodied refugees from various religious systems—and began to shape us. . . ."[35]

Thumma's observations about megachurch demographics and message also link these influential institutions to countercultural Christianity. In terms of membership, for example, he observed that most megachurches catered to well-educated, middle-class families of suburban America. In their doctrine, the megachurches had a conservative theological orientation, but a nontraditional approach to religious expression that communicated "a message that religion is not a thing apart from daily life."[36] One recalls that when Glenn Kittler visited the Jesus people at the height of the Jesus movement, he had taken note of Chuck Smith's message to the congregation that God is "talking to you all the time." Kittler found this a rather odd formulation, coming as he did from the mainstream paradigm that compartmentalized religion. But he remarked that this seamless spirituality was "the general conviction of the Jesus People."[37] It is no coincidence that the megachurches declaimed the same doctrine; it is simply a matter of origins.

More pertinent to the topic at hand, however, Thumma's study also revealed that megachurches leaned rightward in their politics. In Atlanta, where fundamentalism and the Jesus movement had both thrived, a megachurch publicly advertised its links to "Promisekeepers, the Pre-Tribulation Research Center, and the Christian Coalition." In 2005 the vast majority of megachurches were not politically active, but 83 percent said they were "somewhat" or "predominantly" conservative, and only 6 percent considered themselves liberal or somewhat liberal.[38]

Here, where baby-boomer liberal Christians and secular humanists often ended up as converts, Republicanism, which had given way to the Christian Right agenda, was the order of the day. It was more so in the churches of the greater evangelical movement. Admittedly, the churches themselves may not have technically been politically active, but when a minister promotes homeschooling, pro-life ideology, abstinence, and family values as part and parcel of the biblical message, he does not have to say the word "Republican."

Conclusion

It does not take one long to realize that many of the voters and activists of the Christian Right did not have an immediate fundamentalist, Pentecostal, or new evangelical background; rather, many were products of the counterculture.[39] Even those who had had a biblically grounded past had often gone into the counterculture before reemerging as Christian Right activists. One of the most surprising of these young people was, of course, Billy Graham's own son, Franklin. Some Christian Right activists, like Benham, had not been idealists when they practiced countercultural habits, but others like McMillan were steeped in sixties' idealism. Some important countercultural figures, like Bob Dylan or Eldridge Cleaver, did not become radical Christian Right activists in the late 1980s, but the fact that they had been symbols of the counterculture and then embraced evangelicalism (as when Dylan denounced homosexuality and Cleaver spoke at Falwell's church) furthered the melding of countercultural Christianity within evangelicalism and the Christian Right.[40]

The common denominator shared by many people voting with the Christian Right during the 1980s and into the 1990s was that they owed a debt to the counterculture inasmuch as they upheld, in their minds, the golden rule ideal, expressive individualism, intellectual sophistication, and an all-season antitechnocratic spirituality. They did not compartmentalize their faith, or cut off the spiritual dialogue with popular culture, or restrict themselves to customs of yesteryear, or neglect brothers and sisters in Central America who needed a church or home constructed. They had rejected the old mainstream, broken loose of the shackles of modernism, and reclaimed themselves and their godly potential in biblically grounded Christianity. They were heirs of the counterculture.

The radical connection between hippies and the Religious Right has not been considered in previous histories, and because of this, there is need of a careful restatement of what has been argued so that the claims presented here will not be misconstrued, exaggerated, or otherwise set up as straw men and casually dismissed.

Quite simply, it has been proposed that youth who engaged in the counterculture and eventually became Christians joined the larger evangelical community with their countercultural ideals intact and later supported and participated in the Christian Right. The counterculture was defined as a rejection of the modernist establishment, and it encompassed most of the baby boomers to some degree. Some of these rebels were political activists, most were simply trying to "do their own thing," to find themselves. As Barry Melton, guitarist for the politically attuned sixties' rock group Country Joe and The Fish, put it,

"There were two very different movements going on at this time. One was a political movement dedicated almost entirely to ending the war in Vietnam; the other movement was, if you will, a consciousness movement." And he observed that "the musicians in effect bridged the two movements."[41] There was protest music and there was music about love, peace, happiness, and the meaning of life, and so it was with the Jesus People music.

The Jesus movement, obviously, had much more to do with the second movement, the "consciousness movement." For the most part, then, we have not been following the radical political "fists," the Tom Haydens of the day, but rather the young people from all sorts of households who were seeking spiritual fulfillment. These youth, for the most part, rejected the science-calibrated establishment religion; they wanted the supernatural always present in their lives. This does not mean they rejected intellectual sophistication; in fact, they wanted their faith to flow logically and seamlessly into their everyday lives and be existentially and eternally authentic. Their rebellion consisted of throwing off secular humanism, liberal theology, and, yes, the establishment trappings of conservative churches, wherever religion had been cut off and compartmentalized; this is why they seized upon the "hippie Jesus" they found in Scripture.

Once born again, these Christians insisted on an approach to Scripture that focused on its authentic relevance and on the perennial significance of their Lord. Francis Schaeffer showed them how this could be so, and in a manner they had never been shown before. Young people from non-evangelical homes had never heard this presentation, this intellectually sophisticated blending of faith and life; for them it was revolutionary, it overturned the older generation's doctrines. For youth who had been raised as fundamentalists or Pentecostals, but who had rejected their parents' ways as too stifling and had abandoned themselves to the counterculture, Schaeffer's proclamation that the Christian could engage all of life was literally music to their ears, even if that music was initially discordant to their parents' ears.

These youths, with all their struggles with the older generation, were certainly committed to the counterculture and to rock 'n' roll, drugs, and premarital sex as a form of protest. But they did not cease being countercultural simply because they found religion, any more than a Hare Krishna did, or a Timothy Leary steeped in his acid enlightenment. On the contrary, one might better make the argument that the countercultural Christians had done what few other hippies accomplished: in converting, most countercultural Christians claimed that they fulfilled their spiritual quest.

Born again, the Jesus Freaks carried forth their countercultural ideals, living for the golden rule and expressive individualism; now converted, they lived these things in a way that they interpreted to be infinitely and eternally liberating and meaningful because they experienced them through the infinite, creative, eternal, and very personal spirit of God. The first Jesus People had, before their born-again experience, indulged in free love and drugs and found such things binding and limiting. Upon conversion, they passionately argued that anyone addicted to sex or drugs was not free but enslaved. One may or may not agree with this rendition of expressive individualism and freedom, but no one ought to deny that countercultural Christians held this perspective.

Once we established that the Jesus people, these hippie Christians, were indeed countercultural, clung to their values, and lived out their faith in a way that defied mainstream religion, we next considered their catalytic effect on traditional evangelicalism. Their impact was immediate. Once born again, Jesus People by and large attended local evangelical churches. As the Eskridge-Sabatino survey indicated, over 80 percent of the Jesus People respondents admitted that upon conversion they entered into a local church.[42] Only a small percentage actually lived in communes, but many of these were affiliated with a church. Within greater evangelicalism, the Jesus People impacted like-minded Christians. They were the pop stars of sixties' and seventies' Christianity, and evangelically raised youth wanted not only to bask in their light, they wanted to be stars themselves.

These churched youth, however, did not need to go on a spiritual quest in the same manner as their heroes had done. Biblically grounded young people were already outsiders to mainstream religion; they already understood the supernatural as being active within their daily life; but they were uncomfortable with the unnecessary kowtowing their parents did to the establishment: the predictable music, the conventional suit and tie, the conformist short hair, etc. Their rebellion was against outward appearances rather than against the inward spirituality. These fellow travelers quickly became influential in the Jesus movement because they were well read in the Bible and understood spiritual living; it must not be denied, however, that they too, in their defiance and in their spirituality, partook of countercultural Christianity.

By the late 1970s, churches across the country had been altered by the Jesus movement effect. Liberal churches lost younger members to biblically grounded ones and biblically grounded ones had begun exchanging organs for guitars and hymns for praise music. If not members of evangelical churches, the countercultural Christians formed their own assemblies, some of which became megachurches that reflected, in a way, the Woodstock spirit of the sixties.

By this time in our narrative, however, it was hard to keep thinking of this new generation of believers as "countercultural Christians." The counterculture faded after Watergate. A better term with which to denote countercultural Christianity was "baby boomer Christianity," because many of the new converts, though indelibly marked by their counterculture experience, never encountered street evangelists or Christian nightclubs and only found Jesus after the counterculture's demise, that is, in the late seventies, eighties, and even in the nineties. Nevertheless, the baby boomer who came to know Christ in this period believed, just as the Jesus People had, that he or she too, though perhaps "as one untimely born," had finally ended a spiritual quest and begun life anew.

It would be naive to maintain that the countercultural values first espoused by the Jesus People remained inviolate during the eighties and nineties. For one thing, when Christ failed to make a reappearance on earth forty years after the prophetic reestablishment of the state of Israel, the feeling of urgency, common among baby boomer evangelicals, dissipated. Then, as these Christians aged, left campuses and street life, and took on familial, household, and bread-winning responsibilities, their connection to popular youth culture waned. Under these new conditions, certain aspects of the technocracy lost their threatening edge and became tolerable. Even in church, baby-boomer Christians were now in charge of such mundane things as personnel management, building maintenance, and budget considerations; here, they too could reproduce or maintain the trappings of the old ecclesiastical establishment.

Furthermore, as much as the baby-boomer Christians had wanted to dispense with unnecessary customs in the traditional evangelical churches, they often found themselves accommodating a more conventional style as the years passed. This was perhaps less of a fact in the denominational churches directly born of countercultural Christianity—such as the Vineyard fellowship and the nondenominational churches—than it was in long-established and proudly denominational ones. Nonetheless, the nature of the movement shifted as time went on. By the nineties, country communes were definitely out and suburban megachurches were in and growing.

Along with this phenomenal evangelical growth came the Christian Right. Here too we need to define rather carefully what we are talking about. By "Christian Right" I have referred to two interlinked phenomena, one specific in nature and the other general. In the first instance, the designation referred to a religio-political movement launched by leaders of political organizations, such as Robert Grant of Christian Voice, Jerry Falwell of Moral Majority, and Pat Robertson of the Christian Coalition. Secondly, the Christian Right denoted people and organizations who endorsed or voted for issues that the Christian Right political organizations generally promoted. With this larger definition, churches, parachurch ministries, and missions were considered part of the Christian Right movement. In both definitions, I have focused on the evangelical aspect of the Christian Right (as opposed to the Catholic aspect) not because evangelicals dominated the Christian Right, though they did, but because it was through evangelicalism that the hippie Jesus Freaks and their fellow travelers entered into Religious Right politics.

Now with the arguments restated, it is important to insist upon the fact that there are, indeed, good reasons for properly understanding the nature and development of biblically grounded Christianity. Historians and political observers have misread biblically grounded Christianity before and tossed it off as a cultural dinosaur well on its way to extinction. Then came Jimmy Carter who raised more than a few eyebrows with his "born again" confession. Then came Jerry Falwell with his Moral Majority that left mainstream America agape. If we fail to understand the countercultural ideals that have made their way into the religio-political world of biblically grounded Christianity, historians and political scientists may well be surprised yet again. One can see the possibility dawning upon the political horizon of this new century.

Epilogue

In the turmoil of the sixties, there were, of course, countercultural Christians who expressed their faith through leftist political activism. Theirs is a fascinating history, but it is not part of this story. Here, we have been solely interested in countercultural Christians who contributed to the Religious Right.

Nevertheless, mention should be made of the evangelical left because the evangelical left and the evangelical right are both part of biblically grounded Christianity. Indeed, just as mainstream political observers of the 1960s should not have overlooked the culturally astute message of new evangelicals at that time, so we ought not ignore alternative biblically grounded Christian voices in our own day.

In analyzing the two sorts of evangelical socio-political expressions coming out of the counterculture, one might suggest that countercultural youth who went into the Christian Right were drawn by the "do your own thing" side of the counterculture while the leftists were partial to the "commune" mentality. The first group would be happy with affluence, vote down tax increases, and doggedly defend their individual rights; the second would feel guilty about being wealthy, vote for more government programs to help the poor, and defend pluralism. The radical evangelical Jim Wallis might agree with this description, but it falls short. It fails to highlight the underlying compatibility between the two groups.

Another spokesman for the evangelical left, Ron Sider, had better insight into the relationship between these two socio-political expressions of evangelicalism after having attempted to win over the other side to his views. Sider had gone to L'Abri and discussed his vision of a community-oriented, empathetic, and committed evangelicalism with Schaeffer's successors. His arguments were not persuasive, and he lamented this fact because, as he put it, "Francis Schaeffer—I'm so *close* to him!" What Sider meant by this is that all biblically grounded Christians are obliged to engage their faith in every aspect of life, being responsible to God, to each other, and to the world. This is what Schaeffer preached, and this concept is resident in greater evangelicalism. Sider's belief, then, was that if all evangelicals focused on the Bible in their socio-political life, they would find much common ground. Sider was right, but it is only in understanding the Christian Right with its countercultural inheritance that the shared values can be fully appreciated and perhaps exploited by the left.

Indeed, because of the legacy, the possibility for a renewal of the social gospel as Quebedeaux had once hoped for is not gone. Even back in 1988, Robert Wuthnow recognized the neo-conservative interest in social action, prompted no doubt by the evangelical constituency.[1] By 1997 the Christian Coalition launched the Samaritan Project which called for, among other things, legislation to give taxpayers a five hundred-dollar tax credit for helping the poor, and to provide public money for poor children to attend private schools.[2]

In sum, social justice has become a subject of religio-political concern for post-sixties' evangelicals. Prior to the advent of countercultural Christians, evangelicals separated themselves from liberals by focusing almost solely on evangelism and by generally ignoring religio-political activism for social causes. Liberal clergy, on the other hand, ignored evangelism and devoted themselves to promoting social justice.[3] The definition of evangelicalism is no longer so clear-cut.

It is the countercultural roots of the Christian Right that explain the renewed interest in social causes by evangelicals.

Evangelist Leighton Ford had picked up on this in the early seventies and wrote *One Way to Change the World* to tap into this compassionate sensitivity that emanated from the younger generation. In his well-attended Rochester crusade he preached, "I believe the 'sweet bye and bye' and the nasty here and now belong together."[4] This is why the enemies of the Christian Right—who deplored its defense spending, tax cutting, welfare-stripping mentality—if they had better understood the countercultural inspiration coursing through the evangelical spirit, might have redirected the political activism of some of those evangelicals toward an agenda more favorable to the Left. Republicans understood this vulnerability, and this is why, in part, presidential candidate George W. Bush deemed it wise in 2000 to campaign on behalf of "compassionate conservatism."

In spite of what Wallis may say to the contrary, the evangelical who lives in the suburb is usually community-oriented; the community is the church, the immediate neighborhood, and the mission field. It is true that these suburbanite Christians are not living amongst the poor and donating all their time and money to the least well off, but they are nonetheless community-oriented and ministering to the needs of those around them as well as to the distant poor. Large minded evangelical, political leaders who realize that all biblically grounded Christians are concerned about their communities, even if the communities differ in terms of material well-being, will have the potential to generate a new socio-political movement.

Given the fact that the postmodern era, with its fragmentation and lack of direction, has now been supplanted by the 9/11 world, there is motive and opportunity for the launching of another campaign. In the 9/11 world, society is searching for a new propriety, not a Victorian one to be sure, but a global propriety, wherein citizens of the world will observe a common ethics based upon a common values system. What this value system will be and what the derivative ethics might be are unknown.

Given, however, the Western shadow over the world, and its promotion of fundamental political concepts such as the separation of church and state and the respect for opposing views within the body politic, the evangelicals are not poorly positioned. Such concepts, derived, as they can be, from scriptural principles, "give to Caesar what is Caesar's, and to God what is God's" and "turn the other cheek" or "love your enemies," can be given an anchor by a people who believe in a biblically grounded God, but only if they also give voice and deed to the scriptural injunctions to care for the hungry, the thirsty, the stranger, the naked, the sick, and imprisoned. If they do not focus on these evangelical commandments, the less impoverished nations will be tempted to develop or nurture an alternative worldview and ethics system. Evangelicals, left or right, will need to convince themselves and others that these are principles to advocate and practice.

If evangelicals do recalibrate their biblically grounded message for the twenty-first century, they may not necessarily abandon their suburbs for the inner cities. But in light of their countercultural inheritance, they will ask that they as Christians be allowed to live out their faith in word and deed whether on a mission field, on a school board, on a judicial bench, in the Peace Corps, or with a United Nations agency. Because of the counterculture, this world is their world, and today's biblically grounded Christians do not appear to be on the verge of sequestering themselves as they did after the Scopes Trial.

One might argue that the Christian Right rejects the separation of church and state and democratic values and seeks to reconstruct the United States as an Old Testament-styled theocracy, and take dominion over every aspect of Americans' lives. As sociologist Sara Diamond pointed out in the early 1990s, however, this is not mainstream evangelicalism. Indeed, such theocratic ideas emerged from the writings of Rousas John Rushdoony, who founded a reactionary organization, the Chalcedonian Foundation, in California during the sixties in order to counter the counterculture by reconstructing society within a biblical framework. Baby-boomer Christians, however, are predominantly conversionists, wholly committed to the idea that people must, of their own free will, select their freedom in Christ.[5] Most evangelicals, in fact, know less about the reconstructionists than do liberal opponents who fear the worst, in part because liberal alarmists do not fully understand the nature of greater evangelicalism.

Are there signs of a socio-political reformulation of evangelicalism? There are. Allowance for homeschooling and the expansion of tuition vouchers, which makes it possible for poorer children to attend private schools, shows the government is willing to negotiate.[6] Obviously judicial appointments to the Supreme Court will be the determining factor in how quickly and radically laws will be interpreted or reinterpreted to allow for society to accommodate today's politically savvy religionists. But if compassionate conservatism is to keep evangelicalism leaning rightward, it will have to make a greater demonstration of its capacity to mind the needs of the sick and impoverished.

As mentioned above, the attempt to attune the political right to social needs has been made. Marvin Olasky, former countercultural communist who converted during the Jesus movement era, became an advisor to George W. Bush and promoted the idea of compassionate conservatism in Bush's first presidential campaign.[7] However, the Bush administration has so far failed to convince most Americans, including most evangelicals, that it has successfully empowered local, faith-based ministries to solve the country's social dilemmas.

To the delight of biblically grounded Christians on the left, certain megachurches, those institutions most immediately shaped by countercultural Christianity, have already begun to raise a new standard. Ted Haggard, pastor of a megachurch and president of the NAE, voiced his support for initiatives to address global warming. Such a position, of course, might lead evangelicals to support increased taxes to address global warming, greater government control over businesses, and a willingness to partnership with non-evangelicals in a worldwide community. When informed of this in 2004, Jim Wallis wrote with enthusiasm that "the NAE adopted a new policy statement 'For the Health of the Nation: An Evangelical Call to Civic Responsibility,' which included a principle titled 'We

Labor to Protect God's Creation.'"[8] Although Haggard would lose both his pastorship and presidency due to his involvement in a drug and sex scandal, his socio-political ideas would live on, especially in certain megachurches.

Complementing this openness to the notion of solidarity, which could lead to a leftist reorientation of evangelicalism, is the factor of hispanic immigration. The new Americans tend not only to be more religious, on the whole, than the American population at large, but their Catholicism is not far removed from Arminianism. This has provoked a tremendous number of conversions in Latin America to Pentecostal and charismatic churches, which means that many of the new arrivals are already a part of evangelicalism, and through proselytism the number of Hispanic evangelicals is growing on this side of the border. Furthermore, the hispanics' cultural connections to Latin America's less developed countries will reinforce the commitment to solidarity.

The number of hispanic converts into the charismatic expression of Christianity will reshape evangelicalism and bolster the number and political power of biblically grounded Christians. The irony of this immigration phenomenon is that traditional evangelicals look askance at the newcomers, believing that they will water down and ultimately dismantle the few remaining biblical principles that inform American government and culture. Most evangelicals object to the immigration because it is illegal, but at the same time they are not lobbying to increase the number of legal immigrants, and many are adamantly opposed to Spanish becoming commonplace, especially for voting purposes. When the Family Research Council polled its readers in 2006, over 91 percent of its eight thousand respondents believed that "illegal immigrants should be returned to their country of origin." Ninety-two percent thought "that election ballots should be printed only in English."[9]

Coinciding with this demographic shift is the emergence of the next generation of evangelicals. The baby-boomer evangelicals will leave their heritage, and evangelicalism will be intellectually sophisticated as well as practical in answering needs, but the new generation is likely to emphasize inclusion, taking care of the outsiders, the poor, the aged, and those unjustly disenfranchised because of their ethnicity, all of which will mesh well with hispanic-influenced evangelicalism.[10] It is even foreseeable that a global evangelical culture will be a force to be reckoned with.

This may mean a left-leaning, but no less dynamic and zealous, political expression of evangelicalism. The shift, however, is possible because of the conversionist emphasis of evangelicalism. If the choice is between remaining faithful to a political expression or bringing salvation to a greater number of individuals by abandoning that expression, the latter course will be followed if well articulated by an evangelical leader with a socio-political vision. One must never forget that biblically grounded Christians are not only devoted to God and the church but also to those they consider spiritually astray. If socio-political activism is proven to them to be not only biblical but also necessary to win the souls of the lost, they will endorse it, just as Billy Graham gave his blessing to the Jesus Generation in the early 1970s.

Ever since the coming of the Jesus Freaks, born of the generation gap and the rebellion against the technocratic establishment, evangelicalism has been injected with an activist fervor that encompasses the whole of life. That activism and commitment stimulated and nurtured the Christian Right.[11] This has been the argument.[12] The Christian Right, therefore, should not be simply viewed as a reactionary movement fomented by enraged fundamentalists who had finally come round to rebelling against the sixties. Although this was true for some, the Christian Right was also an extension of the sixties' counterculture, and without this perspective we cannot adequately explain the all-encompassing activism of the Religious Right.[13]

The greatest irony of the traditional interpretation of the Christian Right as a negative reaction to the sixties' counterculture is that most evangelicals agreed with such a definition in the late 1970s and still agree with it today. And with this understanding, they confidently stand dismissive of the sixties' counterculture. But if it had not been for the counterculture, there may never have been a Christian Right, because the counterculture gave to evangelicalism the rebellious spirit, the youthful activists, and the committed voters it so needed. Given this fact, since biblically grounded Christians apply all Scripture to their own condition, they might do well, when considering the counterculture, and perhaps the latest wave of immigration, to heed the Apostle Paul's words to the first Christians of Rome, "We know that in all things God works for the good of those who love him, who have been called according to his purpose."[14] In the sixties, the counterculture indeed appeared as a threat to biblically grounded Christians, but in the end it turned out to be an agent for future success.

Notes

Introduction

1 Billy Graham, *Just As I Am: The Autobiography of Billy Graham* (New York: HarperPaperBacks, 1997), 835.

2 For an excellent treatment of the term "counterculture," see Arthur Marwick, *The Sixties* (New York: Oxford University Press, 1998). Marwick emphasizes that "countercultural" youth were also part and parcel of mainstream society. I would agree with this assessment, but I am underscoring their conscious and sometimes subconscious objections to certain aspects of mainstream culture, especially its spirituality.

3 See Nina Easton, *Gang of Five: Leaders at the Center of the Conservative Crusade* (New York: Simon & Schuster, 2000), 147.

4 Historians generally do recognize a relationship between the mood of the sixties and the spiritually inspired politics of the seventies and eighties, but they view the Christian Right as reactionary. See, for example: Kenneth Wald, *Religion and Politics in the United States* (New York: St. Martin's, 1987), 210; Robert Wuthnow, *The Restructuring of American Religion: Society and Faith since World War II* (Princeton: Princeton University Press, 1988), 245; George Marsden, *Religion and American Culture* (New York: Harcourt Brace Jovanovich, 1990), 262; Mark Noll, *A History of Christianity in the United States and Canada* (Grand Rapids: Eerdmans, 1992), 445; and Robert Ellwood, *The Sixties Spiritual Awakening: American Religion Moving from Modern to Postmodern* (New Brunswick: Rutgers University Press, 1994), 39. In summarizing the rise of the Christian Right in 2001, Dale McConkey wrote, "After a half-century of self-imposed exile from

American politics, culturally conservative Christians came out of the political closet in the 1970s, attempting to counter what they saw as the country's steady drift away from traditional values toward moral relativism" ("Whither Hunter's Culture War? Shifts in Evangelical Morality, 1988–1998," *Sociology of Religion* 62 [2001]: 152).

Chapter 1

1 Stromberg (1916–2004) extended his critique of *neophilia* to Europe and described it as a plague that by the 1980s had infected most traditional university departments. See Roland Stromberg, *European Intellectual History since 1789* (Englewood Cliffs, N.J.: Prentice Hall, 1994), 313.

2 Vance Packard in *The Status Seekers* (1959) described the conformity prevalent in American society. He also described the American desire for individualism. Although Packard objected to status lines in society aimed at maintaining stability, he did so only because he believed they denied many talented Americans, black Americans especially, the possibility of achieving the American Dream. See Daniel Horowitz, ed., *American Social Classes in the 1950s: Selections from Vance Packard's "The Status Seekers"* (Boston: Bedford/St. Martin's, 1995), 173–90.

3 David Farber correctly observes that even the older generation was pushing apart the seams of convention by 1960, but it should be underscored that the youth of the sixties took their "ideal of unrestrained pleasure" to a height that most of the older generation would not have dared (*The Age of Great Dreams* [New York: Hill & Wang, 1994], 17).

4 Thomas Bailey, David Kennedy, and Lizabeth Cohen, *The American Pageant*, vol. 2, *Since 1865*, 11th ed. (New York: Houghton Mifflin, 1998), 544–55.

5 On the "shifting emphasis of the nation's economy from production to consumption," see Benjamin Rader, *American Ways: A Brief History of American Cultures* (New York: Harcourt College, 2001), 185–92.

6 This was especially true among middle-class women. Two well-known works of the era that make a statement against conventional restraints upon behavior are Charlotte Gilman's "The Yellow Wallpaper" (1892) and Kate Chopin's *The Awakening* (1899). (It should be noted that I extend the Victorian era past the death of Queen Victoria [1901] up to the First World War, because, as others have noted, modernism did not emerge with full vigor until the advent and aftermath of the Great War.)

7 Otis Graham Jr., *A Limited Bounty: The United States since World War II* (New York: McGraw-Hill, 1996), 80–81.

8 The preoccupation with growth and prosperity as a prerequisite to social and political stability can be found in the works of scholars of the 1950s and 1960s, including Daniel Bell, W. W. Rostow, C. E. Black, and Robert Lane. See David Hollinger and Charles Capper, eds., *The American Intellectual Tradition*, vol. 2, *1865 to the Present* (New York: Oxford University Press, 1993), 286.

9 On the ethical assumptions of the leaders of mainstream culture, see Amanda Porterfield, *The Transformation of American Religion* (Oxford: Oxford University Press, 2001), 2–3.

10 Robert Ellwood observes that modernism "requires an elite vanguard that most completely fulfills its requisites for education, scientific/technological expertise, and the management of a complex unitary state, marginalizing many other people in terms of where the action is, and where the rewards are" (*Sixties Spiritual Awakening*, 22). He also points out that the media generally ran favorable stories on mainline churches and respectable mainline clergy (48).

11 My definition is in agreement with that of Ellwood: "A major sixties theme was the human against the System. . . . [And] . . . the System inevitably meant what was created by modern ideals of unity, rationalization, and scientific/technological progress—all of which were now seen, as in Vietnam, as having become a mechanical monster out of all human control" (*Sixties Spiritual Awakening*, 29).

12 For a discussion of the background of this term and its usage, see the "Translator's Introduction" in Jacques Ellul, *The Technological Society*, trans. by John Wilkinson (New York: Vintage Books, 1964), ix–xx. Of course Ellul himself provides an excellent discussion in his opening notes, preface, and first chapter.

13 It is of interest that many biblically grounded Americans considered Ellul to be in some ways an evangelical, although perhaps less so than C. S. Lewis.

14 Howard Brick gives a list of stereotypical features often attributed to modern society. The list spells out what is referred to here as the technocratic ideal and includes "science over religion, technical specialization over generalized knowledge, individualism over solidarity, impersonal efficiency over sentimental ties" (*Age of Contradiction* [Ithaca: Cornell University Press, 1998], 65).

15 On the elite, see Ellwood, *Sixties Spiritual Awakening*, 12.

16 David Farber argues that the theme of "efficient economic production" was at odds with another theme in society during the fifties and sixties, that of "expansive personal consumption" (*Age*

of Great Dreams, 4). I do not disagree with this analysis, and I refer to the latter theme as part of the inspiration behind expressive individualism. Larry Eskridge points out that films of the 1950s depicted non-conforming youth sympathetically "while parents and other authority figures came off as materialistic, self-absorbed, inflexible and small-minded" ("God's Forever Family: the Jesus People Movement in America, 1966–1977" [Ph.D. diss., University of Stirling, 2005], 47).

17 William Link and Arthur Link, *American Epoch: A History of the United States since 1900*, vol. 2, *Affluence and Anxiety: 1940–1992* (New York: McGraw-Hill, 1993), 509–10. Gilbreth's children Frank Gilbreth Jr. and Ernestine Carey published *Cheaper by the Dozen* in 1949; their amusing reminiscences of their childhood with parents devoted to time-and-motion study came out as a film in 1950. For the parents' work see Frank Gilbreth, *Motion Study: A Method for Increasing the Efficiency of the Workman* (New York: D. Van Nostrand, 1911).

18 Theological liberals denounced pure scientism, as will be pointed out. The definition given here is consistent with that of J. Edward Carothers, former head of the national missions agency of the United Methodist Church. See his *The Paralysis of Mainstream Protestant Leadership* (Nashville: Abingdon Press, 1990), 12.

19 By the early years of the twentieth century, Ronald Numbers observes, "scientifically trained creationists . . . had become an endangered species. . . ." (*The Creationists: The Evolution of Scientific Creationism* [Berkeley: University of California Press, 1992], xiv).

20 The Enlightenment thinkers in America did not generally criticize religion, but they did disdain superstition. See Lewis Perry, *Intellectual Life in America* (Chicago: University of Chicago Press, 1989), 149–56. See also Marsden, *Religion and American Culture*, 31–34.

21 On the secularization of American culture, see Marsden, *Religion and American Culture*, 101–4. On the conception of a scientific objectivity until the 1960s, see Allan Megill, ed., *Rethinking Objectivity* (London: Duke University Press, 1994), 3.

22 Marsden, *Religion and American Culture*, 129.

23 An exposition of this view was again given in 1993 by Karl Giberson, then teaching the history of science at Eastern Nazarene College near Boston. Giberson's fundamental opinion does not seem to differ from that of most Victorian Christians. Karl Giberson, *Worlds Apart: The Unholy War Between Religion and Science* (Kansas City, Mo: Beacon Hill Press, 1993), 216–21.

24 On the dichotomous style of Victorian thinking, see Rader, *American Ways*, 150–51.

25 The success of this natural law approach by Christians was marked early on by William Paley's *Evidences of the Existence and Attributes of the Deity*, published in 1802. Also associated with liberals in twentieth-century mainstream culture were the agnostics, such as Clarence Darrow, who stated that there was no purpose or design for forms and formations. See his "The Delusion of Design and Purpose," in *A Modern Introduction to Philosophy: Readings from Classical and Contemporary Sources*, 3rd ed., ed. Paul Edwards and Arthur Pap (New York: The Free Press, 1973), 446–53.

26 Examples of mainstream churchmen who attempted to humanize modern society are many. Liberal Christians, for example, pushed for legislation to bring about desegregation. See Ronnie Dugger, "Texas Christians Stem the Tide," *The Christian Century* 74 (July 31, 1957): 912–15. But see also: Leonard Duhl, "Urbanization and Human Needs," *The Christian Century* 81 (July 22, 1964): 930–33, and Wayne Hartmire Jr., "Farm Workers on the Fringe," *The Christian Century* 81 (July 29, 1964): 959–62.

27 Daniele Hervieu-Leger argues that religion cannot be bottled up into a tidy sphere; certain aspects of it will always spill out into areas of life normally thought to be secular. See her *Religion as a Chain of Memory* (New Brunswick: Rutgers University Press, 2000), 108–11.

28 In 1924 E. Y. Mullins, president of Southern Baptist Theological Seminary, Louisville, argued in *Christianity at the Cross Roads* (1924) that religion was concerned with "personal relation" and not with philosophy and science. See George Marsden, *Fundamentalism and American Culture: The Shaping of Twentieth-Century Evangelicalism, 1870–1925*, new edition (New York: Oxford University Press, 2006), 216. [All citations to Marsden, *Fundamentalism* in the notes is from the 2006 edition].

29 It is interesting to note that the erudite theological conservative J. Gresham Machen equivocated between calling his opponents' religion liberalism or modernism. He apparently felt more comfortable when he defined it, in his seminal 1923 work, by the phrase "modern naturalistic liberalism," which wording emphasized liberalism's warm relationship with a radically secular practice of scientific inquiry. See his *Christianity and Liberalism* (Grand Rapids: Eerdmans, 1923; repr. 1946), 2–3.

30 An interesting article in *The Christian Century* demonstrates that liberals recognized that mainstream culture reflected their religious thinking. According to Virgil Rogers, "It must be concluded

that the churches and the schools have separate functions. . . ." Then he adds "no principle underlying the American public school system is in conflict at any point with the Judeo-Christian ethic" ("Are the Public Schools 'Godless?'" *The Christian Century* 74 [September 11, 1957]: 1067).

31 Biblically grounded believers often argued that their intellectual decision to believe in the authority and inerrancy of the Bible was corroborated by a religious experience wherein God confirmed their decision. Liberals believed in religious experiences but did not believe such experiences validated a belief in biblical inerrancy. Secular humanists believed religious experiences to be of wholly human origin. A curious account is given by the secular humanist art historian Kenneth Clark, author and narrator of the influential television series entitled *Civilization* (1969). Clark claimed he underwent "a kind of heavenly joy, far more intense than anything I had known before. This state of mind lasted for several minutes, and, wonderful though it was, posed an awkward problem in terms of action. . . . I would have to reform. . . . Gradually the effect wore off and I made no effort to retain it. I think I was right: I was too deeply embedded in the world to change course. But that I had 'felt the finger of God' I am quite sure and, although the memory of this experience has faded, it still helps me to understand the joys of the saints." See Stuart Babbage, "Lord Kenneth Clark's Encounter with 'The Motions of Grace,'" *Christianity Today* 23 (June 8, 1979): 28.

32 For a comment on this technique of rationalizing miracles, see C. Milo Connick's college textbook, *The New Testament: An Introduction to Its History, Literature, and Thought*, 2nd ed. (Encino, Calif.: Dickenson, 1972), 173–74. Also, it should be added that liberals believed the symbolism of a myth or miracle had importance for guiding faith. According to Morton Kelsey, the "mythological elements [of the New Testament] can be understood as intrusions by the objective nonphysical world into the physical one." See his "Is the World View of Jesus Outmoded?" *The Christian Century* 86 (January 22, 1969): 115.

33 J. V. Langmead Casserley, *The Death of Man: A Critique of Christian Atheism* (New York: Morehouse-Barlow, 1967), 144.

34 Herbert Welch, "Do You Believe in Love?" in *Best Sermons,* ed. G. Paul Butler (New York: MacMillan, 1952), 161, 163.

35 Reinhold Niebuhr, *Faith and History* (New York: Charles Scribner's Sons, 1951), 233–34.

36 Harry Fosdick, "The Fundamentalist Controversy," in *Memoirs of the Spirit*, ed. Edwin Gaustad (Grand Rapids: Eerdmans, 1999), 134.

37 Reinhold Niebuhr, *Leaves From the Notebook of a Tamed Cynic [1929]* (Louisville: Westminster/John Knox, 1990), 76–77. I include the neo-orthodox theologians within liberalism not only because of their ultimate belief in the potential of the individual to overcome evil, but also because neo-orthodox and liberal theologians alike viewed the Bible in symbolic terms and used modern scientific understanding to help them understand and express faith. See Porterfield, *Transformation of American Religion*, 3–4, 36. Parenthetically, Niebuhr's insistence on selfless love that "did not expect a return in kind" is a Protestant and especially Calvinist emphasis that is found in both biblically grounded and liberal Christianity. Faith and works soteriologies, such as that taught by the Catholic Church, emphasize a give-and-receive understanding of love that is more akin to the European concept of solidarity, so dear to the new immigrant community in late Victorian America.

38 Bernard Meland, professor of constructive theology at the University of Chicago's Divinity School, also saw grace and forgiveness, as symbolized in the crucifixion, as the foundation of ethics. Reviewing Meland's book, *Higher Education and the Human Spirit*, Union Theological Seminary's Daniel Williams noted that Meland "moved within the liberal stream of theology but that his development follows the tendencies of theology in our time. He has come to assert that the Christian message of divine grace and forgiveness affords the real foundation of meaningful existence" ("Liberal Theology Reconstructed," *The Christian Century* 81 [December 2, 1964]: 1496).

39 For an example of this, see Wayne Hartmire Jr., "Farm Workers on the Fringe," *The Christian Century* 81 (July 29, 1964): 959–62.

40 Arnold Toynbee, *An Historian's Approach to Religion* (New York: Oxford University Press, 1956), 143–44.

41 Liberals maintained their focus on love, as summed up in the golden rule, throughout the period under study. Liberal Robert Kysar even suggested that Christians be concerned about ethics first and theology second. "In comparison with the question of the value of man," he wrote, "the theistic question seems secondary or even irrelevant." Robert Kysar, "Toward a Christian Humanism," *The Christian Century* 86 (May 21, 1969): 706.

42 G. Wright and Reginald Fuller, *The Book of the Acts of God: Contemporary Scholarship Interprets the Bible* (Garden City, N.Y.: Anchor Books, 1960), 405.

43 See chapter 4, "The Golden Rule," in Paul Tillich, *The New Being* (New York: Charles Scribner's Sons, 1955): 30–33.

44 Marsden, *Religion and American Culture*, 26.

45 For a discussion of golden rule Christianity, see Nancy Ammerman's "Golden Rule Christianity," in *Lived Religion in America*, ed. David D. Hall (Princeton: Princeton University Press, 1997): 196–216. Ammerman specifically studies "lay liberals" to define mainstream religious practice. According to Ammerman, "Most important to Golden Rule Christians is care for relationships, doing good deeds, and looking for opportunities to provide care and comfort for people in need." Ammerman also noted that even though liberals differed amongst themselves on certain issues, their "pictures of God as loving, caring, comforting, and protecting largely transcended ideological lines" (203–4). Supporting this doctrine is the liberal Christian belief that human beings have the innate capacity to practice selfless love, even if they often fail. This optimistic assessment of human nature can be traced back to the Enlightenment and was incorporated into liberal Christianity during the nineteenth century. "In more modern views," writes George Marsden, "humans were not regarded as naturally depraved or sinful. Rather, they were seen as potentially good, though often misguided. In the new liberal or modernist theologies, Christian teaching blended with such emphases" (*Religion and American Culture*, 128). What mattered, then, was not so much the theological dogma, but how successfully one lived out the golden rule. By the second half of the twentieth-century, liberal Christians "typically subordinated theology to ethical concerns" (238).

46 Even the rather pessimistic neo-orthodox theologians believed individuals had the capacity to rise above evil, even if as a whole humankind probably would not. As Reinhold Niebuhr put it in 1932, "For what the individual conscience feels when it *lifts itself* [italics mine] above the world of nature and the system of collective relationships in which the human spirit remains under the power of nature, is not a luxury but a necessity of the soul" (*Moral Man and Immoral Society* [New York: Charles Scribner's Sons, 1960], 276–77).

47 The pedigree of expressive individualism is complicated and can be claimed by both liberal and biblically grounded Christianity. Arminianism obviously highlighted the capacity of the individual to participate in his or her state of salvation, and Arminianism contributed its notion of perfectibility to both liberal and biblically grounded Christians. For liberals, Friedrich Schleiermacher also influenced the development of expressive individualism by centering religion on the subjective experience (Noll, *History of Christianity*, 372), while for biblically grounded Christians, Charles Finney contributed to the ideal of freedom by championing the idea that the individual could choose to receive or reject

salvation and a Christian lifestyle. On Finney, see Marsden, *Religion and American Culture*, 53.

48 On the primacy of tolerance in liberal thought and the blending of secular and religious humanitarian ideals, see Marsden, *Religion and American Culture*, 215. Also, Porterfield, *Transformation of American Religion*, 4.

49 Edwin Gaustad, ed., *Memoirs of the Spirit* (Grand Rapids: Eerdmans, 1999), 134. Samuel Chapman Armstrong (1839–1893) was a Civil War hero who established the Hampton Normal and Industrial Institution for African Americans. He was much admired by Booker T. Washington.

50 Larry Eskridge also states, "much of the impetus of the hippie quest was distinctly religious in its motivation and concerns" ("God's Forever Family," 66).

51 The liberal clergy had taken the lead in civil rights and naturally linked the movement with love, as expressed in the golden rule, and faith. In 1957 the liberal Theodore Braun wrote that pioneering work in race relations "will take a person theologically into a realm of faith, where he must seek ultimate answers to life and a new humility. But such a pioneering will . . . take a person into the joy and peace which the world can neither give nor take away, and into a divine content which surely must be the first taste of eternal life" ("The New American Frontier," *The Christian Century* 74 [July 17, 1957]: 867). Most American middle-class youth respected this liberal commitment to the golden rule ethic.

52 Even while recognizing Graham's success in the mid-1950s, liberals, who understood Graham as a fundamentalist, still insisted that Fundamentalism, as Graham expressed it, was an anachronism. "Fundamentalism as doctrine and revivalism as method," a liberal editorialist wrote, "were out of date and irrelevant to the real needs of the churches and the nation in 1917 when Billy Sunday held the last great revival in New York. They are even more outmoded and irrelevant in 1957 when Billy Graham addresses the same city with essentially the same message" ("Fundamentalist Revival," *The Christian Century* 74 [June 19, 1957]: 749–51). A follow-up article proclaimed that Graham's New York campaign "will probably stand as the high-water mark of the Billy Graham phenomenon in America" ("The Long Anticlimax," *The Christian Century* 74 [August 7, 1957]: 933). Even as late as 1969, *The Christian Century* still could not refrain from deriding Graham as it referred to his inaugural prayer for President Nixon as one of "those awful prayers" and a "raucous harangue" ("Nixon as Peacemaker," *The Christian Century* 86 [February 5, 1969]: 171). See also Marsden, *Fundamentalism*, 256.

53 Porterfield, *Transformation of American Religion*, 2.
54 *Mr. Deeds Goes to Town*, produced and directed by Frank Capra, 115 min., Columbia Pictures, 1936, videocassette.
55 *Spellbound*, produced by David Selznick and directed by Alfred Hitchcock, 111 min., Twentieth Century Fox, 1945, videocassette.
56 Albert Einstein, *Science, Philosophy and Religion, A Symposium* (New York: Conference on Science, Philosophy and Religion in Their Relation to the Democratic Way of Life, 1941). http://www.sacred-texts.com/aor/einstein/einsci.htm. Accessed April 13, 2006.
57 Peter Nichols, ed., *The New York Times Guide to the Best 1,000 Movies Ever Made* (New York: Times Books, 1999), 428–29. It is a worthwhile exercise to compare this movie with the actual trial transcript to see how the modernist filmmakers modified the courtroom dialogue and proceedings in order to discredit Fundamentalism and lionize humanism and liberalism on the silver screen. For a detailed discussion on the discrepancies between the trial transcript and the film, see Thomas Taylor's "Tennessee v. Scopes," *Fides et Historia* 37, no. 2 (2005); 38, no. 1 (2006): 165–75.
58 An excellent treatment of how liberalism survived the sixties and contributed in a positive way to American spirituality in the last decades of the twentieth century is found in Amanda Porterfield's *Transformation of American Religion*. Porterfield takes Robert Bellah to task for condemning personalized spirituality as unsupportive of the social order (18).
59 Robert Wuthnow discusses the rejection of both Fundamentalism and liberalism in the sixties. See his *Restructuring of American Religion*, 37.

Chapter 2

1 As pointed out in the previous chapter, the golden rule ideal was a central tenet of liberalism. And as liberals worked out their religious practice in the sixties, they were able to rid themselves of much of the perceived hypocrisy. See Nancy Ammerman's "Golden Rule Christianity," 196–214.
2 Matthew 5:43 and 7:1 [RSV].
3 In an autobiographical note, Amanda Porterfield confesses that she rebelled against her theologically liberal upbringing. See Porterfield, *Transformation of American Religion*, 8.
4 Robert Wuthnow notes that between 1960 and 1970 the number of students in higher education grew 139 percent (*Restructuring*

of American Religion, 155). David Farber states that while 16 percent of all high school graduates went on to college in 1940, about 50 percent did so by the mid-1960s (*Age of Great Dreams*, 57).

5 Amanda Porterfield presents an insightful discussion of this topic, noting that certain baby boomers expected an attunement between belief and socially approved behavior lest such behavior be conformist and thus hypocritical. In pointing this out, she classifies Robert Bellah as a moralist who "weighed the value of religion in terms of its contribution to a humane and civilized social order," an attitude countercultural youth would have seen as fertile ground for hypocrisy, since it did not demand an "attunement to an inner voice." See Porterfield, *Transformation of American Religion*, 18.

6 On individualism in the sixties and seventies, see Rader, *American Ways*, 237.

7 Howard Brick gives a nuanced definition of the counterculture that should always be kept in mind. The counterculture, he points out, was variegate and evolved with time (*Age of Contradiction*, 113–19). Although I identify themes pertinent to those countercultural youth who were sensitive to things spiritual—intellectual sophistication, the golden rule ideal, affluence, and expressive individualism—I recognize that there were variations upon these themes throughout the sixties and early seventies.

8 Sara Evans, in her book *Personal Politics: The Roots of Women's Liberation in the Civil Rights Movement and the New Left* (New York: Vintage Books, 1979), particularly in the chapter entitled "A Reassertion of the Personal," discusses the hypocrisy young people felt resided in their churches during the era of the civil rights movement.

9 *The Declaration of Independence* is referred to as a paradox in American society by Tom Hayden in his Port Huron Statement of 1962. The Port Huron Statement is reprinted in *The American Spirit: United States as Seen by Contemporaries*, vol. 2, *Since 1865*, 10th ed., eds. David Kennedy and Thomas Bailey (New York: Houghton Mifflin, 2002), 505–7. In his letter from a Birmingham jail in 1963, Martin Luther King Jr. countered fellow clergymen who denounced his nonviolent protests with the argument that America needed to live up to its Declaration of Independence ("Martin Luther King Jr. Writes from a Birmingham Jail [1963]," in Kennedy and Bailey, *American Spirit*, 485–87).

10 A useful treatment of this topic is found in Heather Warren's "The Shift from Character to Personality in Mainline Protestant Thought, 1935–1945," *Church History* 67, no. 3 (1998): 537–56.

She notes that even Harry Fosdick, "like the theologians and educators he fed upon . . . advanced the separation of private and public morality in Protestant America" (555).

11 Farber, *Age of Great Dreams*, 183.

12 Bailey, Kennedy, and Cohen, *The American Pageant*, 1041.

13 On the close relationship between the Beats and the counterculture, see Park Puterbaugh, "The Beats and the Birth of the Counterculture," in *The Rolling Stone Book of the Beats: The Beat Generation and American Culture*, ed. Holly George-Warren (New York: Rolling Stone Press, 1999), 357–63.

14 The Port Huron Statement was apparently drafted in 1961 and adopted by the Students for a Democratic Society at the organization's national convention in 1962 (Kennedy and Bailey, *American Spirit*, 505). See also Link and Link, *American Epoch*, 655.

15 Farber, *Age of Great Dreams*, 195–98.

16 Farber, *Age of Great Dreams*, 58.

17 *Auntie Mame*, directed by Morton Da Costa, 144 min., Warner Home Video, 1958, videocassette.

18 Joseph Krutch's *The Modern Temper* (New York: Harcourt, Brace & World, 1929 and 1956) gives perhaps the best description of modern man's obliged submission to scientism. In spite of Krutch's verdict, however, Americans were still reluctant to let science dictate ethics, which they believed should come, somehow, from religion. See James Gilbert's *Redeeming Culture: American Religion in an Age of Science* (Chicago: University of Chicago Press, 1997).

19 Amanda Porterfield, writing about the upheaval of the sixties, refers to "millions of rebellious and religiously inspired college students" (*Transformation of American Religion*, 14).

20 As quoted in Herbert Stroup, "The Privatist Ethic and Self-Fulfillment," *The Christian Century* 81 (August 19, 1964): 1033.

21 There were liberals who began moving back toward the idea of gospel-type miracles occurring in the twentieth century. The liberal Episcopalian clergyman Alfred Price, for example, who initiated healing prayer meetings at his church, was "ready to speak of 'miracles' in some sense or other." See Martin Marty, "Healing Ministry—Historic Church: St. Stephen's Episcopal Church, Philadelphia," *The Christian Century* 74 (August 28, 1957): 1010–13. The movement of such clergymen was initiated too late and seemed too half-hearted, however, to stall the defection of young people from mainline churches.

22 Herbert Stroup, "The Privatist Ethic and Self-Fulfillment," *The Christian Century* 81 (August 19, 1964): 1033..

23 Robert Wuthnow, *After Heaven: Spirituality in America since the 1950s* (Berkeley: University of California Press, 1998), 76. The baby boom itself can be dated from 1946 to 1964. See Eskridge, "God's Forever Family", 340, n. 26.

24 The need for a radical spiritual or psychic dimension to modern life had been argued by many prior to the sixties. Bernard Meland, for example, wrote in 1957 that Americans needed the "Christian mythos as a counterpart of the Christian ethic." In other words, the golden rule alone was not enough. See his "New Dimensions of Liberal Faith," *The Christian Century* 74 (August 14, 1957): 963.

25 Ellul, *Technological Society*, xxx.

26 Herbert Marcuse, *One Dimensional Man* (Boston: Beacon Press, 1964). On the influence of Marcuse, see Ellwood, *Sixties Spiritual Awakening*, 18.

27 Theodore Roszak, *The Making of a Counter Culture* (Garden City, N.Y.: Doubleday, 1969), 148, 56.

28 Roszak, *Making of a Counter Culture*, 158.

29 Roszak, *Making of a Counter Culture*, 124–25.

30 Roszak, *Making of a Counter Culture*, 138.

31 On Graham's disparaging comments about the hippies' physical appearance, see Eskridge, "God's Forever Family," 56, 83.

32 The spirituality of the sixties is recognized in a later analysis of the era by Robert Ellwood who observes, "The sixties did not so much secularize the sacred as sacralize the secular . . ." (*Sixties Spiritual Awakening*, 19).

33 Michel Lancelot, *Je veux regarder dieu en face* (Paris: editions j'ai lu, 196 ; rev. 1971), 39. My translation of "Tandis que leurs aînés parcourent l'espace ou violent les fonds sous-marins, ces jeunes explorent leurs entrailles, et se font des lavages de cerveau volontaires pour retrouver une pureté de pensée et de perception."

34 Lancelot, *Je veux regarder*, 50–51.

35 This analysis was shared by evangelicals. Graduate assistant James Moore of Trinity Evangelical Divinity School wrote in 1972: "Committed students of the seventies will be more easily radicalized for Jesus than their 'beat' predecessors of a decade ago because the idea of commitment need no longer be argued in addition to the faith. Moreover, in an atmosphere of universal commitment—where the pressure exists for each to do his own 'thing'—biblical Christianity, like other religious options, can be presented boldly as a legitimate, credible, and necessary ideology for the foment of the moment" ("The Literature of Countercultural Religion," *Christianity Today* 16 [April 28, 1972]: 14).

36 Lancelot, *Je veux regarder,* 109: "Prêcher et pratiquer l'Amour sous toutes ses formes individuelles et universelles. . . ."
37 *Time* magazine published an article on the Death of God in the fall of 1965: "Christian Atheism: The 'God Is Dead' Movement," *Time* 86 (October 22, 1965): 62. Other news magazines (*Newsweek, U.S. News and World Report*) followed suit. But already in the spring of 1969 *Time* issued an article "Is 'God Is Dead' Dead?" *Time* 93 (May 2, 1969): 44. For some of the Death of God writings, see Thomas Altizer and William Hamilton's *Radical Theology and the Death of God* (Indianapolis: Bobbs-Merrill, 1966).
38 Farber, *Age of Great Dreams,* 180–81.
39 Farber, *Age of Great Dreams,* 188.
40 Allen Ginsberg, "Footnote to Howl," in *The Portable Beat Reader,* ed. Ann Charters (New York: Penguin Books, 1992), 70–71.
41 John Suiter, "Rolling Towards the Moon," *Sierra* 83, no. 2 (1998): 78.
42 Robert Pirsig, *Zen and the Art of Motorcycle Maintenance* (New York: William Morro, 1974), 402, 286, and 412.
43 Don Giller and Ed Lozano, eds., *The Definitive Dylan Songbook* (New York: Amsco Publications, 2001), 70–71.
44 Fred Bronson, *The Billboard Book of Number One Hits,* 4th ed. (New York: Billboard Books, 1997), 253. For lyrics, see Carol Cuellar, ed., *Eighty Years of Popular Music: The Sixties* (Miami: Warner Brothers, 1999), 205.
45 *The Complete Beatles,* vol. 2 (Milwaukee: Hal Leonard, 1988), 315.
46 Bronson, *Billboard Book,* 274. Lyrics are found at http://www.getlyrics.com.
47 See Bosley Crowther's *New York Times* review of February 15, 1963, reprinted in Nichols, *The New York Times Guide,* 885–86.
48 See Charles Marsh's *God's Long Summer: Stories of Faith and Civil Rights* (Princeton: Princeton University Press, 1997).
49 *Mary Poppins,* directed by Robert Stevenson, 140 min., Buena Vista Home Entertainment, 1964, videocassette.
50 *Guess Who's Coming to Dinner,* directed by Stanley Kramer, 108 min., Columbia TriStar Home Entertainment, 1967, videocassette. *Love Story,* directed by Arthur Hiller, 100 min., Paramount Home Entertainment, 1970, videocassette.
51 *Jesus Christ Superstar,* directed by Norman Jewison, 107 min., Universal Studios Home Video, 1973, videocassette. Lyrics to "I Don't Know How to Love Him" are found at http://members.tripod.com/~JCSKelly/lyrics.html. Accessed April 13, 2006. *Godspell* was another musical that highlighted the life of Jesus

Christ, but in a modern, hippie setting. On the somewhat positive response to *Godspell* by new evangelicals, see "Godspell," *Campus Life* (December 1973): 48–52.

52 *The Best Rock Songs Ever,* 2nd ed. (Milwaukee: Hal Leonard, n.d.), 146.

53 Bronson, *Billboard Book,* 186.

54 *Best Rock Songs Ever,* 29.

55 *The Groovy Years: 53 Songs of the Hippie Era* (Milwaukee: Hal Leonard, 1996), 152.

56 *The Graduate,* directed by Mike Nichols, 120 min., MGM Home Entertainment, 1967, videocassette. For a review, see Nichols, *The New York Times Guide,* 349–50.

57 "Mrs. Robinson," in *Paul Simon: Complete Music from 1957–1993* (New York: Amsco Publications, 2000), 318.

58 *Easy Rider,* directed by Dennis Hopper, 94 min., Columbia Tri-Star Home Entertainment, 1969, videocassette.

59 *Midnight Cowboy,* directed by John Schlesinger, 113 min., MGM Home Entertainment, 1969, videocassette. *M*A*S*H,* directed by Robert Altman, 116 min., Twentieth Century Fox Home Entertainment, 1970, videocassette.

60 *Beach Blanket Bingo,* directed by William Asher, 97 min., HBO Home Video, 1965, videocassette.

61 There are antecedents to this form of American spirituality, but they did not dominate mainstream culture in the fifties and sixties. Young people wanted an all-encompassing spirituality from whence would issue a compassion for others. As Amanda Porterfield puts it, "Socially approved behavior not animated by this sense of attunement amounted to conformity and thus to hypocrisy" (*Transformation of American Religion,* 18).

Chapter 3

1 This division of biblically grounded Christianity in America is not uncommon, see Mark Shibley, *Resurgent Evangelicalism in the United States: Mapping Cultural Changes since 1970* (Columbia: University of South Carolina Press, 1996), 20. I use the term new evangelical much the way George Marsden does in *Reforming Fundamentalism* (Grand Rapids: Eerdmans, 1987), 153–71. By using the adjective biblically based, I do not intend to suggest that other Christians who fell (or fall) outside of the four rubrics here listed thought the Bible unimportant or not inspired by God. Marsden notes that those referred to here as biblically grounded have also been designated as biblically based or Bible-based in the past. See Marsden, *Fundamentalism,* 207.

2 W. A. Criswell, *The Bible for Today's World* (Grand Rapids: Zondervan, 1965), 117.
3 Lyle Dorsett, *Billy Sunday and the Redemption of Urban America* (Grand Rapids: Eerdmans, 1991), 128.
4 For an account of the southernization of American religion in the twentieth century, see Shibley, *Resurgent Evangelicalism.* Shibley argues that southern religious ways penetrated greater America and contributed to the rise of evangelicalism. He also notes the near simultaneous transformation of evangelicalism, as it encountered pluralism, into something different yet. While Shibley focuses on the fundamentalist influence, I focus on the countercultural, which Shibley would call the "Californication of conservative Protestantism" (1).
5 Walter Elwell, ed., *Evangelical Dictionary of Theology,* 2nd ed. (Grand Rapids: Baker Books, 1984), 435. Elwell lists various fundamentalist taboos.
6 Glenn Utter and John Storey, eds., *The Religious Right: A Reference Handbook* (Santa Barbara: ABC CLIO, 1995), 48, 56.
7 John Stormer, *The Death of a Nation* (Florissant, Mo.: Liberty Bell Press, 1968), 22.
8 Richard Quebedeaux, *The Young Evangelicals* (New York: Harper & Row, 1974), 22. Some of the essays in this work appeared in 1971.
9 Elwell, *Evangelical Dictionary of Theology,* 435.
10 The Federal Council of Churches, established in 1908, became the National Council of Churches in 1950.
11 Joel Carpenter, *Revive Us Again: The Reawakening of American Fundamentalism* (New York: Oxford University Press, 1997), 147–52.
12 For a treatment of these youth organizations, see Bruce Shelley, "The Rise of Evangelical Youth Movements," *Fides et Historia* 18 (1986): 47–63.
13 For a history of Fuller Theological Seminary and its relationship to evangelicalism, see Marsden, *Reforming Fundamentalism.*
14 Marsden, *Reforming Fundamentalism,* 53.
15 The "Foreword" was penned by Gordon College of Theology President T. Leonard Lewis. Carl Henry, *Giving a Reason for Our Hope* (Boston: W. A. Wilde, 1949), 5.
16 Marsden, *Fundamentalism,* 233.
17 Marsden, *Reforming Fundamentalism,* 67. See also Carpenter, *Revive Us Again,* 140. Evangelicals usually maintained a small but active presence in mainline denominations. In 1970 United Methodists for Evangelical Christianity held their first annual

convocation. In 1972 the countercultural Christian leader Jack Sparks was in attendance as a speaker. See Cheryl Forbes, "'Good News' Turns Inward," *Christianity Today* 16 (September 15, 1972): 53–56.

18 James V. Heidinger II, "The History of Renewal in the United Methodist Church." See http://www.goodnewsmag.org/renewal/30years.htmChtt. Accessed April 12, 2006.

19 It is noteworthy, inasmuch as it emphasizes the highbrow intent of the journal's creators that the name of the journal was the same as one once published by the new evangelicals' intellectual hero, J. Gresham Machen. For a list of Machen's major works and periodicals, see Elwell, *Evangelical Dictionary of Theology*, 724.

20 Marsden, *Reforming Fundamentalism*, 158.

21 Marsden, *Reforming Fundamentalism*, 165.

22 *Time* magazine printed a piece on Francis Schaeffer in its religion section: "Mission to Intellectuals," *Time* 75 (January 11, 1960): 62.

23 Schaeffer stated that his books were derived from his lectures at universities in England and America. See his *Introduction to Francis Schaeffer* (Downers Grove, Ill.: InterVarsity, 1974), 37; Edith Schaeffer, *Dear Family: The L'Abri Family Letters, 1961–1986* (San Francisco: Harper & Row, 1989), 114–18.

24 Edith Schaeffer, *Dear Family*, 127. See also her *The Tapestry: The Life and Times of Francis and Edith Schaeffer* (Waco: Word Books, 1984), 527.

25 Machen was the first twentieth-century theologian to argue poignantly that modernism was in fact anti-intellectualism. This argument would be picked up and ably handled by Francis Schaeffer in the 1960s and 1970s with great effect. For a concise recapitulation of Machen's argument, see Marsden, *Fundamentalism*, 216–17.

26 Hal Lindsey, who began evangelizing youth in 1958, noted in 1971 that for evangelistic purposes "the high school student is about where the college student was when I started." In fact, he claimed, the optimum age to reach a person was at about his or her sophomore year of high school. "Interview—Hal Lindsey," *The Wittenburg Door* 1 (1971): 8.

27 Schaeffer's argument does not differ from that found in the "Foreword" of Carl Henry's *Giving A Reason for Our Hope*, published in 1949.

28 Francis Schaeffer, *He Is There and He Is Not Silent* (Wheaton: Tyndale House, 1972), 64–65.

29 For an explanation of the Common Sense position as posited by J. Gresham Machen, a position retained by Carl F. H. Henry and Schaeffer, see Marsden, *Fundamentalism*, 216–17.

30 Ron Ruegsegger, in his article "Francis Schaeffer on Philosophy," *Christian Scholar's Review* 10 (1981): 253, wrote that Schaeffer relied on secondary sources when dealing with the history of ideas and often oversimplified the philosophical issues he claimed to adroitly critique. George Marsden noted that many academic Christians, in the end, rued Schaeffer for his philosophical naiveté, but Marsden also noted that such criticism did not take into account that Schaeffer's real objective was to evangelize. See Marsden, "Francis A. Schaeffer," *The Reformed Journal 34* (June 1984): 2–3. It is true that in an interview in 1976 Schaeffer defined himself as an evangelist and not as a theologian or philosopher. See "How Should We Then Live?" *Christianity Today* 21 (October 8, 1976): 20.

31 Allowing a greater role for the spiritual and supernatural in one's worldview would become increasingly popular for American religionists in general during the latter part of the twentieth century. Concerning this reordering in American religious thought during the twentieth century, Wuthnow notes, "Thus the world of facts with which the empirical sciences deal must be seen ultimately in another context—a context given meaning by religious symbols—which is beyond the scope of the empirical sciences" (*Restructuring of American Religion*, 302). Schaeffer, of course, argued that religious (biblically grounded) presuppositions are a prerequisite for the empirical sciences to have anything substantial to say.

32 Francis Schaeffer, *A Christian View of Spirituality*, vol. 3 of *The Complete Works of Francis A. Schaeffer*, 3rd ed. (Wheaton: Crossway Books, 1982), 263–64.

33 Francis Schaeffer, *The God Who Is There: Speaking Historic Christianity into the Twentieth Century* (Downers Grove, Ill.: InterVarsity, 1968), 55, 143. The argument that reason does not lead one to a decision in favor of faith dates back, in its modern existential form, to Kierkegaard, who wrote that "Reason has brought God as near as possible, and yet he is as far away as ever," from a selected passage of Kierkegaard's *Philosophical Fragments*, found in Needleman et al., *Religion for a New Generation* (New York: Macmillan, 1973, 1977), 530. Also, Niebuhr called upon the individual to become involved in the world in spite of humankind's inescapable imperfections, and Tillich suggested that faith came when one recognized the meaninglessness of existence. See

William Graebner, *The Age of Doubt: American Thought and Culture in the 1940s* (Boston: Twayne, 1991), 62.

34 Graham, *Just as I Am*, 188.

35 Graham, *Just as I Am*, 321.

36 Carpenter, *Revive Us Again*, 153.

37 Graham, *Just As I Am*, 452.

38 A chronology (1947–1996) of Graham's significant crusades or evangelistic campaigns, listed by year and city visited, is found as an appendix to his autobiography, *Just As I Am*, 866–69.

39 Graham, *Just As I Am*, 235.

40 Graham, *Just As I Am*, 370.

41 Graham, *Just As I Am*, 236.

42 Graham, *Just As I Am*, 416.

43 Graham, *Just As I Am*, 427. It should be noted that although Southern Baptists generally endorsed segregation, they did support black ministries. In 1954 Southern Baptists helped launch a campaign in Mississippi "to place a Bible in every Bibleless home among the Negroes of the state, provided each recipient [would] promise to read it." See "Bibles for Mississippi Negroes," *The Pentecostal Evangel* (October 17, 1954): 2. For a thorough treatment of southern religion and civil rights, see Paul Harvey's *Freedom's Coming: Religious Culture and the Shaping of the South from the Civil War through the Civil Rights Era* (Chapel Hill: University of North Carolina Press, 2005).

44 Mark Noll notes that Graham "had been a pioneer in integrating blacks and whites in his crusades, even in the South." He also points out that he had been "unusually eager to cooperate with a wide range of Christian groups," which won him the ire of separatistic fundamentalists. Finally, writes Noll, Graham "even won the guarded support of various Catholic bishops" (*A History of Christianity*, 510–11).

45 Carl Henry, "Turning Time for America," *Christianity Today* 16 (September 15, 1972): 44.

46 A good example of a new evangelical college student's influence upon coeds who were not biblically grounded is found in a special later sixties issue of Campus Life, where student recounts how two of her roommates ultimately convert to biblically grounded Christianity. See Alvina Ewing, "First Year at the U," *Campus Life* (special issue, 1968): 22–23+.

Chapter 4

1 For a brief history of this movement, see John Melton, *Encyclopedia of American Religions* (New York: Gale, 1989), 79–84.

For a more lengthy treatment, see Vinson Synan, *The Holiness-Pentecostal Tradition* (Grand Rapids: Eerdmans, 1971; repr. 1991).

2 On the baptism of the Spirit, see Gary McGee, ed., *Initial Evidence: Historical and Biblical Perspectives on the Pentecostal Doctrine of Spirit Baptism* (Peabody, Mass.: Hendrickson, 1991). For a more complete definition and explanation of glossolalia, see Stanley Burgess and Gary McGee, eds., *Dictionary of Pentecostal and Charismatic Movements* (Grand Rapids: Zondervan, 1988), 335–41.

3 Pentecostals believed that "all believers may and ought to be anointed with the Spirit." Furthermore, even though baptism in the Spirit was regarded as the end of a quest to radically connect with or be filled with God, it was also "the starting point of the real spiritual life" (W. E. Moody, "A Fresh Anointing," *The Pentecostal Evangel* [February 28, 1931]: 2). In other words, believers who had not received the second blessing were still Christians, though not deeply spiritual. This is not to say that Pentecostals believed that those openly and knowledgeably committed to liberalism were Christian. In *The Pentecostal Evangel*, for example, a story is told of a modernist (liberal) minister who was unable to communicate the Christian message of salvation to a dying man. See Harold Horton, "Some Other Time," *The Pentecostal Evangel* (January 18, 1936): 13.

4 A Pentecostal, such as the editor of *The Pentecostal Evangel*, might, for example, attend a religious service at a synagogue and comment on it for the benefit of his readers ("United Jewry," *The Pentecostal Evangel* [February 28, 1931]: 4). See also Marsden, *Religion and American Culture*, 156.

5 On the importance of African-American spirituality in the origins of Pentecostalism, see W. J. Hollenweger, "Priorities of Pentecostal Research," in *Experiences of the Spirit: Conference on Pentecostal and Charismatic Research in Europe at Utrecht University, 1989*, ed. Jan Jongeneel (Frankfurt am Main: Peter Lang, 1991), 8–9.

6 Burgess and McGee, *Dictionary of Pentecostal and Charismatic Movements*, 910.

7 Synan, *Holiness-Pentecostal Tradition*, 224–26; and Burgess and McGee, *Dictionary of Pentecostal and Charismatic Movements*, 252.

8 Oral Roberts, *Expect a Miracle* (Nashville: Thomas Nelson, 1995), 75.

9 Burgess and McGee, *Dictionary of Pentecostal and Charismatic Movements*, 97–98.

10 To those not familiar with Pentecostalism, certain rubrics in the Assemblies of God journal *The Pentecostal Evangel* read something like those of the *National Enquirer*. Article titles include "Alive after 7,200 Volts Pass through His Body" and "Lump on Back Disappears—Pain Gone Too." See "Testimonies of Healing" *The Pentecostal Evangel* (January 30, 1972): 20–21.

11 David Wilkerson, *The Cross and the Switchblade* (New York: Jove Books, 1962), 169.

12 Eskridge, "God's Forever Family," 364.

13 Synan, *Holiness-Pentecostal Tradition*, 243–45.

14 Synan, *Holiness-Pentecostal Tradition*, 254.

15 More than charismatic Christians, Pentecostals retained their Victorian taboos against drinking and gambling and the like and condemned such things in quaint Victorian style. An article in *The Pentecostal Evangel* of 1969, for example, intones: "A man liquored up is the devil's pawn" (Lowell Lundstrom, "Private Enemy Number One," *The Pentecostal Evangel* [June 29, 1969]: 8).

16 Marsden, *Fundamentalism*, 243.

17 Donald Miller, *Reinventing American Protestantism: Christianity in the New Millennium* (Berkeley: University of Carolina Press, 1997), 8.

18 Burgess and McGee, *Dictionary of Pentecostal and Charismatic Movements*, 136.

19 Synan, *Holiness-Pentecostal Tradition*, 257–58.

20 Burgess and McGee, *Dictionary of Pentecostal and Charismatic Movements*, 136.

21 Pat Robertson and Jamie Buckingham, *The Autobiography of Pat Robertson: Shout It from the Housetops* (Plainfield, N.J.: Logos International, 1972; rev. 1995), 84.

22 Burgess and McGee, *Dictionary of Pentecostal and Charismatic Movements*, 140.

23 Synan, *Holiness-Pentecostal Tradition*, 257.

24 Peter Hocken, "The Challenge of Non-Denominational Charismatic Christianity," in Jongeneel, *Experiences of the Spirit*, 221 and 231. Although this number includes Canada and Mexico, it still is indicative of the extraordinary growth of the charismatic renewal in the United States.

CHAPTER 5

1 For an article discussing an evangelical view of capitalism, see Kenneth Elzinga, associate professor of economics at the University of Virginia, Charlottesville, who argues in *Christianity*

Today: "Consumer sovereignty means goods and services will be promoted and sold that will provide great temptations for Christians. But inherent in the market system is also the freedom to procure goods and services that can facilitate the Christian life" ("The Demise of Capitalism and the Christian's Response," *Christianity Today* 16 [July 7, 1972]: 14).

2 Political observers will also extend the term to include other biblically grounded Christians of the 1970s and 1980s who were willing to be grouped, especially politically, with new evangelicals and charismatics. Jerry Falwell, who is normally understood as a fundamentalist, is therefore included in discussions of evangelicalism in the late 1970s because he freely associated, for politico-religious purposes, with new evangelicals and charismatics. The historian George Marsden refers to this latter phenomenon as fundamentalistic evangelicalism. See Marsden, *Fundamentalism*, 234–35.

3 Robertson and Buckingham, *Shout It from the Housetops*, 80.

4 Robertson and Buckingham, *Shout It from the Housetops*, 109, 114.

5 Robertson and Buckingham, *Shout It from the Housetops*, 310–11.

6 Graham, *Just As I Am*, 470.

7 Dinesh D'Souza, *Falwell Before the Millennium: A Critical Biography* (Chicago: Regnery Gateway, 1984), 48.

8 On Schaeffer's conversion, see *Introduction to Francis Schaeffer*, 34–35. For his critique of liberalism as leading to meaninglessness, see *Escape from Reason* (Downers Grove, Ill.: InterVarsity, 1968), 74–75.

9 Scott Burson and Jerry Walls, *C. S. Lewis and Francis Schaeffer* (Downers Grove, Ill.: InterVarsity, 1998), 36–37.

10 Robertson and Buckingham, *Shout It from the Housetops*, 138. This is not to say Robertson's father did not support traditional southern religious practices. He authored a unanimous Senate resolution that urged Americans to protect the nation and preserve peace. This was read at a Graham crusade. See William Martin, *With God on Our Side: The Rise of the Religious Right in America* (New York: Broadway Books, 1996), 31.

11 Marsden, *Reforming Fundamentalism*, 24–25. These men considered such answers as "fleeces" set out before God. The idea is taken from Judges 6:36-40, in which Gideon lays out a fleece, seeking a definitive sign of God's intent to, through him, lead Israel to victory. This was a common approach used often by biblically grounded people when considering what decisions to make.

Cf. the narrative of Oral Roberts and his "three fleeces" that formally convinced him to devote himself to a healing ministry (Roberts, *Expect a Miracle*, 78).

12 Marsden, *Reforming Fundamentalism*, 51–54.

13 Burson, *C. S. Lewis and Francis Schaeffer*, 65–66.

14 Michael Richardson, *Amazing Faith: The Authorized Biography of Bill Bright, Founder of Campus Crusade for Christ* (Colorado Springs: WaterBrook Press, 2000), 105.

15 Roberts, *Expect a Miracle*, 123–24.

16 Charles Colson, *Born Again* (Old Tappan, N.J.: Spire Books, 1976), 110.

17 Richardson, *Amazing Faith*, 83.

18 Graham, *Just As I Am*, 162.

19 Graham, *Just As I Am, 164.*

20 Richardson, *Amazing Faith*, 22–23.

21 As quoted in Richardson, *Amazing Faith*, 36.

22 Richardson, *Amazing Faith*, 37.

23 Richardson, *Amazing Faith*, 61–65.

24 Schaeffer, *Introduction to Francis Schaeffer*, 36.

25 Graham, *Just As I Am*, 96; Roberts, *Expect a Miracle*, 48; Robertson and Buckingham, *Shout It from the Housetops*, 109, 114.

26 Roberts, *Expect a Miracle*, 126.

27 Graham, *Just As I Am*, 150.

28 Robertson and Buckingham, *Shout It from the Housetops*, 11.

29 Robertson and Buckingham, *Shout It from the Housetops*, 92–93.

30 Robertson and Buckingham, *Shout It from the Housetops*, 138.

31 James Bakker, *I Was Wrong* (Nashville: Thomas Nelson, 1996), 467.

32 The Four Spiritual Laws are listed in Richardson, *Amazing Faith*, 271–77.

33 This concept was not original with Bright. Fundamentalists and Pentecostals also taught as much. In 1936 an article in *The Pentecostal Evangel* remonstrated that all things belonged to the believer. "Life is yours, and you can multiply and extend the description of all that it means. Life now, life eternal, abundant life, victorious life" ("All Things Are Yours," [January 18, 1936]: 1).

34 Eskridge, "God's Forever Family," 241.

35 Wuthnow, *Restructuring of American Religion*, 194.

36 Richardson, *Amazing Faith*, 97.

37 Eskridge, "God's Forever Family," 215.

38 Richardson, *Amazing Faith*, 271–77.

39 A 1968 edition of *Campus Life* encouraged students to take an active role in evangelizing their schoolmates. "Your group of teen

men and women like yourself who have met Jesus Christ in a vital, life-changing experience is probably outnumbered by far. But remember, Jesus Christ changed the world with a small group of men and women. Forget the martyr pills and remember Luke 1:37 'For with God nothing shall be impossible.'" ("Doin' Your Thing," 18).

40 Mention of Leary's visit to L'Abri is in Michael S. Hamilton, "The Dissatisfaction of Francis Schaeffer," *Christianity Today* 41 (March 3, 1997): 22.

41 Perhaps his rejection of sectarianism and its legalisms was due to his having lived in a non-American culture and to the fact that his wife had grown up in China. Missionaries often drop some of their cultural biases.

42 Schaeffer referred to L'Abri as a community rather than as a commune. See Philip Yancey, "Schaeffer on Schaeffer, Part II," *Christianity Today* 23 (April 6, 1979): 21.

43 "Mission to Intellectuals," *Time* 75 (January 11, 1960): 62.

44 J. A. Kirk, professor of New Testament at the Union Theological Seminary, Buenos Aires, noted as early as 1963 that Schaeffer had a unique capacity to relate to youth. After observing Schaeffer for three years, he stated, "I began to realize that we had, amongst those of us who accepted the inerrancy of Scripture, a man to whom God had given a special gift of understanding the mentality of the twentieth century and of identifying himself with people affected by it." The complete essay by Kirk, "A Word Concerning L'Abri," is found in Schaeffer's *The God Who Is There*, 171–76.

45 Kenneth Woodward, "Guru of Fundamentalism," *Newsweek* 100 (November 1, 1982): 88

46 Fritz Detwiler recognizes that Schaeffer played a key in establishing the ideological framework for the Christian Right's sociopolitical agenda. See his *Standing on the Premises of God: The Christian Right's Fight to Redefine America's Public Schools* (New York: New York University Press, 1999).

Chapter 6

1 Some scholars have a difficult time accepting that Jesus People were bona fide hippies. Even Robert Ellwood writes of the Jesus movement among "ex-hippies." See his *Sixties Spiritual Awakening*, 35. I think this is a mistake. Countercultural youth did not miraculously lose their counterculture the day they became Christian. Ira Gallaway, in the United Methodist publication *Engage* (March, 1972), recognized that youth from the counterculture were turning to Jesus Christ (reprinted in "Liberation

and Revolution," *Christianity Today* 16 [August 25, 1972]: 20). A good summary of the Jesus People movement is found in David Di Sabatino, *The Jesus People Movement: An Annotated Bibliography and General Resource* (Westport: Greenwood Press, 1999).

2 The proof that youth were rebelling against their parents' religion when they became Jesus followers was evident in the objections parents exhibited toward their children's religious conversion. Armand Nicholi II, M.D. and Harvard faculty member, noted that parents were startled by their children joining the Jesus movement. See his "Why Jesus Attracts Today's Youth," *Christianity Today* 16 (June 9, 1972): 4. Although most of the deprogramming efforts of the 1970s were aimed at sects that were not biblically grounded (according to evangelicals), these efforts were nonetheless evidences that parents realized that they were losing their children to rebel religions.

3 An evangelist working among hippies at a music festival was convinced that "young people are hungry to know reality in this life and the life to come." He reported that though they could not find that reality in liquor, drugs, and sex, "after accepting Christ, they state 'This is what I was always searching for.'" (Brentice Bush, "Christian Witness at Hippie Festival," *The Pentecostal Evangel* [September 27, 1970]: 18).

4 Glenn Kittler, *The Jesus Kids and Their Leaders* (New York: Warner Paperback Library, 1972), 62–63.

5 Eskridge, "God's Forever Family," 149–50

6 Eskridge, "God's Forever Family," 130.

7 Eskridge, "God's Forever Family," 169–70.

8 Kittler, *Jesus Kids*, 140–41. In 1975 Edward Plowman judged that the Jesus movement in the Midwest was stronger than it had been in California. See Eskridge, "God's Forever Family," 212.

9 Eskridge, "God's Forever Family," 5.

10 Kittler, *Jesus Kids*, 62, 25–27.

11 Reprinted in Duane Pederson, *Jesus People* (Glendale, Calif.: G/L Regal Books, 1971), 30–31.

12 Keith Green's popularity was attested to by a full-page advertisement promoting his music placed in *Campus Life* (July 1980): 17. In 2000 *Christianity Today* reported that "Keith Green tied for eighth on the online readers' most personally influential list" of Christians. Readers were asked to list five Christians they believed were most personally influential. See "Survey Results: What Do You Think?" *Christianity Today*.com. http://www.christianity-today.com/ch/2000/001/12.42.html; and http://www.ctlibrary.com. Accessed in 2002 and April 12, 2006 respectively.

13 Quoted in Melody Green, *No Compromise*, revised and expanded (Eugene, Ore.: Harvest House Publishers, 2000), 43–44.

14 New evangelical and charismatic churches responded favorably to the folk rock music. During the Jesus movement, an Assemblies of God parent wrote, "There is a BEAUTIFUL new folk-type music now. It has a sweet, simple quality I really love. Even the humble old guitar has made a great recovery." He urged his fellow believers, "Let's not be afraid of innovation when you look at the faces of the teen-agers who are leading the revival." See Emil Balliet, "Sing a New Song," *The Pentecostal Evangel* (January 30, 1972): 18–19.

15 Arthur Blessitt, *Arthur, A Pilgrim* (Hollywood: Blessitt, 1985), 67.

16 Street ministries existed throughout the United States. Teen Challenge worker Richard Turgeon, for example, worked among street people in Boston and Pittsburgh and participated in the Jesus Festival in Pittsburgh with fifteen-hundred youth. See his "1,500 Youth Join in Walkathon, Teen Challenge 'Jesus Festival'," *The Pentecostal Evangel* (January 30, 1972): 30.

17 Eskridge, "God's Forever Family," 258.

18 Erling Jorstad, observing the Jesus movement in its later stage, remarked, "the teen-age Jesus People, Catholic charismatics, and evangelical students are united in their dedication to the teachings, ministry, and redemptive life of Jesus. They find in him the authority, direction, and love they consider completely adequate for their lives" ("Unity of the Jesus Movement," *Christianity Today* 16 [August 11, 1972]: 15). I include all three groups referred to by Jorstad as participants, to varying degrees, in the counterculture.

19 Duane Pederson, as quoted in Kittler, *Jesus Kids*, 32–33.

20 Linked to the countercultural Christian's radical spirituality was his or her informed aversion to naturalistic evolutionary theory and his or her receptivity to what evangelicals labeled scientific creationism. I say informed because the middle-class youth who rejected evolutionary theory after his or her conversion to Christianity had learned evolutionary theory in high school and college and had once believed in it. Significantly, Henry Morris founded the Institute for Creation Research in 1970 in southern California; and works such as Norman Macbeth's *Darwin Retried* (London: Garnstone Press, 1971) appeared and grew in popularity at the height of the Jesus movement. The creation science movement practiced a measure of intellectual sophistication that pleased many counterculture Christians seeking to radically undo naturalistic evolutionary theory, which they believed to be the main buttress of scientism. Even Dean Kenyon, profes-

sor of biology and coordinator of the general biology program at San Francisco State University commended the volume by Henry Morris and Gary Parker, *What Is Creation Science?* (Green Forest, Ariz.: Master Books, 1982 and 1987) when he penned the foreword to it. For a scholarly history of the movement see Numbers, *The Creationists*.

21 Blessitt, *Arthur*, 74.

22 The Jesus movement people "are sharing the new birth in communes, group witnessing, and group Bible study. They submerge their individual preferences into the redemptive power of their chosen community" (Jorstad, "Unity of the Jesus Movement," *Christianity Today* 16 [August 11, 1972]: 16).

23 Kittler, *Jesus Kids*, 68–71.

24 There was also a connection between Teen Challenge and college students. Many centers (there were twenty-four in the United States and Puerto Rico by 1969) were basically run by college students. As one college student testified, "The cry of college students all over this nation is to have a cause, I found mine in Teen Challenge" ("Apostles of the Streets," *The Pentecostal Evangel* [June 29, 1969]: 19).

25 Evangelical youth would continue their interest in missions. At Urbana '76, sponsored by InterVarsity Christian Fellowship, some 14,000 collegians gathered to hear about missions. They donated $23,000 for hunger relief to World Vision, Food for the Hungry, and the Voice of Calvary in Mississippi. See the report by Arthur Matthews, "Urbana '76: Declaring God's Glory and Word," *Christianity Today* 21 (January 21, 1977): 38–40.

26 As the Jesus movement gained momentum, black evangelist Tom Skinner became increasingly popular among American youth. At Flint, Michigan, in 1972, some 30,000 attended Skinner's crusade ("Skinner Gets Them Together," *Christianity Today* 16 [June 9, 1972]: 45).

27 Blessitt, *Arthur*, 80–81.

28 The biblical orientation of Jesus People caught the attention of Billy Graham, who stated in his 1971 book, *The Jesus Generation*, that the movement was "Bible-based." See his *The Jesus Generation* (Minneapolis: World Wide Publications, 1971), 18.

29 Kittler, *Jesus Kids*, 12.

30 Kittler, *Jesus Kids*, 21.

31 On the Death of God movement, see Ellwood, *Sixties Spiritual Awakening*, 136–42.

32 Kittler, *Jesus Kids*, 82–84.

33 Roger Bennett, "The New Propriety," *Christianity Today* 16 (June 23, 1972): 11.

34 In reviewing Roger Palms's *The Jesus Kids* (Valley Forge: Judson Press, 1971), Donald Williams, minister to college students at the Hollywood Presbyterian Church, noted, "Palms rightly distinguishes between Fundamentalism and the Jesus movement by the movement's absence of legalism in the living and witnessing and by the corporate Christian life-style" ("Getting It All Together," *Christianity Today* 16 [January 7, 1972]: 28). This book should not be confused with that by Glenn Kittler, *Jesus Kids*, cited above in n. 4, and passim.
35 Kittler, *Jesus Kids*, 42.
36 Pederson, *Jesus People*, 30–31.
37 Mary Pikrone, "Evangelism Plus: Ford Reaches Out," *Christianity Today* 16 (June 9, 1972): 43.
38 Green, *No Compromise*, 75–76.
39 Melody Green described her visit to a home Bible study, where she found thirty-five people seated on couches, chairs, and plush carpeting. See her *No Compromise*, 118.
40 Kittler, *Jesus Kids*, 26.
41 In the early seventies Revell published Arthur Blessitt's *Tell the World: A Jesus People Manual* (Old Tappan, N.J.: Fleming H. Revell, 1973). This was a guide to aggressive proselytism.
42 Eskridge, "God's Forever Family," 114.
43 Kittler, *Jesus Kids*, 42–44.
44 Kittler, *Jesus Kids*, 50.
45 In delineating Jesus People characteristics, Larry Eskridge notes that they "inhabited a supernaturally charged world chock-full of signs and wonders and a steady outpouring of what they perceived to be divine intervention in their lives" ("God's Forever Family," 109–10).
46 Kittler claimed, "this is the core of the Jesus People Movement—the Second Coming of Jesus Christ" (*Jesus Kids*, 71–72).
47 The idea of Israel being reestablished was not new with Lindsey or the countercultural Christians. Fundamentalists and Pentecostals talked and wrote of this even prior to World War II. In late 1930 or early 1931, before Hitler's chancellorship, the editor of *The Pentecostal Evangel* attended a service at the Springfield, Missouri, synagogue to hear a Zionist speak about the favorable prospects for reestablishing Israel in Palestine. See "United Jewry," *The Pentecostal Evangel* [February 28, 1931]: 4. A later article in *The Pentecostal Evangel* reported that a Jewish publication in Vienna understood Hitler's persecution of the Jews as a prelude to the creation of a new Jewish state. See "Hitler—A Friend of Israel," *The Pentecostal Evangel* (January 18, 1936): 3.

48 Hal Lindsey and his role in the political thinking of countercultural Christians will be discussed in a later chapter. For his interpretations of prophecy in 1970, see Hal Lindsey, with C. C. Carlson, *The Late Great Planet Earth* (Grand Rapids: Zondervan, 1970).

49 In 1980 a condensed fiction novel on the rapture, which would occur, according to the story, on June 4, 1988, made its way into the youth magazine *Campus Life*. See Carol Balizet, "The Last 7 Years," *Campus Life* (September 1980): 39–41.

50 It should be noted that some countercultural youth in Europe were also receptive to the Jesus movement, demonstrating that technocracy, counterculture, and the Jesus movement were transcultural and symbiotic, at least in the West. For example, Udo Lemke, 24 years old, and Kurt Blumenthal, 20, both German communist journalists converted to the Jesus movement in 1972 in their homeland. Concerning these two conversions, see Edward Plowman "2,000 Christian Youth Reach Out at Olympics," *Christianity Today* 16 (September 29, 1972): 43.

51 The first eight books were reviewed by Donald Williams, "Getting It All Together," *Christianity Today* 16 (January 7, 1972): 28+. Erling Jorstad reviewed the next seven books listed, see Ehrling Jorstad, "Unity of the Jesus Movement," *Christianity Today* 16 [August 11, 1972]: 15–16.

52 Jorstad, "Unity of the Jesus Movement," 15.

53 It is interesting to note that a *Time* magazine article on the Jesus movement talks about converts. One wonders, "Converting from what?" They were certainly not converting from Fundamentalism, Pentecostalism, new evangelicalism, or from charismatic Christianity. They came from secular and liberal homes. And the Time article recognizes this, stating, "Most of them are Middle America, campus types: neatly coiffed hair and Sears, Roebuck clothes styles." But the article also recognizes the radical countercultural population as well, stating, it's a "marriage of conservative religion and the rebellious counterculture, and many of the converts have come to Christ from the fraudulent promises of drugs" ("The New Rebel Cry," *Time* 97 [June 21, 1971]: 59, 56).

54 Edward Plowman, "WCC Central Committee: Fellowship Adrift," *Christianity Today* 16 (September 15, 1972): 46. Ironically, the Committee did give room for the countercultural Children of God, which was deemed a cult by evangelicals because it had extra-biblical sources of authority.

Chapter 7

1 William Martin highlights Ed Dobson's observation that though fundamentalists were absolutists on moral principles, they were always innovative in methodology. See Martin, *With God on Our Side*, 202.

2 Graham noted in his address to the European Congress on Evangelism (1971) that since 1966 his crusades had become "youth crusades." He claimed that 70 percent of the audience at his northern California crusade in the summer of 1971 were under twenty-five years of age. See his "The Marks of the Jesus Movement," *Christianity Today* 16 (November 5, 1971): 4. Graham's observations underscore the spiritual quest many youth pursued and the effects of the Jesus Movement, which was going strong by 1971. Nonetheless, there was an increasing number of youth who, even though they had grown up attending Sunday school, had rejected the church and by the 1960s could not be reached by traditional evangelistic methods.

3 For the conversion and ministry of Ted and Elizabeth Wise, see John MacDonald, *House of Acts* (Carroll Stream, Ill.: Creation House, 1970), 22–35 and "Ted Wise Interview," at http://www.one-way.org/jesusmeovment/index.html. Accessed October 31, 2006.

4 MacDonald, *House of Acts*, 30.

5 Eskridge, "God's Forever Family," 94.

6 Eskridge, "God's Forever Family," 98.

7 MacDonald describes their sometimes rocky relationship in some detail in *House of Acts*, 67–80.

8 MacDonald, *House of Acts*, 69.

9 Kittler, *Jesus Kids*, 64.

10 Kittler, *Jesus Kids*, 66.

11 Blessitt gives a short summary of his childhood upbringing in *Arthur*, 63–66.

12 Blessitt, *Arthur*, 65.

13 Blessitt, *Arthur*, 66.

14 Sparks has had a remarkably diverse career. He was successively associate professor of applied statistics at the University of Northern Colorado; associate professor of educational psychology at Pennsylvania State University; director of the correspondence division for Campus Crusade for Christ; founder and director of Christian World Liberation Front; bishop of the Evangelical Orthodox Church; and dean of St. Athanasius Academy of Orthodox Theology. For a *curriculum vitae* of Jack Sparks, see "Orthodox Study Bible Old Testament Project." http://www.lxx.org/who_d1.htm. Accessed April 12, 2006.

15 Billy Graham agreed with *Time* magazine's assessment of the Jesus movement when he quoted the newsweekly at the European Congress on Evangelism in 1971. The *Time* article quote spoke of Jesus People as full of love, rebelliousness, and a desire to apply their faith to all aspects of life. "There is a morning freshness to it all," Graham quoted, "a buoyant atmosphere of hope and love along with the usual rebel zeal. Most converts seem to enjoy translating their faith into everyday life" ("The Marks of the Jesus Movement," *Christianity Today* 16 [November 5, 1971]: 4).
16 Quebedeaux, *Young Evangelicals*, 94–98.
17 "From Freaks to Followers," *Christianity Today* 16 (October 22, 1971): 33–34.
18 Edward Plowman, "Explo '72: 'Godstock' in Big D," *Christianity Today* 16 (July 7, 1972): 31.
19 "Executive Leadership," http://www.nae.net/index.cfm? FUSE ACTION=nae.staff. Accessed March 23, 2006. Haggard's political clout would suffer when he became implicated in a drug and gay sex scandal in November of 2006. http://news.yahoo.com/s/ap/20061103/ap_on_re_us/haggard_sex_allegations.
20 Other effective street evangelists who did not come from a Pentecostal or charismatic background include Sammy Tippitt in Chicago, Richard Hogue in Houston, and Jack Sparks in Berkeley. See Eskridge, "God's Forever Family," 132.
21 Edward Plowman, "Explo '72: 'Godstock' in Big D," *Christianity Today* 16 (July 7, 1972): 13.
22 MacDonald, *House of Acts*, 12–13.
23 MacDonald, *House of Acts*, 119–20.
24 MacDonald, *House of Acts*, 21.
25 MacDonald, *House of Acts*, 121, 123.
26 Robert Girard, *Brethren, Hang Loose* (Grand Rapids: Zondervan, 1972), 9.
27 Girard, *Brethren*, 181.
28 Girard, *Brethren*, 182.
29 Girard, *Brethren*, 186. One also notes that a countercultural Christian writing style became a part of evangelical journalism by the 1980s. In writing about the golden rule, Verne Becker adopts a style very much in keeping with *The Hollywood Free Paper:* "The kind of love Jesus talked about was different than the mushy expressions found on greeting cards. He talked about a tough kind of love—the giving-your-life-for-someone-else kind of love. A love that means sticking it out with others over the long haul" ("Spark," *Campus Life* [January 1981]: 29).
30 Miller, *Reinventing American Protestantism*, 29–37.

31 Eskridge, "God's Forever Family," 121.
32 Eskridge, "God's Forever Family," 121.
33 Synan, *Holiness-Pentecostal Tradition*, 256.
34 Eskridge, "God's Forever Family," 261.
35 Eskridge, "God's Forever Family," 124, 254.
36 "People and Faces," http://www.one-way.org/jesusmovement/index.html. Accessed April 13, 2006.
37 Miller, *Reinventing American Protestantism*, 94.
38 Miller, *Reinventing American Protestantism*, 47–51.
39 Green, *No Compromise*, 131.
40 Miller, *Reinventing American Protestantism*, 44.
41 Interview with Carol Wimber entitled "The Way It Was: The Roots of Vineyard Worship," found in *Cutting Edge* (Winter 2002). Located at http://www.vineyardusa.org/upload/winter_2002.pdf. Accessed April 11, 2006.
42 Miller, *Reinventing American Protestantism*, 50.
43 The "melding," of course, was slow and difficult. Many traditional evangelicals, for example, had a hard time accepting Christian rock music. In 1979 *Christianity Today* found it necessary to publish an article by Richard Mountford, professor of music at Malone College, Canton, Ohio, which denied that rock music was inherently evil. See Mountford, "Does the Music Make Them Do It?" *Christianity Today* 23 (May 4, 1979): 21–23.
44 Carl Henry, *Answers for the Now Generation* (Chicago: Moody Press, 1969), 9. Also found under the original title *Giving a Reason for Our Hope* (Boston: W. A. Wilde, 1949), 10.
45 Henry, *Answers for the Now Generation*, 8. Henry's analysis of countercultural youth is similar to the one made much later by Dominick Cavallo, who argued that American youth "revived older, pre-industrial visions of work, individualism, self-reliance, community and democracy" (*A Fiction of the Past: The Sixties in American History* [New York: St. Martin's, 1999]: 8).
46 Henry, *Answers for the Now Generation*, 9. Evangelicals generally understood what they considered authentic modern science, as practiced by Newton, as allowing for the supernatural, and modern modern science, as practiced by Darwin, as being a closed naturalistic system.
47 Henry, *Answers for the Now Generation*, 80.
48 Edith Schaeffer, *Tapestry*, 521. In her collected letters Edith Schaeffer mentions some of the Americans visited during their 1966 tour. See Edith Schaeffer, *Dear Family*, 100–103.
49 Martin, *God on Our Side*, 196.
50 Francis Schaeffer, *Escape from Reason*, 7.

51 "Interview—Hal Lindsey," 8.

52 The Children of God was a sect of Jesus People that severed its biblically grounded tether and created its own free-form religion that honored the leader's extra-biblical prophetical writings and promoted the use of sexual favors to gain recruits. See Kittler, *Jesus Kids*, 142. A *Christianity Today* article stated that the missives from the Children of God leader, Moses David Berg, "endorse some totally unbiblical practices" ("The Children of God: Disciples of Deception," *Christianity Today* 21 [February 18, 1977]: 18). David Berg's teachings can be found in "The Family Making a Difference" at http://www.thefamily.org. Accessed April 11, 2006. Schaeffer dealt with this problem early on, even before the Children of God sect materialized in 1968–1969. "The evangelical Christian," wrote Schaeffer in 1968, "needs to be careful because some evangelicals have recently been asserting that what matters is not setting out to prove or disprove propositions; what matters is an encounter with Jesus" (*Escape from Reason*, 76). This was a common fear among evangelicals. See, for example, Paul Marshal, "'Turning on' Is Nothing New," *Christianity Today* 16 (August 11, 1972): 10. Marshal, of the Salvation Army, wrote, "Elation and ecstasy need not be condemned out of hand, but we should evaluate them to see whether they are an integral part of the spiritual life."

53 Francis Schaeffer, *The Church at the End of the Twentieth Century* (Downers Grove, Ill.: InterVarsity, 1970), 103–4.

54 Schaeffer, *The Church*, 19.

55 Schaeffer considered autonomous freedom, where one was cut off from one's Creator and sequestered into the naturalistic worldview, a form of bondage. See *The Church*, 25.

56 Schaeffer, *The Church*, 21.

57 Schaeffer, *The God Who Is There*, 165.

58 Schaeffer, *The God Who Is There*, 165–66.

59 William Martin, referring to Arbitron and Nielsen ratings, states that in 1979 "no television preacher had an audience larger than 2.5 million," and "the audience for [Jerry] Falwell's Old Time Gospel Hour stood at approximately 1.4 million, while James Robison drew less than six hundred thousand" (*God on Our Side*, 213). I suspect Martin includes Robertson amongst the television preachers.

60 Robertson and Buckingham, *Shout It from the Housetops*, 312.

61 Robertson and Buckingham, *Shout It from the Housetops*, 313.

62 Eskridge, "God's Forever Family," 289.

63 Graham, *Just As I Am*, 499.

64 Graham, "The Marks of the Jesus Movement," *Christianity Today* 16 (November 5, 1971): 5.
65 Wuthnow, *Restructuring of American Religion*, 88.
66 Shibley, *Resurgent Evangelicalism*, 28.
67 Wuthnow, *Restructuring of American Religion*, 160.
68 This is particularly surprising in that this occurred prior to the rise or expansion of the many biblically grounded institutions and communes that would have been able to accommodate youth who had converted over to a biblically grounded worldview. In the 1950s only four of the nation's ten most popular seminaries were evangelical, but by the 1980s it would be eight of the ten. See Wuthnow, *Restructuring of American Religion*, 192. Wuthnow also notes that evangelicals who had graduated from college had a more negative attitude toward liberals than did non-college evangelicals (217–18).
69 Wuthnow, *Restructuring of American Religion*, 168, 169.
70 Robert Wuthnow even notes that the new generation of evangelical leaders was "much more comfortable with the label 'neo-fundamentalist,' or simply 'fundamentalist.'" For some, I would argue, this was an expression of their rebellion. See *Restructuring of American Religion*, 195.
71 "From Freaks to Followers," 34.
72 Richardson, *Amazing Faith*, 156–57.
73 Erling Jorstad underscored the merging of the Jesus movement into evangelicalism as early as 1972 when he noted, "The movement clearly is moving into a new phase, one that will mean closer association with established congregations. The Jesus People and those in the establishment bear the responsibility of sharing their resources with one another and with non-believers" ("Unity of the Jesus Movement," *Christianity Today* 16 [August 11, 1972]: 16). One particularly symbolic demonstration of the merger of countercultural Christianity and evangelicalism was that the Jesus People's "one way" sign, an uplifted index finger, became common among regular evangelicals by the mid 1970s. The sign figures in an advertisement in Campus Life promoting folk rock music (*Campus Life* [January 1974]: 2). It was adopted by Billy Graham during the 1971 Tournament of Roses Parade. See Eskridge, "God's Forever Family," 185.
74 Arthur Matthews, "Urbana '76: Declaring God's Glory and Word," *Christianity Today* 21 (January 21, 1977): 38–40.
75 "We Poll the Pollster," *Christianity Today* 23 (December 21, 1979): 10. The Gallup poll conducted for *Christianity Today* indicated that while youth aged from eighteen to twenty-four were not well represented in evangelicalism, those aged twenty-five to

twenty-nine "nearly caught up with the general profile." Evangelicals thirty years old and older were 4 percent above. See "We Poll the Pollster," 17.

76 "Jesus '76: Love in a Pasture," *Christianity Today* 20 (April 23, 1976): 53.

77 Larry Eskridge underscores the importance of aging in the dissolution of the Jesus movement. See his "God's Forever Family," 7–8.

78 Eldridge Cleaver, *Soul on Fire* (Waco: Word Books, 1978), 236.

79 John Maust "Cleaver: Gazing at a Different Moon," *Christianity Today* 23 (December 7, 1979): 49.

80 Another spectacularly symbolic convert was the son of arch-liberal Episcopal Bishop James Pike, Chris Pike. See Billy Graham, "The Marks of the Jesus Movement," *Christianity Today* 16 (November 5, 1971): 4.

81 Robert Shelton, *No Direction Home* (New York: Ballantine Books, 1986), 562.

82 Shelton, *No Direction Home*, 563.

83 Armand Nicholi II, "Why Jesus Attracts Today's Youth," *Christianity Today* 16 (June 9, 1972): 4.

Chapter 8

1 In 1975 Harold O. J. Brown, associate editor for *Christianity Today*, observed that evangelical leaders were more than reluctant to mix religion and politics. As he put it, they were "still of the older non-interventionist persuasion." As quoted in Martin, *With God on Our Side*, 193.

2 The Goldwater campaign of 1964 made many liberal clergymen nervous because Goldwater supported school prayer as a political issue. In the pages of *The Christian Century* they freely spoke out against Goldwater. Once Goldwater had been defeated, liberals wished to return to normalcy, which translated into the "politics and religion don't mix" formula. Churches, one liberal article read, "have no interest in and no ties to the Democratic party, the Republican party or any other party as such" ("The Churches' Mandate," *The Christian Century* 81 [November 18, 1964]: 1419). Robert Wuthnow contends that liberal clerical zeal provoked the creation of conservative special interest groups, giving a "new impetus to conservative inclinations that had long failed to gain organizational expression" (*Restructuring of American Religion*, 186). This certainly was true by the 1970s, but should not obscure the fact that countercultural Christians also contributed to both a religious and political resurgence.

3 George Marsden argues that political activism in the North would be occasioned by southern fundamentalists who moved north and

there could not bear the modernist threat to their way of life. See his *Fundamentalism*, 237. I would add that liberal Christian converts to evangelicalism carried with them a tradition of protest and activism, dating from abolitionism and through prohibition, women's suffrage, ERA, and right into the civil rights movement.

4 It is also argued that fundamentalists believed societal problems had a spiritual origin that could only be remedied by an individual's conversion to Jesus Christ, and that for this reason fundamentalists did not participate in political solutions. See Carpenter, *Revive Us Again*, 118–19. The problem with this approach, however, is that fundamentalists had strongly supported certain types of social legislation in the past, most notably that concerning Prohibition.

5 Carl Henry set the tone publicly in 1957 when he called upon biblically grounded Christians to tone down their rhetoric and exhibit a spirit of love. See Marsden, *Reforming Fundamentalism*, 165. A good example of the new evangelical approach as it had matured by 1972 was presented by E. Mansell Pattison, associate professor of psychology at the University of California at Irvine. Pattison discoursed on homosexuality, and though he did not think it right, he asked the church "to find out how it can assume its appropriate responsibility for the humanity of the homosexual" ("Defrocking the Stereotypes," *Christianity Today* 16 [May 12, 1972]: 21).

6 Marsden refers to this as "social displacement." In 1900 theologically conservative Christians believed they were the dominant force in American culture, but after the Scopes Trial they had become "a laughingstock" and were forever banned from taking center stage again. See Marsden, *Fundamentalism*, 218–19.

7 Wald, *Religion and Politics in the United States*, 210.

8 Albert Menendez, "The Faithful: How They Voted," *Christianity Today* 21 (December 3, 1976): 60.

9 Arthur Matthews, "Crusade for the White House: Skirmishes in a 'Holy War,'" *Christianity Today* 21 (November 19, 1976): 48.

10 Arthur Matthews, "Religious Broadcasters: Pressing the Issues," *Christianity Today* 21 (February 18, 1977): 56.

11 N.a. "The Political Peak Is Also the Brink," *Christianity Today* 21 (November 19, 1976): 33.

12 Andrew Young, *A Way out of No Way: The Spiritual Memoirs of Andrew Young* (Nashville: Thomas Nelson Publishers, 1994), 9 (on rebellion), 21 (on being born-again), 41 (on liberal theologians) and 68 (on the National Council of Churches).

13 John Warwick Montgomery, "Will an Evangelical President Usher In the Millennium?" *Christianity Today* 21 (October 22, 1976): 66.

14 Marsden notes that Carter did not appeal to the antiliberal side of the evangelical constituency, but he seems to overlook the countercultural character of young evangelicals, who were in revolt against theological liberalism. See Marsden, *Religion and American Culture*, 262. For Wuthnow's assessment of Carter's influence on evangelical political behavior see *Restructuring of American Religion*, 204.

15 Some evangelicals, like Carl Henry, demonstrated a sharp interest in social causes. *The Christian Century*, the liberal journal, published an article by Henry wherein he explained his "mind-shifts" and his desire for "evangelical humanitarianism." Henry, however, remained thoroughly evangelical. See Henry, "American Evangelicals in a Turning Time," *The Christian Century* 97 (November 5, 1980): 1059. On Henry, see also Robert Fowler, *A New Engagement: Evangelical Political Thought, 1966–1976* (Grand Rapids: Eerdmans, 1982), 81.

16 Many people who were to emerge as evangelicals during the late seventies and eighties were affluent, educated, and Republican religious conservatives who had resided in the liberal mainline denominations until the liberal pressure became too much to bear and the presence of alternative evangelical churches too alluring to pass up. Also, Marsden notes that fundamentalists, who in the North and West would tend toward evangelicalism by the 1960s on, "drifted in a politically conservative direction" without any "theoretical preparation to guide them." In other words, they were focused on individual salvation rather than group socio-political action and moved rightward while liberal theology and liberal politics became bedfellows. See Marsden, *Fundamentalism*, 208.

17 N.a., "Plain Talk on Viet Nam," *Christianity Today* 16 (May 26, 1972): 27. See also the editorial "Viet Nam: A Presidential Dilemma," *Christianity Today* 16 (May 12, 1972): 27.

18 N.a., "Election Promises: Counting the Cost," *Christianity Today* 16 (July 28, 1972): 22.

19 "Campus Crusade: Into All the World," *Christianity Today* 16 (June 9, 1972): 38.

20 Wuthnow, *Restructuring of American Religion*, 188.

21 Cheryl Forbes, "Campaign 72: Confrontation for Christ," *Christianity Today* 16 (July 7, 1972): 38.

22 Edward Plowman, "Along the Blessitt Trail," *Christianity Today* 16 (January 21, 1972): 35–36. President Reagan would sign a bill for a specific National Day of Prayer in 1987. A 1952 law had allowed the President to select a day of his own choosing each year as a day of prayer.

23 "Demo 72" stood for Demonstration 72. See Adon Taft, "The World at Miami," *Christianity Today* 16 (August 11, 1972): 33.
24 Taft, "The World at Miami," 33–34.
25 Jack Kerouac, *Tristessa* (New York: Penguin Books, 1960; repr. 1992), 52.
26 Taft, "The World at Miami," 34.
27 George Marsden, "Evangelical Social Concern—Dusting Off the Heritage," *Christianity Today* 16 (May 12, 1972): 8. It is interesting, if not ironic (because he is asking traditional evangelicals to become like countercultural Christians who have no conscious link with the evangelical Victorian past) that in order to entice traditional evangelicals into becoming progressive, Marsden has to remind them that nineteenth-century evangelicals concerned themselves with social causes.
28 Other evangelical scholars hoped for this. See, for example, Timothy Smith, professor of history at Johns Hopkins, "A 'Fortress Mentality,'" *Christianity Today* 21 (November 19, 1976): 22–26.
29 As quoted in Richard Hasler, "John Witherspoon, Pastor in Politics," *Christianity Today* 16 (September 29, 1972): 11.
30 Quebedeaux, *Young Evangelicals*, 134.
31 Wuthnow identifies Mark Hatfield as a political liberal. See his *Restructuring of American Religion*, 255. In 1979 the biblically grounded Hatfield spoke to three thousand evangelical college students and, according to *Christianity Today* "told the students to provide the world with 'a new vision,' a new stewardship model for God-given resources. Students should live that model, he said, and seek 'global economic justice' and an end to the nuclear arms race." See John Maust, "Low-Profile Coalition Grows Behind Scenes," *Christianity Today* 23 (April 20, 1979): 45.
32 "Stacking Sandbags against a Conservative Flood," *Christianity Today* 23 (November 2, 1979): 76–77.
33 Cheryl Forbes, "Unlisted Bestsellers," *Christianity Today* 16 (June 23, 1972): 40. The article complained that these Christian best-sellers were not listed by *Publisher's Weekly, The New York Times*, or *The Washington Post*. By the 1990s Hal Lindsey's *The Late Great Planet Earth*, according to the claim on its cover, would have sold over 15 million copies.
34 Lindsey wrote, "Let us seek to reach our family, our friends, and our acquaintances with the Gospel with all the strength that He gives us. The time is short" (*Late Great Planet Earth*, 188).
35 Kittler saw the preoccupation with end times as an essential doctrine in the Jesus People movement. "And this is the core of the Jesus People Movement—the Second Coming of Jesus Christ" (*Jesus Kids*, 71–72).

36 Lindsey, *Late Great Planet Earth*, 48.
37 Lindsey, *Late Great Planet Earth*, 65.
38 Lindsey, *Late Great Planet Earth*, 82, 86.
39 Support for Israel was shared by most biblically grounded Christians. Jerry Falwell would claim: "one reason God favors America is that America 'has blessed the Jew—his chosen people'" ("Politicizing the Word," *Time* 114 [October 1, 1979]: 68). This did not mean that biblically grounded Christians believed Jews had the same filial relationship with God that Christians had. *Newsweek* pointed this out poignantly by reporting the Southern Baptist Convention President's remark that "God Almighty does not hear the prayer of the Jew" in its issue distributed just prior to the November 1980 elections. See Kenneth Woodward and Stryker McGuire, "The Fundamentalists and the Jews," *Newsweek* 96 (November 10, 1980): 76.
40 It is interesting that Jimmy Carter, as an outspoken evangelical candidate for the U.S. presidency in 1976, stated that "a basic cornerstone of our foreign policy should be preservation of the nation of Israel," and that the establishment of Israel in 1948 was a "fulfillment of Bible prophecy." As quoted from an interview in *Liberty*. See "Campaign Countdown: 'Bloc Busters,'" *Christianity Today* 21 (October 22, 1976): 47.
41 Evangelicals did not condemn Israel for its kibbutz system, which, although not antireligious, certainly had communistic features.

CHAPTER 9

1 On Schaeffer's talent in communicating Machen's arguments to the world of the 1960s and 1970s, see Marsden, *Fundamentalism*, 245.
2 Marsden, *Fundamentalism*, 241.
3 Indeed, in the evangelically politically charged year of 1979, Harold Brown, professor of theology at Trinity Evangelical Divinity School, Deerfield, Illinois, recognized Schaeffer's influence when he wrote, "It is Francis Schaeffer . . . who is challenging American evangelicals to choose with care the new battles they will fight." At the end of his presentations, Brown added, Schaeffer calls "on audiences to do everything in their power to change the present situation of evangelical inaction, including, 'if necessary, even removing our leaders'" ("The Church of the 1970s: A Decade of Flux?" *Christianity Today* 23 [December 21, 1979]: 22–23).
4 Schaeffer treated these topics in his first works of 1968. On the importance of intellectual integrity and freedom, see his *Escape from Reason*, 82 and 84 respectively. On the centrality of love, see Schaeffer, *The God Who Is There*, 97.

5 Wuthnow discusses the liberal concern for peace and social justice. See hise *Restructuring of American Religion*, 250–51.
6 Marsden writes, "Even those who most dislike the Religious Right and its simple either/or choices might recognize that it has been responding to a real crisis in a culture that has lost its moral compass—or, more precisely, finds itself with too many competing moral compasses" (*Fundamentalism*, 257).
7 Marsden, *Fundamentalism*, 246.
8 Schaeffer, *The Church at the End of the Twentieth Century*, 37. Although Wuthnow contends that Schaeffer belatedly concerned himself with ethics, such a claim seems exaggerated, since Schaeffer, from the beginning, insisted on applying one's faith to all of life, and hence to all ethical choices. Certainly in this 1970 book, published only two years after his first book and before *Roe v Wade*, he was calling for social justice. See Wuthnow, *Restructuring of American Religion*, 206.
9 Fowler, *A New Engagement: Evangelical Political Thought*, 68–71.
10 Advertised in *Christianity Today* 21 (November 19, 1976): 210–11.
11 Francis Schaeffer, *How Should We Then Live? The Rise and Decline of Western Thought and Culture* (Old Tappan, N.J.: Fleming H. Revell, 1976), 223–24.
12 Schaeffer, *How Should We Then Live?* 256.
13 Schaeffer, *How Should We Then Live?* 227.
14 Schaeffer and Koop apparently conducted twenty seminars, each being two to three days in length, on the subject in twenty major American cities in the fall of 1979. Taken from a four-page advertisement for the seminars, found in *Christianity Today* 23 (May 4, 1979).
15 Francis Schaeffer, *A Christian View of the West*, vol. 5 of *The Complete Works of Francis A. Schaeffer*, 281. It should be noted that this postulation presupposes that the golden rule ideal is an immutable truth imprinted on the heart of all humankind for all times.
16 As reproduced in PBS's *With God on Our Side: The Rise of the Religious Right: Prophets and Advisors: 1979–1984*, produced and directed by Calvin Skaggs and David Van Taylor, 55 min., Lumiere Production, 1996, DVD.
17 Schaeffer, of course, was not the only one among evangelicals to trumpet the sanctity of human life. The respected English evangelical, John Stott, rector of All Souls Church, delivered a message entitled "Reverence for Human Life" to a service held for doctors in October of 1971. Although nuanced, Stott's message suggested it best to err on the side of caution and to consider the embryo

as created in the image of God and possessing human life and, therefore, to allow it to live. See his "Reverence for Life," *Christianity Today* 16 (June 9, 1972): 8–12. Also, the theologian Harold O. J. Brown opposed abortion early on. He, along with Graham, Schaeffer, and C. Everett Koop formed the anti-abortion Christian Action Council in 1975. See Martin, *With God on Our Side*, 156.

18 Sociologist of religion Robert Wuthnow recognized this biblically grounded Christian conception of things in the political history of the Christian Right. He observed, "The religious right consistently used the language of morality to present its claims, arguing that morality was a very large domain and that liberals were simply amoral or immoral rather than merely holding different political views" (*Restructuring of American Religion*, 210).

19 Schaeffer, *Complete Works*, vol. 5, 426. It is true that liberal denominations generally supported the pro-choice position. Liberal denominations, such as the American Baptist Churches, Church of the Brethren, and the United Church of Christ filed a friend-of-the court brief against the Hyde Amendment, an amendment to disallow Medicaid payment for abortions. See "Aborting the Law," *Christianity Today* 21 (November 19, 1976): 54.

20 Burson and Walls, *C.S. Lewis and Francis Schaeffer*, 43.

21 Edward Plowman, "Is Morality All Right?" *Christianity Today* 23 (November 2, 1979): 76.

22 Plowman, "Is Morality All Right?" 77.

23 Duane Oldfield, *The Right and the Righteous: The Christian Right Confronts the Republican Party* (New York: Rowman & Littlefield, 1996), 100.

24 Oldfield, *Right and Righteous*, 96.

25 Easton, *Gang of Five*, 178.

26 Easton, *Gang of Five*, 41.

27 A 1979 poll by Gallup indicated that "evangelicals are Democrats, better than three to two, over Republicans." Also, although the South contained only 28 percent of the national population, it possessed 43 percent of the evangelical population. See "Who and Where Are the Evangelicals?" *Christianity Today* 23 (December 21, 1979): 18.

28 Marsden, *Fundamentalism*, 237.

29 For a discussion of the contradictions residing within modern conservatism, see Theodore Lowi, *The End of the Republican Era* (Norman: University of Oklahoma Press, 1995).

30 Paul Weyrich, "Honoring a Soldier of the Religious Right." http://www.renewamerica.us/columns/weyrich. Accessed March 29, 2006.

31 Oldfield, *Right and Righteous*, 101.

32 Oldfield, *Right and Righteous*, 102.
33 Oldfield, *Right and Righteous*, 140.
34 D'Souza, *Falwell Before the Millennium*, 111.
35 Wuthnow observes that in 1982 only one of seven evangelicals ever considered joining Moral Majority. See his *Restructuring of American Religion*, 205.
36 Oldfield, *Right and Righteous*, 139.
37 As quoted in Oldfield, *Right and Righteous*, 140.
38 Oldfield, *Right and Righteous*, 143–44.
39 Fritz Detwiler points out that the success of the Christian Right should not be gauged by the success or failure of any particular evangelical political organization. The success, rather, should be measured by the effectiveness of their ideology which has proven resilient in spite of the failure of particular Christian Right organizations. See his *Standing on the Premises of God*, 159.
40 Oldfield, *Right and Righteous*, 146.
41 Marsden points out that Pat Robertson "was charismatic in his theology, but fundamentalistic in his politics" (*Fundamentalism*, 236). What this meant to the born-again boomer generation, of course, was freedom and seamless authenticity in its religious and daily life, including a political activism consistent with that life.
42 Oldfield, *Right and Righteous*, 189.
43 Robertson's decision to pick a young political activist to direct his political outreach is reminiscent of his decision to pick the young disc jockey, Scott Ross, during the sixties to direct his youth outreach. See chapter 7, above.
44 Easton, *Gang of Five*, 129.
45 As quoted in Easton, *Gang of Five*, 200.
46 According to an unscientific *Christianity Today* poll, James Dobson remained popular with its readership, among scholars and general readers alike. Among general readers (408 replies) and scholars (155 replies) Billy Graham received most votes as the most influential Christian of the twentieth century. James Dobson placed sixth among general readers but not at all among scholars. But as most personally influential, Dobson placed fourth, while C. S. Lewis, Billy Graham, Francis Schaeffer placed first, second, and third respectively among general readers. Among scholars, Dobson placed seventh as personally influential and C. S. Lewis, Francis Schaeffer, Billy Graham, Martin Luther King Jr., Dietrich Bonhoeffer, and Reinhold Niebuhr placed first, second, third, fourth, fifth, and sixth. http://www.christianitytoday.com/ ch/2000/ 001/12.42.html. Accessed July 26, 2002.

47 The "culture war" idea was popularized by James Davison Hunter's *Culture Wars: The Struggle to Define America* (New York: BasicBooks, 1991).
48 Oldfield, *Right and Righteous,* 191.

Chapter 10

1 On the importance of the abortion issue, see Wuthnow, *Restructuring of American Religion*, 13.
2 As quoted in Patrick Allitt, ed., *Major Problems in American Religious History* (New York: Houghton Mifflin, 2000), 377–78. Also, see Tina Bell, "Operation Rescue," *Human Life Review* 14 (1988): 37–42.
3 "Former Abortionists Become Pro-life," May 1989. Located at *The Forerunner.* http://www.forerunner.com/forerunner/X0438_Former_Abortionists.html. Accessed April 13, 2006.
4 "Former Abortionists Become Pro-life."
5 Last Days Ministries Website. http://www.lastdaysministries.org/about/about.html. Accessed April 6, 2006.
6 Melody Green, *No Compromise*, 377.
7 Lyrics and comment both at http://www.sockheaven.org. Accessed March 22, 2006.
8 Lyrics at www.tabcrawler.com/lyrics. Accessed March 22, 2006.
9 E-mail from James Muffet. Accessed March 28, 2006.
10 Student Statesmanship Institute Online Homepage. http://www.ssi-online.org/index1.html. Accessed April 12, 2006.
11 In an interview with *Christianity Today*, Schaeffer stated in reference to his support of revolution, "I am a radical in this sense. Most people don't realize that" (Philip Yancey, "Schaeffer on Schaeffer, Part II," *Christianity Today* 23 (April 6, 1979): 21).
12 As quoted in Jim Henderson, "Bio: Flip Benham," *Houston Chronicle*, May 31, 1998. Reprinted at http://www.gayday.com/news/1998/houston_chronicle_980531.asp. Accessed April 13, 2006.
13 Neal Horsley, as quoted at http://www.adl.org/poisoning_web/anti_abortion.html. Accessed April 1, 2002.
14 Neal Horsley, "Talk Is Cheap." http://www.christiangallery.com/pictures.html. Accessed March 9, 2006.
15 As quoted on the Anti-Defamation League's Website in "Anti-Abortion Extremism in Cyberspace: The Creator's Rights Party," located at http://www.adl.org/poisoning_web/anti_abortion.asp. Accessed April 13, 2006.
16 Henderson, "Bio: Flip Benham."
17 Benham's remarks are found in Henderson, "Bio: Flip Benham."
18 Henderson, "Bio: Flip Benham."

19 Martin, *With God on Our Side*, 182.
20 Shelton, *No Direction Home*, 563.
21 "Oregon Citizens Alliance." http://www.webpan.com/dsinclair/rright.html. Accessed April 13, 2006.
22 "Oregon Citizens Alliance."
23 "United States Senator." http://www.sos.state.or.us/elections/nov52002/guide/candidates/mabonl.htm. Accessed April 13, 2006.
24 "Oregon Citizens Alliance."
25 "Oregon Citizens Alliance." Prior to founding the Christian Action Network, Mawyer had worked for Jerry Falwell.
26 David Kyle Foster, "Finding Real Life." http://www.exodus.to/testimonials_left_homosexuality_11.shtml. Accessed April 4, 2006.
27 Taft, "The World at Miami," 34.
28 "The History of Promise Keepers." http://www.promisekeepers.org/genrl2. Accessed April 4, 2006.
29 "The History of Promise Keepers," http://www.promisekeepers.org/genrl2.
30 http://www.promisekeepers.org/faqs/core/faqscore26.htm. Accessed March 31, 2002. See also "Promise Keepers/Bill McCartney" at the Ministry Watch website located at http://www.ministrywatch.com/mw2.1/F_MinDesc.asp?EIN=841157834. Accessed April 13, 2006.
31 The biblically grounded concept of freedom is somewhat analogous to what Andrew Busch claims was Ronald Reagan's concept of freedom. See his *Ronald Reagan and the Politics of Freedom*, 237. What Reagan saw as granting freedom to the unborn, of course, others interpreted as taking away freedom from the pregnant woman.
32 In 1988 Peretti also released *Tilly* (Wheaton: Crossways, 1988), a touching pro-life novel about a woman, abortion, and reconciliation.
33 Kimon Sargeant, *Seeker Churches: Promoting Traditional Religion in a Nontraditional Way* (New Brunswick: Rutgers University Press, 2000), 164. As quoted in http://www.findarticles.com/p/articles/mi_m0SOR/is_2_63/ai_89078711. Accessed April 13, 2006.
34 I say a high percentage of countercultural youth because there were a high number of baby boomers in the congregations. Fully 48 percent of the congregants admitted to having smoked marijuana often or a few times. Although less indicative of a countercultural past, 74 percent admitted to having engaged in premarital sex. Most members did not consider themselves Christians prior

to a conversion experience. Most converted after fifteen years of age. See Miller, *Reinventing American Protestantism*, 195–212.

35 http://hirr.hartsem.edu/bookshelf/thumma_article2.html. Accessed April 4, 2006.

36 http://hirr.hartsem.edu/bookshelf/thumma_article2.html.

37 Kittler, *Jesus Kids*, 21.

38 Results of a Hartford Institute for Religion Research and Leadership Network survey. "The perceived political outlook of the majority of megachurch members is much as the popular media portray it. Over 50% were predominantly conservative, with another 33% somewhat conservative. Only 11% chose 'middle of the road,' 4% 'somewhat liberal' and 2% selected 'liberal.'" http://hirr.hartsem.edu/org/megastoday2005_summaryreport.html. Accessed April 5, 2006.

39 I do not include "charismatic" in the background list as no one of the baby-boomer generation can be easily identified as having had a truly charismatic upbringing; the movement only became significant when most baby boomers had already reached high school or college.

40 See Cleaver, *Soul on Fire*, 236.

41 *The Sixties: The Years that Shaped a Generation*, produced and directed by David Davis and Stephen Talbot, 120 min., Oregon Public Broadcasting, 2005, DVD.

42 Eskridge, "God's Forever Family," Appendix A.

Epilogue

1 Wuthnow, *Restructuring of American Religion*, 139.

2 Sara Diamond, *Not by Politics Alone: The enduring Influence of the Christian Right* (New York: Guilford Press, 1998), 110.

3 Wuthnow, *Restructuring of American Religion*, 149.

4 Mary Pikrone, "Evangelism Plus: Ford Reaches Out," *Christianity Today* 16 (June 9, 1972): 43.

5 Sara Diamond, "The Truth About the Christian Right's Bid for Power." http://www.publiceye.org/diamond/sd/_domin.html. Accessed April 15, 2006.

6 In April of 2006, the oldest school voucher program in the United States in Milwaukee, Wisconsin, expanded the number of students eligible from 15,000 to 22,500. Associated Press, "Milwaukee Increases School Vouchers." http://www.thestate.com/mld/thestate/news/nation/14353537.htm?source=rss&channel=thestate_nation. Accessed April 16, 2006.

7 See Marvin Olasky, *Compassionate Conservatism: What It Is, What It Does and How It Can Transform America* (New York: Simon & Schuster, 2000).

8 Jim Wallis, "The Religious Right Is Losing Control." http://jmm.aaa.net.au/articles/17068.htm. Accessed April 16, 2006.

9 Tony Perkins, "Make Your Voice Heard on Immigration Policy." Bulk e-mail from Family Research Council at frcpub@frc.org. Received April 13, 2006.

10 See Robert Webber, *The Younger Evangelicals* (Grand Rapids: Baker Books, 2002).

11 One notes that prior to the merging of countercultural Christianity and evangelicalism, evangelical political activism was hard to come by. Richard Hasler, a Presbyterian pastor, for example, pleaded with evangelical ministers to become involved in politics when he wrote in 1972, "Political activism is needed today more than ever before in the work of the ministry" ("John Witherspoon, Pastor in Politics," *Christianity Today* 16 (September 29, 1972): 14).

12 This conclusion also falls in line with the findings of Jack Whalen and Richard Flacks, *Beyond the Barricades: The Sixties Generation Grows Up* (Philadelphia: Temple University Press, 1989) and Timothy Miller, *The 60s Communes: Hippies and Beyond* (Syracuse: Syracuse University Press, 1999). Both of these studies demonstrate that sixties activists generally continued on in their idealism even after the counterculture had died away.

13 Biblically grounded Christians were certainly shocked and frustrated at times by the youth revolt in the sixties, as evidenced by Navy chaplain David Plank's "Cure for Youth Revolt," *The Pentecostal Evangel* (June 29, 1969): 10–11. His cure was that youth say "Yes Sir to God."

14 Romans 8:28 [NIV].

Bibliography

Books

Abramson, Paul and Ronald Inglehart. *Change in Global Perspective.* University of Michigan Press, 1995.

Altizer, Thomas J. J. and William Hamilton. *Radical Theology and the Death of God.* Indianapolis: Bobbs-Merrill, 1966.

Ammerman, Nancy T. "Golden Rule Christianity." In *Lived Religion in America,* edited by David D. Hall, 196–216. Princeton: Princeton University Press, 1997.

Bakker, James. *I Was Wrong.* Nashville: Thomas Nelson, 1996.

The Best Rock Songs Ever. 2nd ed. Milwaukee, Wisc.: Hal Leonard, n.d.

Blessitt, Arthur. *Arthur, A Pilgrim.* Hollywood: Blessitt, 1985.

———. *Tell the World: A Jesus People Manual.* Old Tappan, N.J.: Fleming H. Revell, 1973.

Blodgett, Jan. *Protestant Evangelical Literary Culture and Contemporary Society.* Westport: Greenwood, 1997.

Bloom, Alexander, ed. *Long Time Gone: Sixties America Then and Now.* New York: Oxford University Press, 2001.

Blumhofer, Edith. *Aimee Semple McPherson: Everybody's Sister.* Grand Rapids: Eerdmans, 1993.

———. *The Assemblies of God: A Chapter in the Story of American Pentecostalism.* Springfield: Gospel Publishing House, 1989.

Boston, Robert. *The Most Dangerous Man in America?: Pat Robertson and the Rise of the Christian Coalition.* Amherst: Prometheus, 1996.

Brick, Howard. *Age of Contradiction*. Ithaca: Cornell University Press, 1998.

Bronson, Fred. *The Billboard Book of Number One Hits*. 4th ed. New York: Billboard Books, 1997.

Brouwer, Steve, Paul Gifford, and Susan Rose. *Exporting the American Gospel: Global Christian Fundamentalism.* New York: Routledge, 1996.

Burgess, Stanley, and Gary McGee, eds. *Dictionary of Pentecostal and Charismatic Movements*. 9th printing. Grand Rapids: Zondervan, 1988.

Burson, Scott, and Jerry Walls. *C.S. Lewis and Francis Schaeffer.* Downers Grove, Ill.: InterVarsity, 1998.

Busch, Andrew. *Ronald Reagan and the Politics of Freedom.* Lanham, Md.: Rowman & Littlefield, 2001.

Butler, Paul, ed. *Best Sermons*. New York: MacMillan, 1952.

Carothers, J. Edward. *The Paralysis of Mainstream Protestant Leadership.* Nashville: Abingdon, 1990.

Carpenter, Joel. *Revive Us Again: The Reawakening of American Fundamentalism.* New York: Oxford University Press, 1997.

Carter, Dan. *The Politics of Rage: George Wallace, the Origins of the New Conservatism, and the Transformation of American Politics*. Baton Rouge: Louisiana State University Press, 1996.

Casserley, J. V. Langmead. *The Death of Man: A Critique of Christian Atheism.* New York: Morehouse-Barlow, 1967.

Cavallo, Dominick. *A Fiction of the Past: The Sixties in American History.* New York: St. Martin's, 1999.

Cleaver, Eldridge. *Soul on Fire.* Waco: Word, 1978.

Collins, Kenneth. *The Evangelical Moment: The Promise of an American Religion*. Grand Rapids: Baker Academic, 2005.

Colson, Charles. *Born Again*. Old Tappan, N.J.: Spire, 1976.

The Complete Beatles. Vol. 2. Milwaukee: Hal Leonard, 1988.

Cox, Harvey. *Fire from Heaven: The Rise of Pentecostal Spirituality and the Reshaping of Religion in the Twenty-first Century.* New York: Addison-Wesley, 1994.

Criswell, W. A. *The Bible for Today's World.* Grand Rapids: Zondervan, 1965.

Cuellar, Carol, ed. *Eighty Years of Popular Music: The Sixties.* Miami: Warner Brothers, 1999.

Detwiler, Fritz. *Standing on the Premises of God: The Christian Right's Fight to Redefine America's Public Schools.* New York: New York University Press, 1999.

Diamond, Sara. *Not by Politics Alone: The Enduring Influence of the Christian Right.* New York: Guilford Press, 1998.

———. *Roads to Dominion.* New York: Guilford Press, 1995.

Di Sabatino, David. *The Jesus People Movement: An Annotated Bibliography and General Resource.* Westport: Greenwood Press, 1999.

Dorsett, Lyle. *Billy Sunday and the Redemption of Urban America.* Grand Rapids: Eerdmans, 1991.

D'Souza, Dinesh. *Falwell Before the Millennium: A Critical Biography.* Chicago: Regnery Gateway, 1984.

Easton, Nina. *Gang of Five: Leaders at the Center of the Conservative Crusade.* New York: Simon & Schuster, 2000.

Edsall, Thomas. *The New Politics of Inequality.* New York: Norton, 1984.

Ellul, Jacques. *The Technological Society,* translated by John Wilkinson. New York: Vintage Books, 1964.

Ellwood, Robert. *The Sixties Spiritual Awakening: American Religion Moving from Modern to Postmodern.* New Brunswick, N.J.: Rutgers University Press, 1994.

Elwell, Walter, ed. *Evangelical Dictionary of Theology.* 2nd ed. Grand Rapids: Baker Books, 2001.

Eskridge, Larry. "God's Forever Family: the Jesus People Movement in America, 1966–1977." Ph.D. diss., University of Stirling, 2005.

Evans, Sara. *Personal Politics: The Roots of Women's Liberation in the Civil Rights Movement and the New Left.* New York: Vintage Books, 1979.

Farber, David. *The Age of Great Dreams.* New York: Hill & Wang, 1994.

Flynt, Wayne. *Alabama Baptists: Southern Baptists in the Heart of Dixie, Religion and American Culture.* Tuscaloosa: University of Alabama Press, 1998.

Fowler, Robert. *A New Engagement: Evangelical Political Thought, 1966–1976*. Grand Rapids: Eerdmans, 1982.

Frady, Marshall. *Billy Graham: A Parable of American Righteousness*. Boston: Little, Brown, 1979.

Frum, David. *How We Got Here: The 70s, The Decade That Brought You Modern Life (For Better or Worse)*. New York: Basic Books, 2000.

Gaustad, Edwin, ed. *Memoirs of the Spirit*. Grand Rapids: Eerdmans, 1999.

George-Warren, Holly. *The Rolling Stone Book of the Beats: The Beat Generation and American Culture*. New York: Rolling Stone Press, 1999.

Giberson, Karl. *Worlds Apart: The Unholy War Between Religion and Science*. Kansas City, Mo.: Beacon Hill Press, 1993.

Gilbert, James. *Redeeming Culture: American Religion in an Age of Science*. Chicago: University of Chicago Press, 1997.

Giller, Don and Ed Lozano. *The Definitive Dylan Songbook*. New York: Amsco, 2001.

Girard, Robert. *Brethren, Hang Loose*. Grand Rapids: Zondervan, 1972.

Graebner, William. *The Age of Doubt: American Thought and Culture in the 1940s*. Boston: Twayne, 1991.

Graham, Billy. *The Jesus Generation*. Minneapolis: World Wide Publications, 1971.

———. *Just As I Am: The Autobiography of Billy Graham*. New York: HarperPaperBacks, 1997.

Graham, Otis, Jr. *A Limited Bounty: The United States Since World War II*. New York: McGraw-Hill, 1996.

Greeley, Andrew. *Religious Change in America*. Cambridge: Harvard University Press, 1989.

Green, Melody. *No Compromise*. Revised and expanded edition. Eugene, Ore.: Harvest House, 2000.

The Groovy Years: 53 Songs of the Hippie Era. Milwaukee: Hal Leonard, 1996.

Hall, David D., ed. *Lived Religion in America*. Princeton: Princeton University Press, 1997.

Hankins, Barry. *God's Rascal: J. Frank Norris and the Beginnings of Southern Fundamentalism*. Lexington: University Press of Kentucky, 1996.

Harrell, David. *All Things Are Possible: The Healing and Charismatic Revivals in Modern America.* Bloomington: Indiana University Press, 1975.

———. *Oral Roberts: An American Life.* Bloomington: University of Indiana Press, 1985.

———. *Pat Robertson: A Personal, Political and Religious Portrait.* San Francisco: Harper & Row, 1987.

Harrison, Everett, Geoffrey Bromiley, and Carl Henry, eds. *Baker's Dictionary of Theology.* Grand Rapids: Baker Books, 1960.

Harvey, Paul. *Freedom's Coming: Religious Culture and the Shaping of the South from the Civil War through the Civil Rights Era.* Chapel Hill: Univeristy of North Carolina Press, 2005.

Hawkins, Merrill. *Will Campbell: Radical Prophet of the South.* Macon: Mercer University Press, 1997.

Henry, Carl. *Answers for the Now Generation.* Chicago: Moody Press, 1969.

———. *Giving a Reason for Our Hope.* Boston: W.A. Wilde, 1949.

Hervieu-Leger, Daniele. *Religion as a Chain of Memory.* New Brunswick: Rutgers University Press, 2000.

Hollenweger, Walter. *The Pentecostals: The Charismatic Movement in the Churches.* Minneapolis: Augsburg, 1972.

Hollinger, David, and Charles Capper, eds. *The American Intellectual Tradition: A Sourcebook.* Vol. 2, *1865 to the Present.* New York: Oxford University Press, 1993.

Hunter, James Davison. *Culture Wars: The Stuffle to Demine America.* New York: BasicBooks, 1991.

Jongeneel, Jan, ed. *Experiences of the Spirit: Conference on Pentecostal and Charismatic Research in Europe at Utrecht University, 1989.* Frankfurt am Main: Peter Lang, 1991.

Jorstad, Erling. *The Politics of Doomsday: Fundamentalists of the Far Right.* Nashville: Abingdon, 1970.

Kent, Stephen. *From Slogans to Mantras: Social Protest and Religious Conversion in the Late Vietnam War Era.* Syracuse: Syracuse University Press, 2001.

Kittler, Glenn. *The Jesus Kids and Their Leaders.* New York: Warner Paperback Library, 1972.

Krutch, Joseph. *The Modern Temper*. New York: Harcourt, Brace & World, 1929; repr. 1956.

Lancelot, Michel. *Je veux regarder dieu en face*. Paris: editions j'ai lu, 1968; rev. ed. 1971.

Leege, David, and Lyman Kellstedt. *Rediscovering the Religious Factor in American Politics*. London: M. E. Sharpe, 1993.

Lindsey, Hal, with C. C. Carlson. *The Late Great Planet Earth*. Grand Rapids: Zondervan, 1970.

———. *The 1980s: Countdown to Armageddon*. New York: Bantam, 1980.

Link, William, and Arthur Link. *American Epoch: A History of the United States since 1900*. Vol. 2, *Affluence and Anxiety: 1940–1992*. New York: McGraw-Hill, 1993.

Lowi, Theodore. *The End of the Republican Era*. Norman: University of Oklahoma Press, 1995.

Macbeth, Norman. *Darwin Retried*. London: Garnstone, 1971.

MacDonald, John. *House of Acts*. Carroll Stream, N.Y.: Creation House, 1970.

Machen, J. Gresham. *Christianity and Liberalism*. Grand Rapids: Eerdmans, 1923; repr. 1946.

Malone, Tom. *Essentials of Evangelism*. Murfreesboro, Tenn.: Sword of the Lord, 1958.

Marcuse, Herbert. *One Dimensional Man*. Boston: Beacon Press, 1964.

Marsden, George. *Fundamentalism and American Culture: The Shaping of Twentieth-Century Evangelicalism, 1870–1925*. New York: Oxford University Press, 1980.

———. *Fundamentalism and American Culture: The Shaping of Twentieth-Century Evangelicalism, 1870–1925*. New Edition. New York: Oxford University Press, 2006.

———. *Reforming Fundamentalism*. Grand Rapids: Eerdmans, 1987.

———. *Religion and American Culture*. New York: Harcourt Brace Jovanovich, 1990.

Marsh, Charles. *God's Long Summer: Stories of Faith and Civil Rights*. Princeton: Princeton University Press, 1997.

Martin, William. *A Prophet with Honor: The Billy Graham Story*. New York: Morrow, William, 1991.

———. *With God on Our Side: The Rise of the Religious Right in America*. New York: Broadway Books, 1996.

Marwick, Arthur. *The Sixties.* New York: Oxford University Press, 1998.

McGee, Gary, ed. *Initial Evidence: Historical and Biblical Perspectives on the Pentecostal Doctrine of Spirit Baptism.* Peabody, Mass.: Hendrickson, 1991.

McIntire, Carl. *Modern Tower of Babel.* Collingswood, N.J.: Christian Beacon Press, 1949.

McKinley, Edward. *Marching to Glory: The History of the Salvation Army in the United States, 1880–1992.* 2nd ed. Grand Rapids: Eerdmans, 1995.

Melton, John. *Encyclopedia of American Religions.* New York: Gale, 1989.

Miller, Donald. *Reinventing American Protestantism: Christianity in the New Millennium.* Berkeley: University of California Press, 1997.

Miller, Timothy. *The 60s Communes: Hippies and Beyond.* Syracuse: Syracuse University Press, 1999.

Morris, Henry, and Gary Parker. *What Is Creation Science?* Green Forest, Ariz.: Master Books, 1982 and 1987.

Needleman, Jacob, A. K. Bierman, and James Gould, eds. *Religion for a New Generation.* New York: Macmillan, 1973; 2nd ed., 1977.

Nichols, Peter M., ed. *The New York Times Guide to the Best 1,000 Movies Ever Made.* New York: Times Books, 1999.

Niebuhr, Reinhold. *Faith and History.* New York: Charles Scribner's Sons, 1951.

———. *Leaves From the Notebook of a Tamed Cynic [1929].* Louisville: Westminster/John Knox, 1990.

———. *Moral Man and Immoral Society.* New York: Charles Scribner's Sons, 1960.

Noll, Mark. *A History of Christianity in the United States and Canada.* Grand Rapids: Eerdmans, 1992.

Numbers, Ronald. *The Creationists: The Evolution of Scientific Creationism.* Berkeley: University of California Press, 1992.

Olasky, Marvin. *Compassionate Conservatism: What It Is, What It Does and How It Can Transform America.* New York: Simon & Schuster, 2000.

Oldfield, Duane. *The Right and the Righteous: The Christian Right Confronts the Republican Party.* New York: Rowman & Littlefield, 1996.

Paul Simon: Complete Music from 1957–1993. New York: Amsco Publications, 2000.

Pederson, Duane. *Jesus People*. Glendale, Calif.: G/L Regal Books, 1971.

Perry, Lewis. *Intellectual Life in America*. Chicago: University of Chicago Press, 1989.

Pirsig, Robert. *Zen and the Art of Motorcycle Maintenance*. New York: William Morrow, 1974.

Pollock, John. *Billy Graham: The Authorized Biography*. Minneapolis: World Wide Publications, 1966; Crusade edition, 1979.

Porterfield, Amanda. *The Transformation of American Religion*. Oxford: Oxford University Press, 2001.

Quebedeaux, Richard. *New Charismatics*. San Francisco: Harper & Row, 1983.

———. *The Young Evangelicals*. New York: Harper & Row, 1974.

Rader, Benjamin. *American Ways: A Brief History of American Cultures*. New York: Harcourt College, 2001.

Richardson, Michael. *Amazing Faith: The Authorized Biography of Bill Bright, Founder of Campus Crusade*. Colorado Springs: WaterBrook Press, 2000.

Roberts, Oral. *Expect a Miracle*. Nashville: Thomas Nelson, 1995.

Robertson, Pat. *The Autobiography of Pat Robertson: Shout It from the Housetops!*. South Plainfield, N.J.: Bridge, 1972; revised 1995.

Rossinow, Doug. *The Politics of Authenticity: Liberalism, Christianity, and the New Left in America*. New York: Columbia University Press, 1998.

Roszak, Theodore. *The Making of a Counter Culture*. Garden City, N.Y.: Doubleday, 1969.

Rozell, Mark, and Clyde Wilcox, *Second Coming: The New Christian Right in Virginia Politics*. Baltimore: The Johns Hopkins University Press, 1996.

Sandeen, Ernest. *The Roots of Fundamentalism: British and American Millenarianism, 1800–1930*. Chicago: University of Chicago Press, 1970.

Sanders, Cheryl. *Saints in Exile: The Holiness–Pentecostal Experience in American Religion and Culture*. New York: Oxford University Press, 1996.

Schaeffer, Edith. *Dear Family: The L'Abri Family Letters, 1961–1986.* San Francisco: Harper & Row, 1989.

———. *The Tapestry: The Life and Times of Francis and Edith Schaeffer.* Waco: Word Books, 1984.

Schaeffer, Francis. *The Church at the End of the Twentieth Century.* Downers Grove, Ill.: InterVarsity, 1970.

———. *The Complete Works of Francis A. Schaeffer.* Vols. 3 & 5. Wheaton: Crossway, 1982.

———. *Escape from Reason.* Downers Grove, Ill.: InterVarsity, 1968.

———. *The God Who Is There: Speaking Historic Christianity into the Twentieth Century.* Downers Grove, Ill.: InterVarsity, 1968.

———. *He Is There and He Is Not Silent.* Wheaton: Tyndale House, 1972.

———. *How Should We Then Live? The Rise and Decline of Western Thought and Culture.* Old Tappan, N.J.: Fleming H. Revell, 1976.

———. *Introduction to Francis Schaeffer.* Downers Grove, Ill.: InterVarsity, 1974.

Schwarz, Fred. *You Can Trust the Communists (...to do exactly as they say!).* Englewood Cliffs, N.J.: Prentice-Hall, 1960.

Shelton, Robert. *No Direction Home.* New York: Ballantine Books, 1986.

Shibley, Mark. *Resurgent Evangelicalism in the United States: Mapping Cultural Change since 1970.* Columbia: University of South Carolina Press, 1996.

Shole, Jerry. *Give Me that Prime Time Religion: An Insider's Report on the Oral Roberts Evangelistic Association.* New York: Hawthorne Books, 1979.

Smith, Christian. *American Evangelicalism: Embattled and Thriving.* Chicago: University of Chicago Press, 1998.

Smith, Oran. *The Rise of Baptist Republicanism.* New York: New York University Press, 1997.

Stoner, Peter. *From Science to Souls.* Chicago: Moody Press, 1944.

Stormer, John. *The Death of a Nation.* Florissant, Mo.: Liberty Bell Press, 1968.

Sweeney, Douglas A. *The American Evangelical Story: A History of the Movement.* Grand Rapids: Baker Academic, 2005.

Synan, Vinson. *The Holiness-Pentecostal Tradition.* Grand Rapids: Eerdmans, 1971, 1991.

Tillich, Paul. *The Courage to Be.* New Haven: Yale University Press, 1952.

———. *The New Being.* New York: Charles Scribner's Sons, 1955.

Toynbee, Arnold. *An Historian's Approach to Religion.* New York: Oxford University Press, 1956.

Utter, Glenn, and John Storey, eds. *The Religious Right: A Reference Handbook.* Santa Barbara: ABC CLIO, 1995.

Wald, Kenneth. *Religion and Politics in the United States.* New York: St. Martin's, 1987.

Wallis, Jim. *Agenda for Biblical People.* New York: Harper & Row, 1976.

———. *The Soul of Politics: Beyond "Religious Right" and "Secular Left."* New York: Harcourt Brace, 1994.

Webber, Robert. *The Younger Evangelicals.* Grand Rapids: Baker Books, 2002.

Whalen, Jack and Richard Flacks. *Beyond the Barricades: The Sixties Generation Grows Up.* Philadelphia: Temple University Press, 1989.

Wilkerson, David. *The Cross and the Switchblade.* New York: Jove Books, 1962.

Wright, G. and Reginald Fuller. *The Book of the Acts of God: Contemporary Scholarship Interprets the Bible.* Garden City, N.Y.: Anchor Books, 1960.

Wuthnow, Robert. *After Heaven: Spirituality in America since the 1950s.* Berkeley: University of California Press, 1998.

———. *The Restructuring of American Religion: Society and Faith since World War II.* Princeton: Princeton University Press, 1988.

Young, Andrew. *A Way Out of No Way: The Spiritual Memoirs of Andrew Young.* Nashville: Thomas Nelson Publishers, 1994.

Articles

Eskridge, Larry. "'One Way': Billy Graham, the Jesus Generation, and the Idea of an Evangelical Youth Culture." *Church History* 67 (1998): 83–107.

Layman, Geoffrey C., and Edward G. Carmines. "Cultural Conflict in American Politics: Religious Traditionalism, Postmaterialism, and U.S. Political Behavior." *Journal of Politics* 59 (1997): 751–78.

McConkey, Dale. "Whither Hunter's Culture War? Shifts in Evangelical Morality, 1988–1998." *Sociology of Religion* 62 (2001): 149–73.

Moen, Matthew. "From the Revolution to Evolution: The Changing Nature of the Christian Right." *Sociology of Religion* 55 (94): 345–58.

Pastor, Gregory S., Walter J. Stone, and Ronald B. Rapoport. "Candidate-Centered Sources of Party Change: The Case of Pat Robertson, 1988." *Journal of Politics* 61 (1999): 423–45.

Shelley, Bruce. "The Rise of Evangelical Youth Movements." *Fides et Historia* 18 (January 1986): 47–63.

Index